PRIMED TO PERFORM

PRIMED TO
PERFORM

**How to Build the Highest Performing Cultures
Through the Science of Total Motivation**

NEEL DOSHI AND LINDSAY McGREGOR

HARPER
BUSINESS

An Imprint of HarperCollins*Publishers*

The authors gratefully acknowledge the Temkin Group and The American Customer Satisfaction Index for allowing us to use their customer experience ratings.

HarperCollins books may be purchased for educational, business, or sales promotional use. For information, please e-mail the Special Markets Department at SPsales@harpercollins.com.

FIRST EDITION

Designed by Renato Stanisic

Library of Congress Cataloging-in-Publication Data has been applied for.

ISBN: 978-0-06-237398-4

15 16 17 18 19 OV/RRD 10 9 8 7 6 5 4

To our parents—Bhanu and Joe, and Elizabeth and Ian—for teaching us the true meaning of play and purpose.

To our mentors and friends who have been extremely generous with their time and support. We hope we can pay it forward.

To all the people whose ToMo we unwittingly destroyed over the years. At least we learned something from it!

Contents

Introduction

Primed to Perform

| *The Science of High-Performing Cultures Demystified*

"It feels like the magic is fading," a senior executive of a prestigious international company explained after he'd summoned us to help rebuild its culture. He knew that culture is critical to success—and over 90 percent of business leaders agree.[1] But he didn't know how to build a great culture. He didn't know how to prove that culture mattered. And he didn't know where to begin.

This executive wasn't alone. We hear similar concerns from leaders across businesses, nonprofits, school systems, and governments. While most people agree that culture is important, building great cultures still feels like magic that only a gifted few are born knowing how to practice.

We wrote *Primed to Perform* to reveal the science behind the magic. Over the last two decades, we built upon a century of academic study with our own original research. We analyzed tens of thousands of workers, from programmers, consultants, teachers, and investment bankers to frontline employees in legendary cultures like Southwest Airlines, the Apple Store, and Starbucks. We found that the magic behind great cultures is actually an elegantly simple science. Since then, we've tested this science around the world, from the Americas to the Middle East to Asia. In each case we found that what it takes to create the highest performing cultures is actually predictable.

Through this science we can systematically build and maintain the highest performing cultures. While culture was once soft and fuzzy, we can now measure the strength of a culture to determine where it's weak and where it's strong. Most importantly, we've developed a set of approaches and tools that help leaders build their own legendary cultures where people are primed to perform.

THE SCIENCE OF PERFORMANCE

It's remarkable how little it can take to enhance or destroy workplace performance. Imagine that it is eight o'clock on a Monday morning. You're at work, trying to read a fax (people do still send them). Somehow it was garbled in transmission, and you can make out only some of its text.

a d _ a n _ _ g _

i _ s p _ r _

_ n _ w _ _ _ g e

Take a moment. Can you figure out what the words are?[2]

The first word is *advantage*. The second is *inspire*. And then *knowledge*. How long did it take you to figure out?

Now imagine that your coworkers are talking all around you, creating a soft background buzz. Could their conversations improve your ability to perform, or would they distract you? Subliminal priming experts conducted an experiment in which test subjects were asked to complete a set of word puzzles like the one above.[3] While they worked in small empty rooms, tape-recorded voices murmured quietly in the background.

For the sake of clarity, let's call one test subject Amy and the other Steve. Test subject Amy and her group heard unintelligible chatter.

Test subject Steve and his group heard the same thing, but it was followed by one minute of real conversation in which the speaker described how much he enjoyed an activity he'd just completed.

The result? Steve's group solved an average of 7 percent more problems than Amy's did. They were 13 percent faster, and they stuck with an impossible problem for 14 percent longer. All after hearing just *one minute* of a specially scripted conversation.

Even more amazing, Steve didn't report hearing that conversation at all. None of the test subjects did. The volume was so low, and they were so focused on the puzzles, that the voices didn't penetrate their conscious minds. But their unconscious minds took note. The overheard voices primed them, unconsciously influencing them to work better, faster, and harder.

What if you could make every single person in your organization solve problems 10 percent better, 10 percent faster, and with 10 percent more persistence?

You can. But before you go and rig your workplace (or your child's bedroom) with hidden loudspeakers, keep reading. *Primed to Perform* isn't about mind control. Tricks don't work over the long haul. *Primed to Perform* shows you how to build a genuinely great culture.

Culture is like the background conversation that neither Steve nor Amy reported hearing. It surrounds you, but it is invisible, hidden in plain sight. You can't escape it. If just one minute of priming can boost Steve and his group's performance, imagine the impact of a culture that has been systematically designed to maximize the performance of every person at every level.

To build a high-performing culture, you must first understand what drives peak performance in individuals. The answer sounds deceptively simple: *why* you work affects how *well* you work.

In the case of this priming experiment, the overheard conversation put the idea of "play" into Steve's head. Play—when you do something simply because you enjoy the activity—is the most powerful motive for working. As you will learn in the next chapter, there are six basic motives behind people's work. Play, purpose, and potential strengthen performance. Emotional pressure, economic pressure, and inertia weaken it. When a culture maximizes the first three and minimizes the last three, it has achieved the highest levels of a phenomenon called total motivation (also known as ToMo). Part I of this book introduces you to this science.[4]

Part II of the book examines what we mean by "performance." Many leaders forget that there are actually two types of performance, both important yet mutually opposed. Most organizations manage *tactical performance*—the ability to execute against a plan. But *adaptive performance*—the ability to diverge from a plan—is just as important. Because tactical performance and adaptive performance are opposites, they live in a tension that few leaders have learned how to balance.

Figure 1: Great cultures fuel total motivation, and total motivation fuels performance. *Primed to Perform* shows you how each step works.

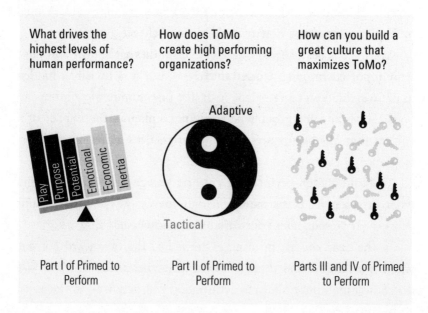

What drives the highest levels of human performance?

How does ToMo create high performing organizations?

How can you build a great culture that maximizes ToMo?

Adaptive

Tactical

Part I of Primed to Perform

Part II of Primed to Perform

Parts III and IV of Primed to Perform

In most organizations, the machinery of performance management, from dashboards to evaluations to compensation, is designed to maximize tactical performance. But a single-minded focus on tactical performance can cripple adaptive performance. In a world of extreme volatility, this misstep can be fatal.

Great leaders must also understand the biases and reflexes that get in the way of building great cultures. Part III turns the microscope on our knee-jerk reactions and mistakes.

Finally, in Part IV, we share a step-by-step guide to culture building, starting with the total motivation (ToMo) factor, a simple, easy, and highly predictive new measurement of the six motives that enables you to see where your culture is weak, where it's strong, and where it needs to change.

The total motivation factor is the ultimate culture-building tool, the compass you've always needed to make sure your culture is heading in the right direction. It has enabled us to find data-driven answers to replace the folklore around questions like:

- What leadership style should you use?
- How do you design motivating jobs and career paths?
- What is the best way to establish core values and build a strong sense of community around them?
- How should you manage the performance of your people?
- What is the fairest and most effective compensation philosophy?
- What are the best processes for managing culture?

And perhaps most important, how do you change a culture that's already in trouble? Using the simple, free survey (which can be found online at www.primedtoperform.com), you can begin to chart your way.

By the time you finish reading *Primed to Perform*, you will not only have the answers to all of these questions and more, but you will be ready to put them into action.

CULTURE MATTERS

For decades, researchers have proven that culture drives performance. Thomas J. Peters and Robert H. Waterman Jr. focused on iconic cultures in their classic book *In Search of Excellence*. If you had bought stock in the companies they profiled when the book was first published in 1982 and held them for twenty years, your portfolio would have returned 1,300 percent (compared to the Dow's 800 percent and the S&P 500's 600 percent).[5]

You can take culture to the bank.

In an unrelated study, the Harvard Business School gurus John Kotter and James Heskett compared the stock market performance of firms with great cultures and leadership to those with middling cultures over an eleven-year period. Share values increased by 901 percent for the first group compared to 74 percent for the second; revenues increased by 682 percent and net incomes by 756 percent (versus 166 percent and 1 percent, respectively).[6]

Even the most talented people will have only half the impact they should if they work in mediocre cultures. Well before writing *Primed to Perform*, Neel learned this lesson when the tech start-up he helped launch lost its early magic as it grew in size. He simply didn't understand how to build a great culture. Lindsay saw this when she worked with teams of teachers and administrators at public schools and universities. Some of the best-laid plans faltered due to cultures of mistrust and blame. As entrepreneurs and consultants who have spent a combined two decades working at firms like McKinsey & Company, Citibank, American Express, and two technology start-ups, we've seen many Fortune 500 companies, educational organizations, and nonprofits design great strategies. But too often they have failed to take because their cultures were not primed to perform.

Most organizations—even legendary ones—have a hard time building, maintaining, and strengthening their cultures. Absent a systematic, psychologically informed understanding of culture, their leaders have relied on intuition and replication. They have tried to copy Apple, Southwest Airlines, Zappos, or the Ritz-Carlton, only to find that the cultures they built weren't consistent and didn't feel genuine. They didn't motivate in the right ways, so they didn't stick.

Total motivation is the missing link.

Many of the most admired organizations already use components of total motivation intuitively. They understand that the best way to motivate people is not through rewards or threats, but by inspiring people to find play, purpose, and potential in their work.

We found evidence of this one evening in Boston on the T (the local train), where two men in their twenties were discussing how to grow their business. One of them was dressed smartly in khakis and a polo shirt. The other sported a fashionably untucked button-down and a week-old beard, expertly groomed to look ungroomed. They spoke passionately about how their personalized customer service made all the difference to their bottom line. They devised plans to visit their competitors, to ferret out their tactics and weak spots. These two men weren't tech CEOs or members of the hottest start-up incubator. They were employees at a local Whole Foods Market grocery store. They wore their Whole Foods hats with pride, and reveled in working for the only store in their neighborhood that still hand-stacked produce.

This really happened. There was no boss standing over them cracking the whip. No talk of how much money their extra work would earn them. They were brainstorming ways to help their company on their own free time, just for the fun of it. This is *adaptive performance* in the flesh. And it was a direct result of the ToMo culture that cofounder John Mackey baked into his business from its very inception.

Though today it has more than 400 locations in three countries,[7] Whole Foods Market was born in 1978 as a 3,000-square-foot

natural foods store.[8] It would be an understatement to say that John
Mackey was deeply committed to his vision. He earned so little in
the early days that he and his cofounder lived in an office above the
store. "There was no shower or bathtub there, so we took 'show-
ers' in the store's Hobart dishwasher when we needed to clean up,"
Mackey related in his book *Conscious Capitalism*.[9]

Most of us know that there is something special about the culture
of Whole Foods. Whole Foods is *Fortune* magazine's most admired
company in its industry in 2015, and has been on the "100 Best Companies to Work For" list for eighteen straight years.[10] Yet few companies have been able to create the culture they have built. Whole Foods'
culture feels like an extension of Mackey's personal brand of magic.

The fact is, Whole Foods is total motivation incarnate. The
phrase "total motivation" didn't exist yet, but John Mackey intuitively grasped its principles from the get-go.

In a 2006 open letter to his employees (or "team members," as
he calls them), Mackey describes how he wanted to work "simply for
the joy of the work itself and to better answer the call to service that
I feel so clearly in my own heart."[11] He perfectly describes play and
purpose, the first two of the six motives.

Using our cultural measurement tool, we tested how much employees at Whole Foods felt each of the six motives.[12] Whole Foods creates
far more play, purpose, and potential (the three direct motivators) and
less emotional pressure, economic pressure, and inertia (the three indirect motivators) than many of its peers. As a result, it produces *triple*
the level of total motivation versus the average of three competitors.
This high level of ToMo is what drove the two Whole Foods team
members to keep thinking about their business even on their commute
home, and it is also what has made Whole Foods a market leader.

Whole Foods' total motivation advantage isn't an accident. It is
intentional. The company purposefully builds direct motives into the
workplace. It increases play through store-level, self-managed teams,

whose members actually get to make decisions.[13] Each department decides who to hire and what to stock. Individual team members have the opportunity to experiment with ways to improve their performance. The company enables this decentralized decision making with unprecedented transparency. Every team knows exactly how comparable groups in other stores are performing. They even know how much everyone in the store is paid. So complete is the information that in the mid-nineties, all 6,500 team members were deemed insiders by the Securities and Exchange Commission, suggesting they had access to privileged company information.[14]

Whole Foods increases the purpose motive through a compelling and credible mission. As Mackey and Rajendra Sisoda wrote in *Conscious Capitalism*, "Business has a much broader positive impact on the world when it is based on a higher purpose that goes beyond only generating profits and creating shareholder value. Purpose is the reason a company exists. A compelling sense of higher purpose creates an extraordinary degree of engagement among all stakeholders and catalyzes creativity, innovation, and organizational commitment."[15]

At Whole Foods, store employees feel the difference. As one team member wrote to us, "I love the company I work for. I can get behind their mission statement, attitude, work ethic, and events. My co-workers are like family to me and the company has gone out of their way to provide for and accommodate me."

Total motivation, however, isn't just about how employees feel. Because total motivation fuels adaptive performance, we can see its effect on how customers feel too. Great customer experience occurs when an organization adapts its approach around each individual. When we look at Whole Foods and other grocers, we can see this connection clearly in the data (see Figure 2).[16]

We found this tight relationship between ToMo and customer experience throughout many industries, including banking, airlines, cable TV, and retail. And this was just the tip of the iceberg. We saw the same relationship between ToMo and salesmanship, problem-solving ability, citizenship, resilience, and creativity—all forms of adaptive performance.

Figure 2: Total motivation drives adaptive performance, which can lead to better experiences for your customers.

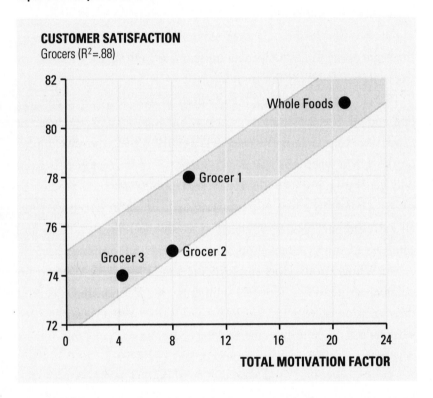

Even professional services firms can thrive or dive based on their total motivation. Dewey & LeBoeuf, founded in 1909, was one of the nation's top law firms.[17] One of its named partners was New York governor and would-be US president Thomas Dewey,[18] of the infamous 1948 *Chicago Daily Tribune* "Dewey defeats Truman" headline.[19] Through a series of mergers, Dewey & LeBoeuf became one of the biggest legal partnerships in the world. Yet the death spiral of emotional pressure, economic pressure, and inertia led to its untimely dissolution in 2012. According to an analysis by the *New York Times:*

> *Many observers say the root causes of Dewey's fall are not unique . . . unfettered growth, often through mergers; the aggressive poaching of lawyers from rivals by offering outsize pay packages; and a widening spread between the salaries of the firm's top partners and its most junior ones.*
>
> *These trends, they say, have destroyed the fabric of a law firm partnership, where a shared sense of purpose once created willingness to weather difficult times. Many large firms have discarded the traditional notions of partnership—loyalty, collegiality, a sense of equality—and instead transformed themselves into bottom-line, profit-maximizing businesses.*[20]

"Because the partnership lacks any shared cultural values or history, money becomes the core value holding the firm together," said William Henderson, a law professor at Indiana University who studies law firms. "Money is weak glue."[21]

Dewey destroyed its adaptability and resilience when it changed its culture to one that focused less on direct motivators, like a "shared sense of purpose," and more on indirect motivators, like money. Predictably, as the total motivation of the Firm decreased, so did its adaptive performance. When the Firm hit a rough patch, partners fled and the Firm collapsed.

Total motivation is so fundamental to who we are as people that it can predict which marriages will be happy,[22] whether you'll lose weight on your new diet,[23] which athletes will stick with their sports,[24] and which students will stay in school.

Researchers measured the total motivation of a group of high school students and, one year later, recorded who had dropped out.[25] The dropouts had a dramatically lower total motivation factor. Imagine what you could do, as an educator, a coach, or a businessperson, if you could tell what motivated each person, and then systematically build cultures to improve performance.

GOING FORWARD

Too many well-laid business plans fall flat because of mediocre cultures. Too many people are miserable at work. Too many cultures, even great ones, atrophy over time. We too have worked in bad cultures, built bad cultures, and in some cases propagated bad cultures, all without understanding what we were doing. We didn't realize that we were causing performance and people to suffer.

While most of us have a hunch that culture is important, few of us can define it, or explain why it matters. We wrote this book to fill that gap.

Total motivation cultures are more productive and more profitable. Their people, their customers, and their shareholders are happier. Our own mission is to help create a world where every person is performing at their highest levels, and where every organization is an inspiring, adaptive, and thriving workplace.

RESOURCES AS YOU READ

As you read, you may find it helpful to understand your own levels of total motivation, and the ToMo of your organization. On our website, www.primedtoperform.com, you can take our brief total motivation quiz to understand what drives you. You can also send a short ToMo survey to your team, division, or entire organization, to understand what drives your culture. The survey is free, and takes only a few minutes to complete. It will help you understand the strengths and weaknesses of your culture, and enable you to track how your culture changes over time. It can be particularly helpful to understand where your culture is today as you read Part IV on how to create transformational change.

We continue to share more insights and research on LinkedIn and Twitter (@NeelVF or @McGregorLE). If you have ideas or questions, or want to share stories of your own culture journeys, feel free to email us at neel@primedtoperform.com or lindsay@primedtoperform.com.

PART I

What Is Total Motivation?

| High-Performing Cultures Begin with a Surprisingly
Simple Building Block: Your People's "Why"

The Motive Spectrum

| *The Six Reasons We Work*

The United Arab Emirates (UAE) has a serious problem: too many of its citizens are overweight or obese.[1] In the summer of 2013, the government of Dubai took action, launching a weight-loss challenge it called "Your Weight in Gold."

Dubai followed a playbook that many companies have used to change people's behavior: it offered a reward. For every kilogram of weight that residents lost between July and mid-August, it would pay them one gram of gold.[2] That seems like a reasonable strategy—after all, people will do a lot more than diet in the pursuit of gold. And sure enough, when the contest ended, about 25 percent of the 10,666[3] people who entered[4] the challenge had lost enough weight to claim a prize. Big success, right?

Not exactly. Scientists have studied what happens when people are paid to lose weight, and the results are not very encouraging. Consider an experiment conducted by four university researchers.[5] Coincidentally, its design is very similar to "Your Weight in Gold."

During a three-week program, test subjects were paid about $50 per week (roughly the value of a gram of gold[6]) to lose weight. After the program ended, their weight was tracked for another four months. But before it all began, the test subjects' motives for joining the program were assessed. Why were they there?

Imagine two hypothetical test subjects, Jake and Christine. Jake sees the flyer for the experiment and decides to sign up because he needs the money. The money is his motive. Christine sees the same flyer and decides it would be a great opportunity to lose weight. For her, the money is not the main factor. She's there for the learning, the coaching, and the community.

Jake and the other test subjects like him formed the financially motivated group. Christine and the other subjects like her formed the nonfinancially motivated group. As you'd expect, Jake and the financially motivated group lost weight—0.25 percent of their weight on average. It looked like the financial reward had somewhat successfully motivated behavior. Mission accomplished!

Not so fast. . . .

After they'd collected their rewards, Jake and his group went on to *gain* weight. Over the next four months, Jake and his group gained back the weight they had lost and added more on top of that. The reward might have instigated behavior, but it didn't build persistence.

Meanwhile, Christine and her group saw better results. On average they lost about 1.5 percent of their weight (six times what Jake and his group lost) during the program. Over the next four months, they kept the weight off and lost even more (another half a percent).

The experiment has a simple yet profound lesson: *why* people participate in an activity affects their performance in that activity. Their motive affects their performance.

Even though many organizations rely on money to drive performance, most of us know from our personal lives that motivation is much more complicated. There is a spectrum of reasons why people do their jobs (or lose weight). Understanding that spectrum is the key to creating the highest levels of performance.

THE MOTIVE SPECTRUM

Before we can explain a phenomenon scientifically, it is easy to mistake it for magic.

When we speak with leaders about culture building, they often tell us that it takes special powers of the kind that only a Steve Jobs (Apple), Herb Kelleher (Southwest Airlines), Phil Jackson (legendary coach of the Chicago Bulls and LA Lakers), or some other wizard is graced with. What hope do mere mortals have?

A good first step to turning magic into science is the creation of a framework that helps make predictions. Ideally, this framework organizes all of your scientific observations in a way that helps you see new patterns. This is what happened with alchemy.

Alchemists believed that all matter was composed of earth, air, fire, and water. For centuries they mixed and remixed materials in an attempt to produce the mythical philosopher's stone, which they believed had the power to transform base metals, like iron, into gold, and to confer immortality. Instead, they discovered chemistry.

Chemistry took its biggest leap forward in 1869 when the Russian chemist Dmitri Mendeleev produced the Periodic Table of Elements. "I saw in a dream a table where all elements fell into place as required," he said later. "Awakening, I immediately wrote it down on a piece of paper."[7] Thanks to this organizing framework, Mendeleev was able to predict the properties of elements that had not yet been discovered.[8] What had once been magic was now firmly in the realm of science.

In our own day, an analogous discovery has sparked a great flowering of the science of human performance. In the mid-1980s, Edward L. Deci and Richard M. Ryan of the University of Rochester published an audacious framework of human motives, a single spectrum cataloging the reasons that people engage in activities. They called it "self-determination theory."[9] Their seminal book *Intrinsic Motivation and Self-Determination in Human Behavior* has been cited over twenty-two thousand times in other research. Compare that to the average number of citations a paper gets after ten years, just twenty.[10] We've been deeply influenced by Deci and Ryan in our own research and practice. (A deeper explanation of how we have built on their and other researchers' work can be found in the Appendix: "The Scientist's Toothbrush").

Figure 3: The motive spectrum in its entirety. The circles symbolically represent a person's motive. For example, the purpose motive is mostly driven by the work itself, and partly by your own beliefs.

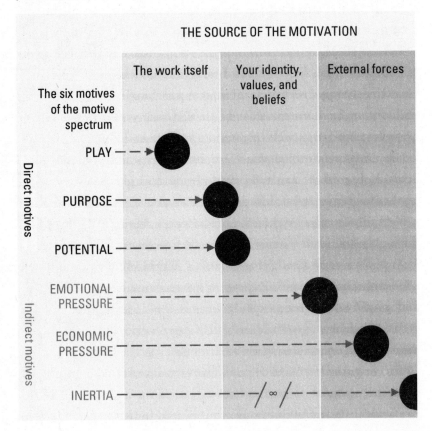

It turns out that there is a spectrum of reasons, or motives, for why people perform an activity. The first three, which we call the direct motives, are directly linked to the activity (in our case, work)

and drive performance. The next three, the indirect motives, are further removed from the work itself and frequently harm performance.

Let's go through the motives one by one, starting with *play*.

THE DIRECT MOTIVES

Play

You're most likely to lose weight—or succeed in any other endeavor—when your motive is play. Play occurs when you're engaging in an activity simply because you enjoy doing it. The work itself is its own reward. Scientists describe this motive as "intrinsic."

Play is what compels you to take up hobbies, from solving crossword puzzles to making scrapbooks to mixing music. You may find play in weight loss by experimenting with healthy recipes or seeking out new restaurants that offer healthy options. Many of us are lucky enough to find play in the workplace too, when we do what we do simply because we enjoy doing it.

Curiosity and experimentation are at the heart of play. People intrinsically enjoy learning and adapting. We instinctively seek out opportunities to play.

Some companies actively encourage their employees to play in their work. Toyota gives factory workers the opportunity to come up with and test new tools and ideas on the assembly line. W. L. Gore & Associates, Google, and a number of other companies encourage play by giving people free time or resources to explore their own ideas. Zappos and Southwest Airlines encourage their people to treat each customer interaction as play. In each case, the organization encourages its people to indulge their curiosity—to play in the work itself.

Play at work should not be confused with your people playing Ping-Pong or foosball in the break room. For your people to feel play at work, the motive must be fueled by the work itself, not the distraction. Because the play motive is created by the work itself, play is the most direct and most powerful driver of high performance.

Purpose

A step away from the work itself is the purpose motive.[11] The purpose motive occurs when you do an activity because you value the *outcome* of the activity (versus the activity itself). You may or may not enjoy the work you do, but you value its impact. You may work as a nurse, for example, because you want to heal patients. You spend your career studying culture because you believe in the impact your work can have on others. Dieters may not enjoy preparing or eating healthy meals, but they deeply value their own health, an outcome of healthy eating.

You feel the purpose motive in the workplace when your values and beliefs align with the impact of the work. Apple creates products that inspire and empower its customers, a purpose that is compelling and credible. The medical devices that Medtronic makes save lives; when its engineers and technicians see their products in action, it has a powerful effect on them.[12] Walmart's financial services division fueled purpose by kicking off its management meetings with a review of how much money the division had saved its customers rather than how much money Walmart had made for itself.[13] As you'll see in the coming chapters, a thoughtful organization can create authentic purpose for just about any type of work. Yet one of the biggest mistakes a company can make is trumpeting a grandiose purpose that isn't authentic. If a purpose doesn't feel credible, it won't improve your motivation.

The purpose motive is one step removed from the work, because the motive isn't the work itself but its outcome. While the purpose motive is a powerful driver of performance, the fact that it's a step removed from the work typically makes it a less powerful motive than play.

Potential

The third motive is potential. The potential motive occurs when you find a *second order* outcome (versus a direct outcome) of the work that aligns with your values or beliefs. You do the work because it will eventually lead to something you believe is important, such as your personal goals.

For example, you may work as a paralegal because it will help you get into law school. You may not enjoy the day-to-day work of filing briefs (no play motive), and you may not care about helping the kinds of clients your firm represents (no purpose motive), but you continue to do the job because you want to be a public defender one day. You are working to bring about a second order outcome that you do believe in.

Dieters motivated by potential eat healthfully to achieve other things they care about—the ability to run faster on the football field, for example, or to keep up with their kids.

When a company describes a job as a good "stepping-stone," they're attempting to instill the potential motive. Some companies go out of their way to enhance the potential motive, offering classes that build skills or knowledge. General Electric draws talent through its reputation as "the leadership factory" for future CEOs.[14]

The potential motive is not as powerful as play or purpose, since it relates to a second order outcome of the work, which is two (or more) steps removed from the work itself.

We call play, purpose, and potential the "direct" motives because they're the most directly connected to the work itself. As a result, they typically result in the highest levels of performance. If you remember only one thing from *Primed to Perform*, it should be that a culture that inspires people to do their jobs for play, purpose, and potential creates the highest and most sustainable performance.

You would think that the more reasons you give someone to work, the more dedicated they would be. But not all motives lead to higher levels of performance. Moving further along the motive spectrum, we reach the "indirect motives," motives that are no longer connected to the work itself. These typically reduce performance.

THE INDIRECT MOTIVES
Emotional Pressure

The first indirect motive, emotional pressure, occurs when emotions such as disappointment, guilt, or shame compel you to perform an activity. These emotions are related to your beliefs (your self-perception) and external forces (the judgments of other people). The work itself is no longer the reason you're working.

You may practice the piano so you don't disappoint your mother.

You may stay in a job because its prestige boosts your self-esteem.

A dieter may eat healthy meals because he's embarrassed by how he looks, or because he feels guilty when his partner catches him with his hand in the cookie jar.

In each case, the motive is not directly connected to the work. It is indirect.

Have you ever looked at your Facebook newsfeed and thought to yourself, "Everyone in the world is having fun right now except for me!" Then you feel compelled to go to a club that evening. Your action—going to the club—isn't driven by the play you feel in dancing or socializing. Instead, it's driven by the emotional pressure created by your newsfeed (a phenomenon known as FoMo or "fear of missing out").

When your motive to work is emotional pressure, your performance tends to suffer.

We see the impact of emotional pressure in workplaces everywhere. For example, a junior employee in a meeting with a senior executive is so worried about what the executive thinks of him that he "chokes under pressure." Emotional pressure can cause fear of public speaking, or writer's block, when the fear of judgment distracts you from the actual activity.

High-performing cultures reduce emotional pressure. Medallia, a fast-growing technology company, teaches people how to be vulnerable in their weeklong onboarding program for new employees. One asset management firm, where financial managers are usually wrong more than 40 percent of the time, brought in an Olympic coach to help them cope with the fear of failure.

When people work because of emotional pressure, their motivation is no longer connected to the work itself, so their performance tends to suffer. But emotional pressure is the weakest of the three indirect motives. The effects of economic pressure can be much worse.

Economic Pressure

Economic pressure is when you do an activity solely to win a reward or avoid punishment. The motive is separate from the work itself and separate from your own identity (see Figure 3 for an illustration of this separation). In business, this often occurs when you're trying to gain a bonus or a promotion, avoid being fired, or escape the bullying of an angry boss. Economic pressure can occur outside the workplace whenever you feel forced to do something.

Put yourself in the place of a marketer who completes what she thinks is a pointless blog post because her bonus requires her to publish ten a quarter. Or a Los Angeles talent agent's assistant who was required to join his boss's training for a marathon. In each case, something separate from the work itself—a bonus, a boss—was compelling behavior.

The biggest misconception about the economic motive is that it is strictly a matter of money. In a study we conducted involving more than ten thousand workers, we looked to see how the economic motive changes with household income. We expected to find that the people with the least income experienced the highest economic pressure. Instead, we learned that income and the economic motive were statistically unrelated. People at any income level can feel economic pressure at work.

This is an important insight. Money alone does not cause the economic motive. We saw this play out with the dieters in the weight-loss experiment. While all of them could earn financial rewards, some were dieting *because* of the reward while others were not. If money is the sole reason you're participating in an activity, it will typically diminish performance. If you're participating for other reasons, money won't cause a problem. This is why we need to understand all the motives together.

Imagine a Boy Scout who learns how to play chess so he can earn a merit badge, for example. He doesn't actually care about chess; he just wants the badge. This Boy Scout has an economic motive. Another Boy Scout may learn chess because he really enjoys learning, or because he's fascinated by chess. This Scout will also earn a badge, but the badge wasn't his reason for learning. His motive was play. All other things being equal, the odds are that the Boy Scout motivated by play will beat the Boy Scout with the economic motive in a match.

As you'll see throughout *Primed to Perform*, money itself is not the core issue. There are situations where money works, and situations where it doesn't. It all depends on whether or not the reward or punishment is the motive behind the activity, and whether the activity would benefit from adaptive performance.

Inertia

The most indirect motive of all is inertia. With inertia, your motive for working is so distant from the work itself that you can no longer say where it comes from—you do what you do simply because you did it yesterday. This leads to the worst performance of all.

A university student may continue to attend school purely because of inertia—he's on the path already, so he just keeps slogging.

An executive continues at his job not because he's engaged in it, but because he can't think of a good reason to leave.

One CEO of a company in the technology industry boasted about his great employee retention. But when we spoke to his employees, it was clear to us that inertia accounted for their retention—not play, purpose, or potential. It isn't enough to have employees who stay. You want them to stay for the right reasons.

As destructive and insidious as it is, inertia is surprisingly common in the workplace. In our research, we've found that a large proportion of the employee population feels like they work in their current job for no good reason. Zappos, the online shoe retailer, has found a clever way to nip this condition in the bud. After four weeks of new-hire training, it offers one month's salary to anyone who quits. Zappos doesn't want anyone hanging around "just because."[15]

WHY WE WORK

If using emotional and economic pressure to inspire weight loss doesn't work, then what does? When human performance expert Luc G. Pelletier and his colleagues conducted a formal study of the relationships between the six motives and dieting, they found that play, purpose, and potential led to better eating behaviors.[16] Emotional pressure, economic pressure, and inertia made things worse.[17]

Their research, and the research of hundreds of others, gives us the two key findings of the motive spectrum:

1. Direct motives typically increase performance and indirect motives typically decrease it. (This point can be difficult to swallow, so Chapter 3, "Rethinking Performance," shares more on why this is true.)
2. The more directly connected the motive is to the activity itself, the better performance becomes. Play is the motive that is closest to the work itself, so it is the most powerful. Purpose is one step removed, so it is the second strongest. Potential is two or more steps removed from the activity, so it is the third strongest (see Figure 3 for an illustration of this distance).

Together, these two insights define total motivation (ToMo, for short). High levels of total motivation occur when a person feels more of the direct motives and less of the indirect motives. Total motivation is the foundation of any high-performing culture.

Author Dan Pink explains this finding eloquently in his bestselling book *Drive*, which introduced a whole generation of leaders to the concept of intrinsic motivation:

In business, we tend to obsess over the "how"— as in "Here's how to do it." Yet we rarely discuss the "why"— as in "Here's why we're doing it." But it's often difficult to do something exceptionally well if we don't know the reasons we're doing it in the first place.[18]

BETTING ON THE UNDERDOG

One of our early breakthrough applications of the science of the motive spectrum to the business world was in the customer service call center of a bank's consumer loans business (we've disguised some details of this story to protect the client's anonymity).

The typical call center isn't known for its warm décor or feng shui. A sign outside this one, which also doubles as a tornado shelter, reminds employees that no guns are allowed inside. Its people work in rows upon rows of cubicles in a space that's big enough to hold several football fields. There's no Ping-Pong table, no fully stocked kitchen, and no official corporate masseuse.

One customer service agent,[19] Eric, had left a career as a schoolteacher to better support his wife and two kids. He spent all day on the phone, sometimes answering in-bound calls, but usually convincing people not to hang up when he dialed them. He spoke to hundreds of people a week. His job, or so he was told, was to handle the calls quickly. He felt like a cog in a giant machine.

The call center used all the "best practices" of the day. Experts had created scripts of talking points, giving the agents the exact words they should use with their customers. The agents themselves had functional specialties so they could focus on only one task. The center as a whole had a bold yet achievable goal that was broken down into specific subgoals for each team and individual. To keep morale high, a stuffed monkey was placed on top of the cube of the worker who'd had the best day. Bonuses were based on performance, which was reviewed by managers in weekly meetings. But none of those practices increased direct motives or reduced indirect ones. Instead, they did exactly the reverse.

We made a bet with our client. We said that by building a team culture that maximized total motivation, we could get the lowest performers in the shop to perform better than the status quo. Due to his own low ToMo, our client was eager to see us lose our bet (another issue with this organization's culture).

The team we put together included not only some of the call center's worst performers, but also some complete newbies who'd never made a professional call in their lives. During our first meeting with the team, we went around the table introducing ourselves. "My name is Rick," said one of our soon-to-be-agents. "You may recognize me because until today, I was the security guard of the building." Our Bad News Bears had six months to beat the incumbents.

To the surprise and chagrin of everyone watching, the first thing we did was reduce the economic pressure. We wouldn't advocate this in every case, but for this experiment we eliminated incentive compensation and increased base pay. We also eliminated all the performance management reviews that were designed to ramp up emotional pressure. Lastly, we gave our team the opportunity to "opt-in," reducing their inertia.

Then we focused on play. Previously, the company had devoted most of its energy to ensuring that employees followed the large number of laws and regulations involved in consumer lending. We too made sure that the rules were clear, but we spent half of our time helping the group understand where they had the freedom to experiment and explore through creativity and problem solving—in other words, where they could play.

We did away with their scripts.

We launched daily huddles in which the agents helped one another figure out complicated cases.

We installed a hotline to get quick approvals for nonstandard courses of action.

The highlight of each week was the Monday working meeting, where agents presented their most difficult cases to three levels of management and collectively brainstormed solutions.

To increase purpose, we gave every agent his own set of customers—two hundred people he would work with from the beginning to the end of their journey. It was the middle of the financial crisis and many of those customers had lost their jobs and were seeking to modify their loans. Each agent could now see the impact his or her work was having on customers' lives. Managers started talking about their group's purpose: helping customers in need. They emphasized new values, like always asking for help if it would benefit a customer. Whenever a customer was helped through some Herculean effort, the story was celebrated.

Eric started hustling to make sure the families he now knew personally got their paperwork in on time. Rick became a master in calming frightened customers. Lakisha beamed when she found a new source of income for a retiree and became an expert in figuring out customer cash flows.

As team members found ways to improve their own performance, they would share their newfound skills with their peers. Their energy was palpable. Better yet, their performance went through the roof. At the end of the day, our team didn't just surpass the status quo—it beat it by 200 percent. All this in an industry known for being slow to change and in a job function whose workers were traditionally treated like automatons.

A senior executive of the bank eventually interviewed the agents to find out how we could have found so much upside in a call center that had supposedly been optimized long before. The most experienced agent told him, "I've been with the bank for fifteen years, and this is the first time I felt like what I did mattered." "For the longest time, what we were doing didn't feel right," another said. "Now our work, the interests of the bank, and the interests of the customer are all the same."

We realized something important: the *why* changes the *how*. When people were driven by the direct motives, they started doing their work differently. They went above and beyond.

These results shouldn't come as a surprise. One of the thinkers who has greatly influenced our work, Adam Grant, a Wharton professor and author of the book *Give and Take*, carried out a formal study of a sales force at a company that had eliminated financial incentives after salespeople falsified data to earn commissions (Chapter 3, "Rethinking Performance," includes more on how the motive spectrum can influence bad behavior).[20] He found that after controlling for tactical performance (for example, the number of calls a person made), those with

Figure 4: Sales representatives with high direct motivation and low indirect motivation dramatically outperformed the rest of the population in revenue generation.

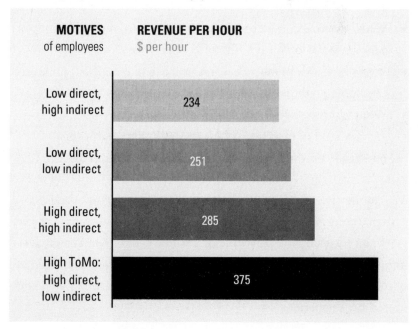

low direct motives and high indirect motives (like a person with little play but lots of economic pressure) produced about $234 in revenue per hour. On the other hand, those with the highest total motivation (like a person with the play motive and little economic pressure) sold $375 per hour. That's a 60 percent difference from a factor that few leaders actively manage and few cultures are designed to encourage.

GOING FORWARD

The first question we now ask anyone who is trying to build a great culture is: *why* do your people come to work every day?

If they come to work because their organization inspires the direct motives—play, purpose, and potential—they are likely performing at their best. If the culture is dominated by indirect motives—emotional pressure, economic pressure, or inertia—their performance is likely to be much worse.

Take a moment to ask yourself how the motive spectrum affects your life as a leader, parent, teacher, or coach:

- Where do you find play, purpose, and potential in your daily activities?
- When have you made a decision because of emotional pressure, economic pressure, or inertia?
- What motivates your colleagues at work?
- Do you tend to motivate others through play, purpose, and potential? Or do you use emotional or economic pressure?

The motive spectrum is the periodic table of great cultures—a systematic organizing framework for the relationships between work, motivation, and performance. While every great culture has a unique personality, behind each and every one of them is the science of the motive spectrum. Using its insights, any culture can be reengineered for the better.

The Total Motivation Factor

"We don't have a culture problem," a CEO we met with two years ago confidently proclaimed. "There's a long line of people who want to work here, so it doesn't matter if my people burn out." He ran a large technology company that had been performing well over the previous few years, although, at the time of this writing, it is stagnating. Good performance can lead to cultural complacency, and this place was no exception.

One of his executives had told us in confidence that the organization's culture was toxic. He hoped we could convince his boss that it was holding the company back. In our hour with the chief executive, it became clear that the very notion of "culture" was voodoo to him.

Two weeks later we met a visionary executive at a Fortune 500 financial institution who believed in the importance of culture, and even had a strong intuitive grasp of the principles of the motive spectrum. About ten minutes into our conversation, she stopped us and said, "You've given me a way to explain everything I've believed in and worked toward my whole professional life."

We asked her what was preventing her from taking the bull by the horns and making her company's culture as high performing as it could be. Clearly it wasn't a lack of understanding or belief. It was simply that she lacked a toolbox. Even a professor of engineering can't repair his car without the right tools.

In this tale of two executives—the skeptic and the believer—we see the biggest barriers that prevent organizations from building high-performing cultures. The skeptics don't understand or believe the science. The believers lack the tools to put the science into practice.

We too were skeptics once. As data-oriented people, we wanted evidence that culture mattered. Then we began to study human performance, and saw how universal the motive spectrum is. We realized that culture can be measured, and that it affects performance. This insight not only turned us into believers, it gave us our most powerful tool.

PREDICTABLE AND UNIVERSAL

Before we could set out to build and rebuild organizations on the principles of total motivation, we needed to know if we could trust it. Did total motivation behave in a predictable way? Was it universal, applicable to all people in all situations, or was it true only some of the time? If it was predictable and universal, we should be able to measure it. As Princeton University physicist John Wheeler said, "No elementary phenomenon is a real phenomenon until it is a measured phenomenon."[1]

There can be no doubt that total motivation is universal. There are literally hundreds of experiments in the academic literature that demonstrate the motive spectrum at work. It has been validated around the world, from China to Canada, Germany to Indonesia.[2] It doesn't just have a bearing on people's jobs, but on their relationships, their parenting skills, and their health.

Take marriage. Four of the leaders in the motivation field surveyed a set of couples who lived together to find out why they stayed together.[3] Most of the couples were married; the average relationship was almost thirteen years. The researchers didn't ask why the couples got together in the first place, or what their best qualities were. The questions were designed to assess the relative strengths of each of the six motives in the motive spectrum at that moment in their relationship. One couple may love doing things together, like hiking, or have the same sense of curiosity for new experiences, like traveling. They share a common form of play. Another couple might share the same deep purpose—perhaps a commitment to raising their children. Still another couple may stay together because their quality of life would decline if they separated (economic pressure), or because they don't want to ruin their reputation in the community (emotional pressure).

Sure enough, the basic principles of the motive spectrum predicted the happiest relationships. First, direct motives (play, purpose, and potential) increased performance (or in this case, the ability of couples to solve problems and sustain a happy marriage). Indirect motives (emotional pressure, economic pressure, and inertia) decreased performance. Second, the closer the motive was to the activity itself, the better performance. Play was more powerful than purpose, followed by potential. Emotional pressure began to have a negative effect, economic pressure was worse, and inertia was at the very bottom. The old adage holds true: couples that play together stay together.[4] But the motive spectrum doesn't just apply to your marriage.

Parents and teachers worry about children's academic success, and wonder how they can influence it. The motive spectrum supplies an answer: by teaching them to associate learning with play.

Researchers asked more than nine hundred high school students "Why do you go to school?"[5] As with the questions the married couples answered, the survey was designed to reveal the relative weight of the motives of the spectrum. At the end of the academic year, they calculated how those motives correlated with their grades. Not surprisingly, direct motives were most strongly correlated with positive academic performance and indirect motives with poorer academic performance.[6]

The motive spectrum applies to health and fitness. When researchers examined physical and emotional exhaustion among elite athletes from fifty-one different sports,[7] the ones who experienced the least amount of burnout weren't necessarily the best athletes. They were the ones who were the most motivated by play, purpose, and potential.[8] On the other hand, those with indirect motives were more likely to feel exhausted.

The motive spectrum applies to anyone trying to stay in shape, not just elite athletes.[9] Play works best. Think about the person you know who tried one sport after another until she discovered how much she loved rock climbing. She's probably much more committed to fitness than your friend who forces himself to run on a basement treadmill.

The second best motivator is purpose—aligning an activity with your values and beliefs. The next time you find yourself flagging toward the end of a run, say to yourself, "I'm the kind of person who believes in going all out." If you convince yourself, you'll get an extra burst of motivation to cross the finish line.

Many of us understand the motive spectrum intuitively; we use it when we try to change the behavior of our children and our spouses. But once we cross the threshold of our workplaces, we seem to forget all about it.

A researcher from the University of Quebec wanted to understand how the motive spectrum affects the performance of high school principals—a job in which creativity and resilience are critical. The work is tough; 15 to 30 percent of principals leave their jobs every year.[10] The researchers studied 570 principals to find out whether their motives for working affected their commitment, satisfaction, and burnout levels.[11]

As predicted, the most committed and satisfied principals were the ones with higher total motivation (higher direct motives and lower indirect motives). They enjoyed their daily activities and were stimulated by them. Some found play in their administrative duties, some in instructional leadership, and still others in their role as community liaisons. They had lower levels of burnout, and were actually better leaders to their people (something we will learn more about in Chapter 8, "The Fire Starters"). They were more likely to engage staff in problem solving, respect the opinions of others, and communicate a vision for the future.

On the other hand, the principals with lower total motivation had the opposite profile. They tended to feel more emotional pressure—the need to prove to themselves that they could do the job. They also tended to feel more inertia—the feeling that their work was pointless. As a result their commitment to the work suffered and they felt more burned out.

Yet despite hundreds of studies, we wanted to test the motive spectrum for ourselves, in the workplace. We surveyed tens of thousands of workers across such diverse organizations as an asset management fund, a professional services firm, school systems, chains of fast-food restaurants, retail stores, and banks. Through our own analysis, we saw that the two principles of total motivation are everywhere, and that they follow a pattern.

First, direct motives typically enhance performance while indirect motives decrease it. Second, the closer the motive is to the work itself, the better the performance. Play is the strongest motive. Then purpose. Then potential. Inertia is the most destructive, then economic pressure, then emotional pressure.

Because these two principles are so common, we can simplify them into a single, measurable concept: the total motivation factor. In the land of the blind, the one-eyed man is king. With the total motivation factor, you'll have two eyes, a microscope, and long-range radar.

With this tool, we can finally turn the art of creating high-performing cultures into an engineering discipline.

WHERE THE RUBBER MEETS THE ROAD

The ToMo factor collapses the six motives of the spectrum into a single metric. To arrive at this number, we add up how much of the direct motives each person in an organization feels, and then we subtract their indirect motives. If play or purpose goes up, for example, ToMo goes up. If emotional or economic pressure goes up, ToMo goes down. Those with a higher total motivation factor usually outperform, as you'll see in the experiments and case studies that follow.

Of course, the math is a little more complicated due to the second principle—the fact that the further your motive is from the activity itself, the lower your level of performance. Because of this, we assign different weights to the motives. Play is about two times more powerful than purpose, which is about three times more powerful than potential. Inertia is about two times more damaging than economic pressure, which is about three times more damaging than emotional pressure. (The exact weights, and a full explanation of how you can calculate your own ToMo, are in Chapter 7, "The Torch of Performance." You can find the free survey online at www.primedtoperform.com.)

The result is a number on a scale from -100 to 100. If your score is positive, you have more direct motives than indirect ones. If your score is negative, you have more indirect motives than direct ones.

This measurement allows us to make some powerful predictions. In still another study of high school students, a leading researcher asked thousands of students why they attended school.[12] His questions were designed to measure the strength of the motives. Using their answers, we were able to calculate the students' ToMo factors.[13] Students who would still be in school a year later had an average ToMo of 17. Students who dropped out had an average ToMo of only 2.

The same thing applies to athletes. Another group of leading total motivation researchers measured the ToMo of elite, nationally ranked swimmers. Two years later, they observed which ones were still competing and which had dropped out. The active athletes had an initial ToMo of 48. The dropouts had an initial ToMo of 23.[14]

Being able to objectively measure the strength of a culture is a true game changer. If you are a school leader, you can track how your students' ToMo is shifting, and adjust your culture to address it. If you are a business leader, you can strategically manage your culture based not just on your gut instincts, but on objective, quantified facts. We once showed the CEO of a multibillion-dollar asset management firm that his highest performing asset managers also had the highest ToMo. His reaction was common: "You just found a factor of performance we have never seen before."

BIRD'S-EYE VIEW

Of all the large organizations whose ToMo we've measured, Southwest Airlines' levels are highest, at 41. That's incredible for a company with over 46,000 employees.[15] Many small companies and start-ups struggle to get that high. The airline with the lowest total motivation in our research had a ToMo of just 22 points. Despite being in a commoditized industry, Southwest was able to double ToMo through its culture.

It's hard to imagine how an airline employee's job would differ that much from one airline to another. The work of flight attendants and gate agents and baggage handlers should be almost identical. Yet when we surveyed employees from Southwest and three other major airlines, we found that Southwest's culture inspired a dramatically higher sense of play, purpose, and potential than the others. So wide is its play, purpose, and potential gap that it offsets the fact that it also creates more emotional and economic pressure than its competitors.

Southwest Airlines achieves its high levels of total motivation even though the cards are stacked against it. It is a low-cost provider, not a high-status, high-end luxury player, like Apple or Nordstrom.

Figure 5: Total motivation and its components measured for Southwest and three competitors.

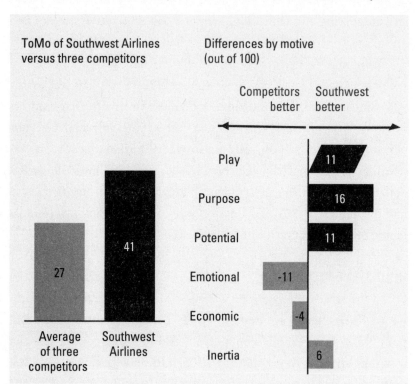

Its flights are mostly short distances, which are more expensive to operate per mile than cross-country flights.[16] Its industry is plagued by bankruptcies. Yet 2014 was Southwest's forty-second consecutive year of profitability.[17]

Southwest's founder and former CEO Herb Kelleher has built play and purpose into the company's DNA. You might have witnessed Southwest's flight attendants at play. Marty Cobb's safety announcement went viral. As colleagues held up life vests, she warned passengers that in the "highly unlikely event" that the plane lands near a "hot tub, everybody gets their very own teeny weeny yellow Southwest bikini."[18] Customers enjoyed themselves, but at the same time they were paying attention to important information.

Fostering play at work has been an explicit part of Southwest's strategy to deliver what they call POS—positively outrageous service. Potential employees have been asked in job interviews: "Tell me how you recently used your sense of humor in a work environment. Tell me how you have used humor to defuse a difficult situation."[19] Play and purpose are also assisted by limiting the number of management layers between the CEO and the front line, and enabling local employees at each airport to make decisions.[20] "We've tried to create an environment where people . . . don't have to convene a meeting of the sages in order to get something done," Kelleher said, according to Southwest researchers Jackie and Kevin Freiberg.[21] By doing so, Southwest inspires curiosity and experimentation.

Southwest's stated mission is "dedication to the highest quality of Customer Service delivered with a sense of warmth, friendliness, individual pride, and Company Spirit."[22] It makes a point of finding, sharing, and celebrating examples of employees who go above and beyond to accomplish the company's purpose. For example, customer service agent Kelli spotted a family in the airport saying goodbye to their dad, a soldier being deployed to Kuwait for six months.[23] She got the whole family through security to the gate so they could spend a little extra time together. Flight attendant Amanda Gauger was off-duty, waiting for a flight, when she noticed a dad with two young daughters juggling car seats, a backpack, and a stroller. She helped them board the plane, and when it landed at its destination, she carried their car seats from one terminal to another to help them make a connection.[24] As another employee told us, "We're a customer service company that happens to be an airline."

Southwest exemplifies a powerful lesson: total motivation not only creates happy employees, it affects customers. We compared the total motivation of four different airlines' employees to their customers' levels of satisfaction.[25] We were blown away by how tightly connected these two measures are.

Figure 6: Higher ToMo for Southwest links to higher customer experience as well.

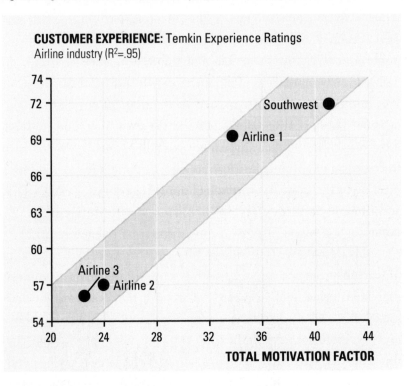

In an industry that many consider to be commoditized with the same planes and terminals, Southwest creates a much better customer experience versus the three competitors whose ToMo we also measured.

Play motivates employees to find unique ways to connect with each customer. Purpose ensures consistency. Everyone works toward the common goal of building customers' trust. When things go wrong, customers are more than willing to give the company the benefit of the doubt.

TOMO AND THE MOST ADMIRED

Take a moment to brainstorm a list of the highest performing cultures you can think of among big companies.

We've led this exercise with thousands of people and we get the same answers again and again. Southwest, Apple Stores, Starbucks, Nordstrom, and Whole Foods are always cited. They are ranked seventh, first, fifth, fourteenth, and eighteenth, respectively, on the *Fortune* Most Admired Companies list in 2015.[26] Yet when you ask people what those companies have in common, their answers become vague. Each organization has its own unique personality, values, beliefs, and traditions, and each sells very different products

Figure 7: Organizations with "magical" cultures produce significantly higher levels of total motivation in their people than their competitors do.

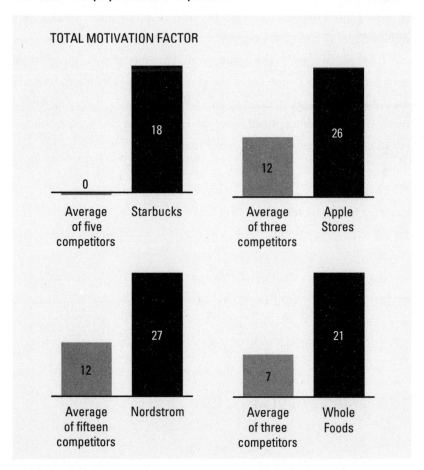

to different types of customers. But measure their total motivation and you'll see that they all outscore their competitors.

The total motivation factor allows us to see which companies are falling short of their peers. It tells us whether a culture is inspiring ToMo in all of its employees, across every factory or store. Most importantly, it allows us to track changes over time.

GOING FORWARD

The science of total motivation has been deeply studied. We've only shared a taste to get you started as culture builders. To learn more, we encourage you to read *Drive* by Dan Pink, which tells the story of how these concepts came to be, and inspired many of our own experiments in the workplace.

Total motivation is the common magic among the organizations we all admire. Fortunately for the rest of us, it is possible to improve an individual's or an organization's total motivation, creating higher levels of performance. But before we can do that, we need to understand exactly what "performance" means.

PART II

How Does Total Motivation Drive Performance?

Total Motivation Is the Missing Link Between Culture and Organizational Performance

Rethinking Performance

| *To Understand How Total Motivation Drives Performance,*
You Need to Look at Performance Through a New Lens

"Your approach is interesting," a red-faced senior executive blurted out, "but I can't believe that emotional pressure and economic pressure reduce performance." The multinational company that he worked for had called us in to introduce its executives to the concept of total motivation. We were in the middle of a three-hour meeting and he had been fidgeting in his seat since we introduced the indirect motives. When the blood rushed to his face, we knew he was about to boil over. "How can you tell me that the indirect motives reduce performance when we've all seen the opposite with our own eyes?" he demanded.

We understood where he was coming from. If someone gave you a million dollars to clean your refrigerator, you would certainly do it. If someone held a gun to your head and ordered you to get them coffee, you would do that too. Doesn't that prove that indirect motivators drive performance? If performance were simply a matter of doing things, yes. But performance is more complicated than that. To understand how the indirect motives destroy performance, we must first understand what performance really is.

CREATIVE DESTRUCTION

Every eight years or so, a sample of children from across the United States are subjected to a battery of tests that were created in 1966 by the "father of creativity," E. Paul Torrance.[1] The professor's audacious goal was to unlock the secrets of creative thought.

The tests are designed to measure creativity through a phenomenon known as divergent thinking. One section may ask you to name the things you could do with an object. Let's use a ladder, for example. The scorer looks at how many different answers you can come up with, how many categories those answers fit into, and how unique your answers are. Perhaps you come up with several uses for a ladder in the category of "reaching for things":

- To paint a wall
- To change a lightbulb
- To dust the ceiling

You may have also thought of answers that have nothing to do with reaching for things. For example, a ladder could be a:

- Bridge for a moat
- Rack for drying clothes
- Exercise station
- Obstacle course component
- Net for a tiny tennis court
- Frame for a giant abacus

Enough time has passed since the test was launched that researchers have been able to study the lifetime achievement of the children whose creativity they measured. "The correlation to lifetime creative accomplishment was more than three times stronger for childhood creativity than childhood IQ," reported *Newsweek*.[2] "Those who came up with more good ideas on Torrance's tasks grew up to be entrepreneurs, inventors, college presidents, authors, doctors, diplomats, and software developers." Creativity is crucial.

They also found that creativity and IQ are not highly linked to each other. According to Kyung Hee Kim, a creativity researcher who examined scores across 46,000 people, "the relationship between creativity test scores and IQ scores is negligible."[3] Classic intelligence alone doesn't always bring out-of-the-box creativity. Creativity is something different.

If creativity is crucial to performance, we would hope that as a society we are increasing the creativity of each new generation. Unfortunately, this is not the case. For the past twenty-five years, average IQ scores have increased while *creativity scores have decreased*.[4] In our fast-moving, globalized, high-tech world in which creativity and innovation are economic imperatives, this is an alarming trend.

At the Harvard Business School, Professor Teresa Amabile has spent the last three decades studying human performance and cracking the code of creativity. For one of her experiments, she recruited a group of poets from the Boston area.[5] All of them were serious about their craft; they typically devoted six hours a week to working on their poems and had published an average of nearly four poems each. One had published seventeen.

Amabile wasn't interested in their poetry, however. She wanted to see if changing their motives could affect their creativity. As part of the experiment, she had them write short, rigidly structured, haiku-like poems about snow and laughter.

After they had written their first poem, used as a creativity baseline, the poets were asked to spend five minutes ranking a list of reasons for why they write poetry in the order in which they found them personally important. This type of ranking exercise is a method that researchers use to temporarily reframe someone's motives.

Some were given a list of direct motives, each linked explicitly to the work of poetry writing. For example:

- "You like to play with words"
- "You enjoy the opportunity for self-expression"
- "You enjoy becoming involved with ideas, characters, events, and images in your writing"

This group felt more play in their craft as they set about composing. This was the high-ToMo group.

The others were asked to rank a different set of reasons for writing poetry. These all fell into the indirect motives camp. For example:

- "Your teachers and parents have encouraged you to go into writing"
- "You have heard of cases where one bestselling novel or collection of poems has made the author financially secure"

This group was primed to feel more emotional and economic pressure during the experiment. This was the low-ToMo group.

When both groups had turned in their work, a panel of twelve judges, also poets, who had not been informed of the details of the experiment, scored all of the poems for their creativity. After only five minutes of priming, the high-ToMo group's poems were rated 26 percent more creative than those of the low-ToMo group.[6]

Amabile was so concerned about the negative effects of the indirect motives that she didn't let the poets whose total motivation had been reduced leave immediately after the experiment. Before she dismissed them, she asked them to review the list of direct motives. She wanted to make sure that they left her lab with the right mindset.

"Managers don't kill creativity on purpose," she wrote in her conclusions. "Yet in the pursuit of productivity, efficiency, and control—all worthy business imperatives—they undermine creativity."[7]

When it comes to performance, productivity and efficiency are only a small part of the picture. When building high-performing organizations, you need to understand and optimize two different, opposing types of performance.

First is *tactical performance*. This represents how well a person executes a plan. Every job requires specific actions to be done in specific ways. For example, a salesperson who works in a call center may have a certain number of calls to make per day. She may be expected to spend a certain number of minutes on each call, and turn a certain number of calls into sales. She may have a script and a process map to follow. Her call "may be monitored for training purposes." All of this machinery serves to increase the tactical performance of an organization—how effectively it sticks to the plan.

Similarly, a business executive may be focused on a quarterly earnings goal, or a market share target, or an efficiency ratio. A computer programmer may be focused on lines of code per day, or milestones on a project plan. An investment analyst may be focused on the number of investment ideas produced each day. Tactical performance is the "productivity, efficiency, and control" that Amabile speaks of.

If tactical performance is a person's ability to execute the plan, then *adaptive performance* is a person's or organization's ability to diverge from the plan. They are opposites.

The military uses the phrase "VUCA" to describe the limitations of tactical performance and why adaptive performance is so crucial. The letters in VUCA stand for volatility, uncertainty, complexity, and ambiguity. Tactical performance is not enough to address VUCA. People and organizations need to adapt. That call center salesperson's script may help some of the time, but she'll need to adapt to serve an angry customer, or solve a technical problem, or help a struggling colleague.

Unfortunately, adaptive performance behaviors are very difficult and sometimes impossible to measure. As a result, they are almost always neglected.

On the contrary, over a hundred years of business practice has developed powerful techniques to manage tactical performance. Most business leaders know how to turn a goal into plans, process maps, dashboards, metrics, and more. But what happens when we overly focus on tactical performance? Think of the times when you called a call center and knew that the person on the other end was reading a script back to you. How did that feel?

Because tactical and adaptive performance are opposites of each other, they exist in tension. Because businesses are so adept at building the systems of tactical performance, they often unknowingly destroy their adaptive performance. Great cultures, however, keep these two opposing forces in balance. But exactly how does total motivation affect performance? Why do the indirect motives reduce adaptability and direct motives increase it? Let's take a look:

THE DISTRACTION EFFECT

Let's start with an exceptionally rare job—one that requires only tactical performance. In a controlled experiment at the Massachusetts Institute of Technology (MIT), students were asked to hit two keys on a keyboard, back and forth as many times as possible in four minutes.[8] This is what they typed:

vnvnvnvnvnvnvnvnvnvnvnvnvnvnvnvnvnvnvnvnvnvnvnvnvnvnv

nvnvnvnvnvnvnvnvnvnvnvnvnvnvnvnvnvnvnvnvnvnvnvnvnvnvnv

nvnvnvnvnvnvnvnvnvnvnvnvnvnvnvnvnvnvnvnvnvnvnvnvnvnv

. . . and so on.

The experiment was designed and conducted by Dan Ariely, a behavioral economics professor at Duke and the author of *Predictably Irrational*, to see how high-IQ students perform under various motivation regimes. One group of students received a large incentive for producing the most text. Their maximum possible payout was a whopping $300, a significant amount for any college student. The other group received a small incentive, a maximum payout of only $30.

Those with the higher payout did hit more keys. Their performance was 95 percent higher.[9] If you stopped there, you would say, "Great! Indirect motivators work and all this talk about direct motives doesn't matter." If a job *only* has tactical performance behaviors, then you can create performance through indirect motivators.

But there's more.

Ariely asked those same students to do math problems. That shouldn't be too taxing for students at MIT, a place where at least

Figure 8: Students were asked to find the two numbers in a grid of numbers, like this, that add up to 10.

9.38	6.74	8.17
5.15	6.61	3.06
9.71	.91	4.88
3.58	4.87	6.42

Dan Ariely, Uri Gneezy, George Loewenstein, Nina Maza, "Large Stakes and Big Mistakes," *Review of Economic Studies*, 2009, 76, 2, 460m, by permission of Oxford University Press.

25 percent of incoming freshmen have perfect math scores on their SATs.[10] The students were asked to find two numbers in a grid of twelve numbers that add up to 10.[11]

Just as with the key-pressers, one group could earn up to $30, and the other up to $300. However, this time, the results painted a completely different picture.

These same MIT students, who were training to be brain surgeons and rocket scientists, performed 32 percent worse[12] when offered high incentives for solving the simple math problems.[13]

Ariely shows that when the job requires only tactical performance, indirect motivators *can* increase performance. He also shows that when the job requires adaptive performance, like problem solving, indirect motivators can make performance worse.

This experiment perfectly illustrates the distraction effect. The students who had the chance to earn a substantial sum of money no doubt *wanted* to perform the task well. However, the economic pressure distracted them because they focused on the stakes, not just the work. When Ariely asked students at the University of Chicago to solve simple anagrams (word scrambles) while other students looked on, they were similarly derailed by the emotional pressure, solving only about half as many problems as they had been able to complete when they were working unobserved.[14]

You can do this for yourself. Ask some of your colleagues to solve a math puzzle while standing up in front of their peers. If you want to add to the emotional pressure, ask them to sit down once they have an answer. The people who remain standing will feel their own brains crumble under the emotional pressure. We've seen this work with CEOs, consultants, and computer scientists who are known for their mathematical acumen.

The further the motive from the activity, the more distracted the subject. "In addition to the narrowing of attention," writes Ariely, "large incentives can simply occupy the mind and attention of the laborer with thoughts about her future should she get the reward and her regrets should she not, distracting her from the task at hand."[15]

We've all experienced what it is to choke. But have you ever stopped to wonder why it is that we are most likely to choke precisely when we need to perform at our best? If we were designing our minds from scratch, I don't think we would make "choking" a functional requirement.

Think about the first time you had to speak in front of a large audience. The stakes were high. Performing well meant big things for your career. Yet, as you began to speak, your mouth felt as if it were stuffed with cotton balls. You were thinking about what the audience was thinking, not just about your speech. We've all been there! Maybe you felt that way before a big exam or job interview. This is the distraction effect.

With very rare exception, every job has areas that require tactical performance and areas that require adaptive performance. When someone has high total motivation, he delivers both. If we reduce his ToMo by adding emotional or economic pressure, his mind's focus shifts from the work to a motive that is disconnected from the work. Because his mind is now divided, his ability to perform adaptively decreases.

At least with the distraction effect, the person is still trying to do all the right things. As a person's total motivation decreases even further, the cancellation effect comes into focus.

THE CANCELLATION EFFECT

Citizenship is an adaptive performance behavior. When an employee helps out another colleague in need, or advocates for the organization when they are unmonitored, the organization does better. But typically, it is very difficult to measure helpfulness in a tactical way. So how can we train people to be more helpful?

In search of an answer, researchers at the Max Planck Institute

in Germany recruited the youngest people they could find to participate in an experiment: twenty-month-old toddlers.[16] At that age,
children can run, but they also fall easily. They can climb stairs but
probably need help getting down. They can speak between twenty
and fifty words. And they have not been exposed to corporate culture (we hope).

Each toddler was placed in a room with a desk. A research assistant, let's call her Anna, sat at the desk writing a letter when—
oops!—she drops her pen. Anna leans over the desk, stretches, and
makes struggling sounds. She can't reach the pen to pick it up.

What does the toddler do? Does he ignore her? Does he laugh?
No. Seventy-eight percent of the toddlers help. They leave their toy,
walk across the room, pick up the pen, and hand it to the woman
they met just a few minutes before. Anna drops her pen, or sometimes a piece of paper or a clothespin, numerous times, and most
toddlers help most of the time, usually without hesitation.

In order to train the helpful kids to always be helpful, the researchers gave some of them a reward for their trouble: a token that
causes a toy to make a jingling sound, the toddler-equivalent of a fat
bonus. Intuitively, this makes sense. How better to train someone
to be helpful than to reward their helpfulness? Other toddlers, the
control group, received nothing.

After a few rounds of training, the researchers wanted to see if
the children had learned the behavior. They continued to test the
children's helpfulness without any rewards. What do you think happened when the very clumsy Anna dropped her pen yet again? Did
the toddlers still leave their toys and help?

The control group, who never received a reward, continued to
help, albeit with a slight decrease. Honestly, we're not sure that *we*
would help Anna after she dropped her pen for the fourteenth time,
but they did, 89 percent of the time.

How about the children who were trained with a reward? They

helped Anna only 53 percent of the time. The other half of the time, they ignored her. They could hear her struggling noises and they could see her imploring looks. But now helping her was a matter of calculation. This is the cancellation effect.

The cancellation effect occurs when a person's total motivation is reduced to the point that they completely stop focusing on adaptive performance. Have you ever described the performance of a colleague (or even yourself) as "checking the box"? In other words, she's doing exactly what's asked of her and nothing more? She's focusing only on the tactical performance behaviors that will reduce whatever pressure she is under. This is a person whose motive to do the right thing has been canceled out.

The toddlers' helpful instinct had been canceled out by the reward. The toddlers were now thinking about the trade-off. They were asking themselves, "Is it really worth helping her when I could be doing other things?"

The cancellation effect happens at work all the time. Perhaps a salesperson is under extreme pressure to meet her quarterly sales target. She stops helping her colleagues, stops problem solving the difficult situations, and gives up more easily on hard-to-serve customers.

Even senior executives are at risk. Under the pressure of a short-term target, how often have you seen executives lose their focus on harder-to-measure but possibly more important long-term goals?

A group of researchers in Tokyo measured the cancellation effect's influence on another form of adaptive performance: persistence. Persistence is the willingness to keep plugging away at something, no matter how hard it is.[17] A persistent employee keeps at a difficult problem or pushes to achieve a high-quality result regardless of the difficulty.

Test subjects were divided into two groups: a "reward group" and a "no-reward group." Then the three-part experiment began.

In the first part, the subjects were given a stopwatch and told to stop it precisely at the five-second mark. The reward group was given $2.20 each time they did it with a margin of error of .05 milliseconds or less. The no-reward group was told that they would receive a sum of money at the end of the experiment just for participating.

In the second part of the experiment, the subjects were sent into a waiting room that was filled with newspapers, magazines, and other sources of distraction for a break. Little did they know that hidden cameras were watching them to see if they would continue practicing with their stopwatches.

Strangely enough, the no-reward group practiced more than twice as much as the reward group during their first trip to the break room (and four times as much in a later trip). You'd think that the reward group would have been more motivated to practice, but that wasn't the case. The reward had canceled out their persistence.

After the break, all of the subjects returned to the stopwatch task, though this time (as in the toddler experiment) neither group received a reward. Something interesting happened. The scientists had been scanning the subjects' brains using functional magnetic resonance imaging (fMRI). In the first phase of the experiment, both groups of stopwatch athletes had been mentally engaged; the parts of their brains that are involved in motivation were clearly activated.

The no-reward group's brains read basically the same, before and after the break. But when the reward group stopped receiving its rewards, their brain activity dropped to almost nothing. The cancellation effect isn't just psychological—it's neurological.

These types of experiments have been conducted hundreds of times by dozens of different researchers. The fathers of motivation theory, Edward Deci and Richard Ryan, analyzed 128 studies to see whether the results were consistent.[18] Like our stopwatch scientists, they found that performance-based rewards tend to cancel out the natural sense of play, thus reducing persistence.[19]

Perhaps more interestingly, they found that while the test subjects' persistence decreased measurably, their self-reported satisfaction mostly stayed the same.[20] In other words, people's own sense of satisfaction is only loosely related to their performance. If you survey workers and ask them if they are satisfied, you might not see the negative impact your culture is having on their performance.

Organizations that use indirect motivators must make trade-offs between tactical and adaptive performance. Those trade-offs will be familiar to most managers, but they are difficult to measure. Here are three of the most important and potentially damaging:

- The trade-off between quantity and quality
- The trade-off between individuality and teamwork
- The trade-off between near-term and long-term results

High-ToMo cultures eliminate those trade-offs, giving you the best of both worlds.

Unfortunately for us, the cancellation effect isn't the worst thing that can happen in a low-ToMo culture. Even worse is the dreaded cobra effect.

THE COBRA EFFECT

Many people travel far and wide to see wild animals, but in the cities of India you can still sometimes see buffalo, leopards, and cobras roaming the streets.[21] During the 1800s, when India was under colonial rule, the British government reportedly set out to reduce the number of cobras in the city of Delhi by paying bounties for dead cobras. At first, the plan went as expected.[22] Dead snakes were exchanged for the bounty and the cobra menace seemed to be under control. But all was not as it seemed.

A few shrewd entrepreneurs realized there was good money to be made from dead cobras. So what did those enterprising citizens do? They built cobra farms to raise more snakes! When the colonial rulers realized what was happening, they canceled the bounty. And when the value of cobras plummeted, the snake farmers had no choice but to release their crop. In the end, the cobra population of Delhi increased.

What the city government failed to realize is that they didn't actually want more dead cobras—they wanted fewer live ones. They had rewarded the wrong thing simply because it was easier to measure. The same thing happens in companies that incentivize narrow metrics such as revenue or "employee satisfaction." Too often the side effects and unintended consequences are worse than the problem they were trying to solve.

While every job has some components that require tactical performance and others that require adaptive performance, every job also creates the opportunity for *maladaptive performance*. When a person's total motivation is low enough, they begin to find the shortest possible path to alleviate the pressure they are feeling, even if that path is contrary to the intent of the plan. This is a cobra effect. Unfortunately, cobra effects are surprisingly common in organizations.

The managers of a call center wanted to make sure that operators helped their customers as quickly as possible, so they indexed their pay to the number of calls they took each hour. When call center reps found themselves with too few calls, a predictable cobra effect would occur. They would hang up on customers as soon as they answered the phone, thus bringing up their number of calls.

Atlas (a codename for a real company) has long been admired for its legacy of success. But its sales data and customer interviews revealed an unsettling undercurrent in one division. About 80 percent of the division's sales came in the last month of each quarter. And each time sales spiked, margins dropped—those sales were occurring at a deep discount on price.

The explanation was found in how Atlas set goals and paid people. Atlas's performance system, like that of many companies, was designed around quarterly earnings goals. Each salesperson was reviewed on his or her ability to meet them. And meet them they did.

While tying sales goals to quarterly earnings goals seems like a "no brainer" best-practice, consider the possible cobra effects. If the total motivation of the sales force is low enough, to achieve the goal salespeople might discount prices, exaggerate claims, and in general find maladaptive ways to game the system. Because salespeople don't actually want to do any of this, they wait until the end of the quarter when the pressure is the highest.

This creates many second-order effects. Cash flow is now lumpy, increasing the borrowing costs of the company. To deliver on these services, the organization will be stretched at the beginning of each quarter, requiring excess capacity that ends up idle at the end of each quarter. Meanwhile, trust begins to erode with customers. We spoke with an Atlas customer who, like others, had caught on to the pattern. "I've learned that if I combine all my purchases and wait until the end of the quarter, prices will drop by around 20 percent," he said. "This isn't ideal, but it is the game I have to play."

An academic study of almost a thousand salespeople at a US-based multinational found that a majority of respondents would engage in some form of customer-unfriendly or company-unfriendly behavior to win a sales contest.[23] About 70 percent would convince customers to make a forward purchase, where the company can book the revenue now and deliver later. This may seem like a benign practice, but it makes the hole only deeper next quarter. Fifty-nine percent said they would set aside their other responsibilities, or in other words their citizenship. Thirty-five percent said they would overemphasize products that the company was incenting. Eighteen percent would help others less, and 13 percent would accept increased credit risk. These are large numbers, especially considering the extent to which people underreport their unethical behavior. If this is what happens because of a relatively low-stakes sales contest, imagine the consequences when bonuses, jobs, and self-esteem are on the line.

Cobra effects are hidden; they're virtually impossible to measure until they're discovered. Once a company spots a cobra farm, it has a choice. It can scrap its indirect motivator strategy and build a culture that enhances total motivation. Or it can build in more controls, hiring people to police those cobra effects. Too often companies choose the second option.

Companies presume (incorrectly) that these cobra effects are a result of bad apples that snuck through the hiring process rather than flaws in the culture. (Chapter 5, "The Blame Bias" explains why we make this error.) These behaviors are then dealt with only when a problem is noticed. They are typically addressed through indirect motives (for example, punishment), almost guaranteeing that they will crop up again and again. The result is an endless game of whack-a-mole (or whack-a-snake) or, worse still, a vicious downward spiral of performance.[24]

THE GREAT WAVE

Figure 9 summarizes the three effects. As ToMo decreases, adaptive performance disappears and is ultimately replaced by maladaptive performance. All the while, tactical performance looks good (dead snakes are still coming in). It's tempting to ignore the distraction, cancellation, and cobra effects, because your tactical performance can still be high. If tactical performance is the only lens of performance that you have, you won't notice that total performance is decreasing until something explodes.

When the distraction, cancellation, and cobra effects come together, you get a perfect storm. This is what happened in the

Figure 9: The distraction, cancellation, and cobra effects.

		TACTICAL PERFORMANCE	ADAPTIVE PERFORMANCE	MALADAPTIVE PERFORMANCE
High ToMo	High-ToMo culture	High	High	None
High ToMo	Distraction effect	High	Medium	Low
Low ToMo	Cancellation effect	High	None	Low
Low ToMo	Cobra effect	High	None	High

mortgage industry leading up to the crisis of 2008. Just before the bubble burst, one particular company tried to create a high-ToMo culture for their mortgage loan officers. But by then it was too late.

The mortgage officers' goal had been to acquire as much work as possible from mortgage brokers, independent agents who worked directly with borrowers.

During the height of the boom, around 2006, when it felt like you could do no wrong in the mortgage industry, this company ramped up the emotional and economic pressure on its loan officers. Low performers were fired; higher performers' earnings were linked to the number of loans they issued. There was a penalty for "bad loans," but it was basically unenforceable—nobody would know if a loan went bad for months or even years. And even then, you couldn't tell exactly why it failed. We interviewed dozens of loan officers, and even spent days on ride-alongs with them, watching them do their work. We witnessed all three effects firsthand.

First, the distraction effect. Near the end of the month, when their performance was about to be tallied, you could see the distraction written all over their faces. They would spend an hour each day tallying their performance. Calls that didn't result in deals clearly irritated them. Stress mounted. Customer experience suffered.

Next, the cancellation effect. The loan officers whose jobs were in the most jeopardy took shortcuts. For example, they wouldn't complete all the fields on an incoming mortgage application, only the ones that were critical. When part of a customer's application seemed dubious, they would let it pass. If a customer genuinely needed help, they wouldn't have the persistence or the creativity to find a solution. Not only did customer experience suffer, loan quality worsened.

Finally, the cobra effect. We watched as the loan officers who stood to gain or lose the most built their own cobra farms. In order to increase their loan volume, they taught the mortgage brokers how to game the system. They knew exactly how applications needed to be written to pass underwriting. They knew which documents to provide, and which ones to leave out. They showed their brokers exactly how to get each loan to pass.

To the credit of the executives of this business, they knew that something was wrong. At first, they did what most companies do— they increased surveillance on their people. Whole teams were built to check the work of the people who were already checking the work of other people. But the loan officers just found new ways to game the system. Within a year, it all came crashing down around them. Too much damage had been done.

GOING FORWARD

Like the executive at the start of this chapter, if you equate all performance with tactical performance, you won't understand why total motivation matters. But as you begin to understand adaptive and maladaptive performance, it becomes quite clear. As total motivation decreases, adaptive performance decreases with it, and maladaptive performance takes its place.

On the other hand, as total motivation increases, so does adaptive performance. Adaptive performance is the secret sauce behind innovation, creativity, great customer experience, distinctive salesmanship, and many other outcomes that have remained a mystery for so long.

Individuals with high total motivation have outstanding performance. But organizations with high–total motivation cultures can achieve even more.

The Yin and Yang of Performance

| *The Balanced Culture, Fueled by Total Motivation,*
Is the Ultimate Competitive Advantage

Up until now, we've focused on the effect that total motivation has on individual performance. But total motivation is even more powerful when it's instilled throughout an entire organization.

ToMo isn't a random psychological trait but a powerful instinct that humans evolved to navigate an ever-changing world. Truly great organizations build cultures that tap into our instinct to adapt. We'll show you how, but first we need to define "culture."

YIN AND YANG

What is strategy? When we ask business leaders this question, most answer in a similar way: "Strategy gives us our destination and the path to get there." When we ask them to define culture, the hands come down. No one shouts out an answer. The silence becomes deafening. Finally, someone brave ventures a try: "Culture is our shared set of values and behaviors."

This answer is a good start—practically the dictionary definition. But it isn't enough if your goal is to build a high-performing culture.[1]

One of the best explanations of the difference between strategy and culture comes from an unlikely source. "Everybody has a plan until they get punched in the mouth. Then, like a rat, they stop in fear and freeze."

Those are not the sage words of a philosopher, but of the boxer Mike Tyson.[2] Tyson knows a thing or two about a punch in the mouth. He holds the record for the fastest knockout in Junior Olympics boxing history (eight seconds), and by age twenty was the youngest heavyweight champion ever.[3] Iron Mike describes how even the best strategies can fall apart in the face of the unexpected. When your plan fails, does your organization freeze or adapt?

Your response depends upon your organization's culture.

The *Oxford English Dictionary* defines strategy as "a plan of action designed to achieve a long-term or overall aim."[4] This plan leads to the machinery of tactical performance: process maps, dashboards, performance management. These tools are important—they keep the organization consistently focused, and can even point out shortcomings of the plan.

Meanwhile, your culture determines how well your people diverge from the plan when VUCA requires it. A high-performing culture fuels the creativity, problem solving, persistence, and citizenship that result in adaptive performance.

Therefore, we define a high-performing culture as the system that maximizes adaptive performance through total motivation.

There is no plan that can properly anticipate or address every form of VUCA that your organization encounters. Each customer is different. Each market is different. Machines break. Technology evolves. A new competitor arrives. The world changes. Not a single moment in your organization is predictable. Your organization needs to adapt at every level all the time. Enter culture.

Together, culture and strategy, and their outcomes—adaptive and tactical performance—are like yin and yang. Like yin and yang, they are two halves of a whole, both important for performance.

Figure 10: The yin and yang of adaptive and tactical performance, culture and strategy.

TACTICAL PERFORMANCE:

- How well you execute the plan

- Comes from strategy

ADAPTIVE PERFORMANCE:

- How well you diverge from the plan

- Comes from culture

Like yin and yang, they may seem like opposing forces, but they are actually complementary.

Strategy helps us focus all our energy on a few critical targets. It is a force of strength. Culture, on the other hand, allows us to react to the unpredictable. It is a force of agility. Together, they create a complete view of performance.

Peter Drucker, one of the most influential management gurus of the last century, once said that "culture eats strategy for breakfast."[5] However, it's not a question of either/or, but of both. Strategy and culture shouldn't cannibalize each other. They should be designed together to eat your competitor's breakfast.

THE FUEL OF ADAPTABILITY

We are frequently asked whether there are workplaces where it is impossible to create total motivation cultures, or where they are unnecessary.

It is easy to assume that a water treatment plant may be just the place. At first, it appears that nothing changes. Machines take water and purify it for human consumption. How would that require total motivation and adaptive performance? Employees just need to follow the right protocols.

Wharton professor Adam Grant and his colleagues conducted a set of experiments that showed how wrong that assumption would be.[6] The pumps in a water treatment plant are active twenty-four hours a day. Heavy rains can overwhelm them. The chlorine gas that's used in water treatment can leak, with potentially deadly consequences. Spotting a potential issue and resolving it early can prevent downtime and even save lives.[7]

Grant surveyed water treatment plant employees to see how strongly they felt the motives of the spectrum.[8] Then their managers rated them for their adaptability.[9] The most adaptive employees were "developing techniques for preventing equipment failures, proposing new pollution control methods, and suggesting new work processes and safety protocols."[10] As you probably expected by now, the direct motives (play, purpose, and potential) were strongly associated with high levels of adaptability. The indirect (emotional and economic pressure) were associated with less.[11]

Interestingly, in a similar study Grant also looked at personality traits, such as how conscientious a security officer was, and how open they were to new ideas. These personality traits did not significantly correlate to their adaptive performance at all. Neither did their feelings of autonomy. But total motivation did.

Correlation, however, does not necessarily mean causation. Grant wanted to prove beyond a shadow of doubt that play and purpose cause adaptive behaviors and not the other way around, with adaptive behaviors causing play and purpose.

Grant recruited students, ostensibly to help a local business solve a problem, and offered them the choice of working on either a fun problem or a boring problem. Naturally every student chose the fun problem, but some were told that the fun group was filled and that they had to work on the boring one. In reality, the fun and the boring problems were exactly the same. Grant had misled some participants so that some would be primed to feel play, and others wouldn't.

Next, Grant had to make some participants feel purpose. All of the participants were asked to help a band of musicians earn more money. Some were told that the band was struggling: "All six members of the band have families to feed, and they are in dire straits; on a weekly basis, they are struggling to make ends meet." Others were told that the band was a hobby for a group of "financially secure" businessmen and lawyers. Some of the participants now felt purpose and play, while some felt neither.

The students' ideas for how the band could make more money were assessed for their creativity by two independent music industry experts. With only a few minutes of priming, the play and purpose group's suggestions were rated 30 percent more creative than the nonplay and nonpurpose group. Since the motives were supplied before the work began, it was clear that the motives caused the change in adaptability, and not the other way around.

Is knowing that total motivation leads to more adaptive individuals enough to create a high-performing organization? Having the most adaptive individuals is a necessary condition, but it is not sufficient. From Nobel Prize–winning experts in chaos and complexity, we've learned that adaptive individuals must work together in a certain way to form truly adaptive organizations.

This concept is called emergence.

EMERGENCE

To explain the concept of emergence, it helps to begin with a simpler example than human organizations. Let's start with termites.

In the world of insects, termites are the nerds. Unlike ants, the go-anywhere, do-anything jocks of the insect world, termites lack a tough exoskeleton. Their bodies are soft and often pale; they burn and die in the sun; those with wings can be carried away by a soft breeze. Yet termites may be the most successful land animals on the planet.

One way to measure the success of an animal is its biomass, the combined weight of every member. From the standpoint of biomass, termites, ants, and humans are the three most successful land animals on the planet today.[12] The biomass of humans amounts to about 350 million tons.[13] Ants are estimated to have a biomass that's somewhere between the same as humans to thirty times larger.[14] The biomass of termites is larger still.[15]

As different as these three creatures may be,[16] they do share one trait in common: all three have developed surprisingly similar instincts to create highly adaptive communities.

The complexity of termite communities is mind-boggling. The mounds they build—some of them thirty feet in height—are giant, temperature-controlled farms where they cultivate the nutritious fungus that helps them digest wood. The fungus isn't easy to grow. To maintain the perfect climate, termites must constantly adapt.[17] Inside their giant earthen chimneys, the termites are continuously adjusting vents to keep the temperature, humidity, and proportion of carbon dioxide gas exactly right. Imagine trying to get everyone in the New York City subway system to open and close their windows to maintain the perfect level of underground humidity on a hot summer day. Sounds impossible, yet termites do this every day. While many of us can barely keep our houseplants alive, termites cope with daily temperature fluctuations, dry spells, and rainy seasons.

They must also adapt to the animals around them. When their nemeses the ant attacks, termite soldiers with giant heads and jaws pour out of the mound while workers seal up the exit holes behind them. Talk about citizenship—those termite soldiers are on a suicide mission.

All of this is self-organized; it is accomplished without a hierarchy. "Termites build the largest structures on earth when compared with the height of the builders, yet there is no CEO termite," writes creativity expert Paul Plsek.[18] Humans named the reproductive termite "the queen," perhaps because of our need to believe that someone is in charge. But the termite queen is every bit as much a citizen of the mound as the rest. She does her job, day in and day out for decades. She doesn't direct the other termites; she doesn't architect the mound. The termites can't call her to adjust the thermostat on a cold winter morning. Each individual termite follows a complex set of instincts that are triggered by the changes in their local environment and positive feedback.

Imagine if we could build organizations that operated like that. Whenever there was a problem, people would spontaneously self-organize to fix it. Whenever a new revenue source was found, resources would shift to take advantage of the new opportunity. Everyone would perform at their personal peak, but the needs of the community would be paramount.

How can we build mounds of our own?

MOUNDS FOR PEOPLE

The termite mound is an example of a phenomenon known as emergence. Emergence occurs when the individual components of a collective are able to organize themselves into a system that is far more complicated than the sum of its parts. These systems are almost always self-organized and have incredible levels of adaptive performance.

Contrast an emergent system to a relatively simple machine like an automobile engine. Each part plays a specific role, working with other parts to drive the car predictably forward or back. The car engine doesn't adapt. In a termite mound, on the other hand, each termite can play multiple roles, depending upon the circumstances.

Examples of emergence are countless when you start to look. Human cities and their economies; flocks of birds and herds of animals; the Internet. The human brain and immune system.[19] Even the broader ecosystems of certain companies. Toyota is justly renowned for its advanced supply chain management practices, yet a complexity researcher wrote that it "cannot begin to fathom the depth and breadth of its supply network."[20]

In each of these cases, the individual units (e.g., people in a company, neurons in a brain, white blood cells in a body, companies in a supply chain) have structured ways to adapt to their local environments and to work with one another. As the individual units become groups of hundreds, thousands, and millions, extremely complicated, often unpredictable ecosystems form.

Think about how emergence applies to your day-to-day life. We're writing this book from an office in New York City. The city's food supply network is an emergent system. No single person oversees it; there is no grand design. Yet there's milk and bread available in every corner grocery. If there is a shortage, industrious self-directed people solve the problem.[21] Like the termite mounds, the city itself seems like a living organism, its people so many cells carrying out their functions.

THE STUDY OF COMPLEXITY

Emergence is studied as part of a field called complexity theory. Among the chief questions that complexity research deals with is "how do simple components self-organize to form incredibly complex and adaptive systems?"[22] One of the hallmark beliefs of complexity theorists is that emergent organizations are the epitome of adaptability. It's no coincidence that the first-, second-, and third-place biomass winners all developed instincts that fuel the adaptive performance of individuals and mechanisms to scale adaptability to the whole community.

What does emergence teach us about the management (and the creation) of great organizations? Imagine three hypothetical companies, all competing in an industry that has complex customer needs that are continually changing.

- The first company has a rigid strategic approach. They have a plan and are highly focused. They are command and control oriented. Everyone sticks to the letter of the plan at all times; no deviation of any kind is tolerated. Many of us have felt the pain of working for this kind of company.
- The second company has a strategy, but it also creates a culture that allows people to be individually adaptive. The employees work hard to find better ways of doing their jobs, but they are unable to shape more than their own immediate surroundings.
- The third company creates a culture where individuals are highly adaptive and are able to spread their ideas to the whole organization. They share their best ideas with one another and are always open to learning from their colleagues. When one identifies a big issue, others jump in to help.

Clearly, the third company will be the most adaptive. Over the long haul, it will be the most successful. Adaptive organizations are truly built to win.

The University of Massachusetts' Benyamin Lichtenstein has argued that complexity theory calls for a different style of leadership. "Traditional, hierarchical views of leadership," he writes, "are less and less useful given the complexities of our modern world."[23] Lichtenstein and his colleagues have identified a set of conditions that are required before high-performing, adaptive organizations can emerge.

First, the individual members of the organization must be adaptive within their environment. Nothing prevents a termite from fixing a hole in the mound one day and creating an air vent the next when one is needed. Their instinct compels them to act and adapt to changing circumstances.

Human organizations must also encourage and allow their people to come up with better ways of performing their jobs and serving their customers.[24] Lichtenstein calls this "encouraging novelty" and "allowing experiments, and fluctuation." Another name for it is play.

Within an emergent organization, the play motive isn't about "gamifying" work or having more parties. Play is directed toward giving people the ability to experiment in the areas that have the greatest needs for adaptability, whether that's customer service, product design, or operations.

Second, emergent organizations must encourage citizenship. Citizens teach and help one another, spread new ideas, and share innovations. When you develop a great new way of working, you should want to share it with the whole organization. Conversely, when you see someone else doing something well, you should feel comfortable asking them to teach you their techniques. When you identify a big problem, others should want to help you solve it.

Termite citizenship expresses itself chemically, through pheromones. When a termite finds food, it lays down a pheromone trail that encourages other termites to follow its path. Humans are a bit more complicated. We rely on tools like money. But we also rely on psychological trails. We give back to our communities when we share a common purpose and identity. Lichtenstein calls this common purpose "sense making and sense giving."[25] Another researcher refers to this as shared meaning and "coherence."[26] This relates directly to the purpose motive, which makes you feel passionate about the impact of your own work, but also about the organization as a whole.

BORN TO ADAPT

"Many people believe, as I do, that when staircases are constructed between psychology and biology, the best strategy is to work from the top down as well as from the bottom up,"[27] wrote Murray Gell-Mann, a Nobel Prize–winning physicist and one of the fathers of complexity theory.

Keeping his counsel in mind, we began this chapter with psychology. Psychological experiments have shown us how ToMo leads to individual adaptability. Complexity theory explains how it also works to produce the most adaptive organizations possible. Biology explains the rest.

We learned in our biology classes *how* humanity came to be—through evolutionary forces—but rarely do we discuss *why* humanity came to be. It isn't obvious why humans exist. While complex life has been around for 550 million years or so, minds like ours have existed for less than one percent of one percent of that time. Large brains are extremely demanding. They need about 15 watts of power, while the brains of other similarly sized mammals need only 3 watts.[28] Even our hearts, which continuously pump blood through roughly 100,000 miles of veins, capillaries, and arteries (the equivalent of four trips around the earth),[29] require only 10 watts.[30] Yet here we are.

Many evolutionary scientists believe that for a long time, the human mind wasn't worth the calories it required. Animals could thrive without our massive brainpower. But starting two million years ago, our environment changed, as average temperatures began to swing by five or six degrees Celsius from year to year, compared to just one or two degrees during the three million years before.[31] University of California researchers Robert Boyd and Peter Richerson propose that our brains evolved in response to this climate variability.[32] "Over the last 6 million years, the climate has gotten . . . more variable," the two scientists wrote. "In many respects, human culture is nothing more than a straightforward adaptation to climate deterioration."[33] We exist *because* of VUCA.

Our larger brains gave us the ability to experiment, learn, communicate, and, ultimately, create cultures. Culture allowed us to adapt via memes instead of genes. "Social learning enhances ability to respond to temporal and spatial variations in the environment," according to Richerson and Boyd. "Cultural evolution allows speedy tracking of a rapidly fluctuating environment because it supplements natural selection with learning and other psychological forces."

Whereas other animals change and adapt from generation to generation, we can change many times in a lifetime. "The advanced cognitive skills of humans and the rich culture that it supports must be driven by the need to adapt to much more rapid variation," according to these scientists.[34] In other words, we are born to be adaptive performers. This is why we have a total motivation instinct.

The evidence for this theory is impressive. While paleontologists have found that many animal brains increased in size during this period, the connection with human evolution is tighter. As climate volatility increased, so did the brain size of human-like species, in almost perfect lockstep, culminating with the ultimate adaptive entity—culture-building humans.[35]

Large brains enable culture formation. Cultures create tribes and civilizations that are more adaptive than any one individual. Nature has spoken—culture is the force of adaptability.

YIN AND YANG IN BALANCE

Humans are capable of creating many forms of our own termite mound when we design the right kind of culture. One of the most interesting exemplars of the yin and yang in balance is Wikipedia, which, while not a business organization, is still perhaps the highest performing organization ever created.

Wikipedia is incredible. If you don't believe us, just ask Wikipedia:

- Wikipedia is one of the top ten most popular sites on the Internet.[36]
- The site has over thirty-four million articles. To put that in perspective, the archive of the *New York Times* (which goes back to 1851) has just thirteen million articles—an impressive feat in and of itself.[37]
- Wikipedia has over 76,000 active volunteer contributors, many of whom write anonymously.[38]

Wikipedia's success can be traced back to a strategy that ensures consistency and a culture that enables adaptability. It adapts to continuously changing information—for example, it kept a real-time tally of game five of the 2013 World Series.[39] Twelve contributors entered the game's scores and stats inning by inning. The contributor who entered the final score—which was added within thirty seconds of the game's last out—has contributed to more than three thousand different pages over the past seven years.

A researcher once tested Wikipedia's adaptability by deliberately introducing thirteen errors into articles on the site (an experiment we do not recommend conducting for the sake of human decency). Every one of them was corrected within three hours. An even more subtle experiment introducing sneakier errors found that "one third to one half of the fibs were corrected within 48 hours."[40] This is a lot like what happens when you poke holes in a termite mound. The termites instantaneously form ad hoc teams to fix it, working together for as long as it takes. If Wikipedia were frozen like ice, this degree of dynamism would be impossible.

But adaptability alone isn't enough to achieve such massive success. You need to balance adaptive performance with tactical performance. Yin and yang. In the case of Wikipedia, tactical performance means consistency across pages that are edited by completely different people from around the world. Despite having no formal structure, the volunteers produce pages that have incredible consistency in their organization.

An example of this tactical performance is a Wikipedia phenomenon called "philosophy is the root of knowledge." Here's how it works:

Start with a random Wikipedia page like the article for "yogurt." Click on the first link in the article (excluding the pronunciation key), which at the time of writing was "bacteria." In the article for "bacteria," the first link is for "domain." Follow the chain of links long enough and you will eventually land on the article for "philosophy."

Now try a completely different page, for example, the article for "stigmergy" (a fancy word for this very phenomenon, initially coined to describe termite behavior).[41] The first link takes you to the page on "coordination." Keep going and, lo and behold, you come to "philosophy," the root of all knowledge. Ninety-five percent of Wikipedia articles eventually link back to the article on "Philosophy," according to Wikipedia.[42] If Wikipedia were chaotic like steam, this degree of consistency would be impossible.

The culture of Wikipedia has been studied deeply to understand what drives volunteers to build something that might be the pinnacle of human performance.[43] In one study, researchers examined the motives that drive Wikipedians to participate on the site, and how satisfied they are with the Wikipedia experience. For example, some Wikipedians edit pages purely because they find it fun. Others are economically motivated to edit (because they are paid to do it by their employer, or believe it improves the reputation of their business).

Consistent with the first principle of the motive spectrum, the direct motives increase Wikipedian performance, and the indirect motives decrease them. Play, purpose, and potential correlate positively to how much Wikipedians contribute, while the economic motive correlates negatively.

Consistent with the second principle of the motive spectrum, the closer the motive is to the activity, the better the performance. For Wikipedians, play is the strongest motive, then purpose, and then potential.

A third insight might be more of a surprise. The researchers found that *all* of the motives lead to higher self-reported satisfaction. People *say* they're satisfied if they do something for the economic motive (the correlation between satisfaction and economic motives is .38). But that doesn't mean they will necessarily contribute (the correlation between economic motives and likeliness to contribute is actually negative, -.28). What people say and what they do are different things.

We've seen this pattern play out in other organizations too, which is why you should never use employee satisfaction as the measure of your culture's strength. It's easy enough to create satisfaction. But satisfaction does not always lead to adaptive performance. In fact, satisfaction (e.g., just satisfied enough) is a great way to create inertia, the most harmful of the motives!

GOING FORWARD

It is not the most intellectual of the species that survives; it is not the strongest that survives; but the species that survives is the one that is able best to adapt and adjust to the changing environment in which it finds itself.[44]

—LEON MEGGINSON, MANAGEMENT GURU

The goal of this chapter was to build a definition for "high-performing culture": A high-performing culture is the system that maximizes adaptive performance in an organization through total motivation. Its goal: adaptive performance. Its mechanism: total motivation. Its tools: the keys of culture, which we'll explore in the second half of *Primed to Perform*.

Armed with this crisp definition of what cultures can accomplish and how, we can start to build and transform them.

Except there's a giant catch. Even while we are biologically coded to want adaptive cultures, misunderstanding and incomplete knowledge have given us dangerous biases. When we lead, these biases quietly whisper in our ears, convincing us to destroy ToMo.

Even the great Wikipedia isn't immune. An in-depth review of the Wikipedia community by *Slate* magazine shows that the well-intentioned desire to protect Wikipedia is causing the community to lose its adaptability. New members do not feel welcome, and existing ones feel under siege. ToMo is dropping, and with it adaptive performance. Unfortunately this outcome is predictable of its life stage (as we will show in Chapter 6, "Frozen or Fluid").

Let's take a look at the insidious biases that can lead even the best organizations astray.

Figure 11: The *Primed to Perform* theory of impact in its totality.

Total motivation maximizes adaptive performance. ToMo requires your people to feel the direct motives and not the indirect motives.

The highest levels of organizational or team performance require a balance between the opposing forces of tactical and adaptive performance.

Culture is the ecosystem that maximizes adaptive performance through total motivation. The many keys to culture must be used together to unlock performance.

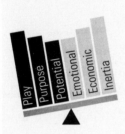

PART III

Why Are There So Few Great Cultures?

Our Biases and Reflexes Get in the Way

The Blame Bias

Our Bias to Blame Causes Us to Lead
Through the Indirect Motives

While we would like to take credit for all of the insights that inform the theories of total motivation and adaptive performance, the truth is that scientists and researchers have been systematically unraveling the Gordian knot of culture for the past seventy years. Even with all of the examples we've shared, you've seen only a small sample of what's out there. However, if there is so much evidence for the power of total motivation, why do the indirect motives hold such sway?

There are a few obvious reasons. Indirect motivators can lead to narrow, short-term increases in tactical performance that are easy to measure. They are like a drug that whole companies can get addicted to. And for all the scientific and management literature that's been devoted to it, few business leaders know about the link between motivation and performance. It's just starting to enter our collective consciousness.

Researchers have uncovered another deeper, more stubborn reason for our resistance. We have a bias that makes us want to use indirect motivators.

The good news is that this bias isn't hardwired. By understanding it, we can eliminate it. To become a leader of great cultures, you will need to start by eliminating this bias within yourself.

TURN ON A DIME

The year is 1972. You're running an errand in a shopping mall when you realize that you've forgotten what you went there to buy. Your smartphone hasn't been invented yet, so you use a phone booth to call your spouse. As you are leaving, a stranger drops a folder full of papers all over the floor. Are you the kind of person who stops to help?

When we put this question to business leaders, almost all claim they are. Two researchers put this same question to the test and found that only 4 percent[1] of people actually helped.[2] When we share their findings with business leaders, they usually ask us about the education and upbringing of the people in the experiment. The 96 percent who didn't help must be lacking in basic human values, they say. One person asked us, only half joking, if the study was conducted in New York City (it wasn't; the malls were in San Francisco and Philadelphia). These executives are doing what we all naturally do—looking for reasons to explain outcomes that don't fit our intuition. Unfortunately, we tend to look in the wrong places.

The researchers made a small change to their experiment. They left a dime in the change receptacle of the phone for the callers to serendipitously discover. Suddenly they were ten cents richer. Did this affect whether or not they helped the person in distress?

If you're like most people, you have a hard time believing that this randomly found dime could change anyone's behavior. We are strongly biased to believe that people's decisions are driven by their innate personalities. We want to believe that by the time you're an adult, you're either a person who helps others or a person who doesn't. Unfortunately, this bias is wrong. The dime made a big difference. Eighty-eight percent of the callers who found a dime helped (versus only 4 percent who helped without the dime).

A few years later the same researchers upped the ante. This time they left an addressed envelope, unstamped, in the phone booth.

Now the question was whether the dime would inspire people to stamp and mail an envelope for a complete stranger.[3] No one would know if they didn't. Again, the results defy intuition. Without the dime, only 10 percent of people mailed the envelope. With the dime, a whopping 76 percent of people stamped and mailed the envelope.

These experiments show how little it takes to make a person feel or not feel citizenship. For the vast majority of people observed in these experiments, their citizenship was inspired by an arbitrary stroke of good fortune, not some immutable aspect of their own personality.

Your reaction to this work is probably a lot like that of our executives. As one of them put it, "There's no way these experiments can be true! There must be something else going on." Our intuition wants to believe that our decisions are a function of our values, our beliefs, or our upbringing. We want to feel in control. Our intuition struggles to believe that people's decisions can be so dramatically affected by small changes to their context.

If context matters so much, then why don't we change it? Why do we spend so much time trying to change the players instead of the game? Rather than poke and prod each person in our organizations, why don't we invest all that time and energy into building cultures that prime everyone to perform?

The answer is our blame bias.

THE BLAME BIAS

The game of Monopoly is a decent simulation of the business world. Players buy, sell, trade, and rent real estate. Luck is involved, of course, but so is a certain measure of skill. Winners are inclined to underestimate the former and overestimate the latter.

To prove this, Paul Piff from the University of California, Berkeley, set up a monopoly game that was blatantly rigged. The scam was hardly subtle. The winning player started out with two times as much money, he related in his TED talk on the experiment.[4] "When they passed Go, they collected twice the salary, and they got to roll both dice instead of one, so they got to move around the board a lot more."

After they completely crushed their opponents, the winners were asked to explain why they won. Given the context, it was clear that they won because the game was rigged. But that's not what they said. "They talked about what they'd done to buy those different properties and earn their success in the game, and they became far less attuned to all those different features of the situation, including the flip of a coin that had randomly gotten them into that privileged position in the first place," Piff observed.

If the winners think they won because of their skill, they implicitly believe their opponents were less skilled. This is an example of the blame bias. Even when the situation makes one outcome far more likely than another, we still believe the individual is to blame.

Let's look at a more troubling life-and-death example. A group of European researchers investigated a number of serious accidents in mines and factories in Ghana to get a better understanding of the ways that managers react to workplace accidents.[5]

First they surveyed people who had worked with the victims of the accidents, some of whom were very familiar with the victims' work situations (for example, they held the same job), and some of whom were not. Only 6 percent of the first group blamed the victim for the accident. But 44 percent of the coworkers who were not directly familiar with the victim's work situation blamed the victim. The more removed we are from someone, the more likely we are to blame them.

If you were the manager in this example and you had a bias to blame the person rather than the situation, what would you do to improve safety? You might require all of your people to take more training courses, or you might tie bonuses to following safety protocols. However, you'd be less likely to try systemic solutions, like painting danger areas yellow, or changing the production process, or scheduling more maintenance for the machines.

The idea that our minds are biased to blame people, even, as in the Monopoly game, when they are clearly not at fault, was a groundbreaking insight in social science. Stanford University's Lee Ross found it so important that he dubbed the blame bias the "fundamental attribution error."[6]

BLAME ROLLS DOWNHILL

Now that you've learned about the blame bias, you'll be surprised by how often you'll see it. For example, the blame bias looms large in education, creeping in whenever the issues of student and teacher performance are debated.

Psychologist Linda Beckman tested the ways that the blame bias affects how we judge educators.[7] She recruited some UCLA education students to teach a lesson, and others to observe and evaluate the lesson. The observers, as fellow education students, should have naturally been sympathetic to those teaching the lesson. Moreover, the evaluators were studying introductory psychology, so they should have been protected against the blame bias. But they weren't.

To prove this, Beckman made the situation obviously bad. The lecturers were trying to give a math lesson to a group of children, but they couldn't see or hear the kids (in fact, there were no real children). They were told that the students were on the other side of a one-way window, the kind you might find in a police department interrogation room. The lecturers had no visual or auditory cues to see if the students were following or not. Furthermore, the lecturers were allowed twenty minutes to prepare for a twenty-minute lesson on content they had never seen before.

Afterward, the lecturers and their evaluators were told that the students had taken a test to measure how effective the lesson had been. Some of the students' scores, they were told, showed that their skills had actually decreased. Then the lecturers and evaluators were asked what had gone wrong. For both groups, blame rolled downhill.

The evaluators attributed 50 percent of the blame to the students and 32 percent of the blame to the lecturers. Though they'd witnessed it themselves, only 18 percent of the blame was assigned to the horrible conditions. Even the lecturers, who had neither seen nor heard the children, and who knew better than anyone how awful the context was, assigned 42 percent of the blame to the students.

If you were one of those evaluators, and you were asked to improve the teaching experience, what would you do? Since you tended not to blame the teaching context, you wouldn't focus on improving it. Instead, you would focus any interventions directly on the lecturers or the students. Rather than changing the game, you'd try to change the players.

DON'T HATE THE PLAYER, HATE THE GAME

We see this in organizations all the time. Why do we believe that someone missed her sales target? Because she's a slacker. Why was his work sloppy? Because he's not smart. Why did that manager cheat? Because she's an unethical person and her mother didn't hold her enough as a baby. We make snap judgments, geared toward blame.

The blame bias affects the way we run organizations. Every leader has limited time to spend on improving performance. Because the blame bias causes us to blame the player, not the game, we focus on prodding the player, not changing the game. The easiest way to prod is through indirect motivators. We concoct more potent sticks and carrots. We spend weeks on performance evaluations, but very little time on culture building. We invest all sorts of energy in hiring the right people and then underestimate the influence of our culture once they arrive.

The distraction effect, cancellation effect, and cobra effect render this strategy of blame and indirect motivators fruitless. But even if you could make a blame-based performance system work, it would still be incredibly inefficient compared to a high-performing culture.

Why would you water one blade of grass at a time when you can make it rain?[8]

BLAME'S IMMUNE SYSTEM

We once led a workshop with a group of senior executives where we discussed the implications of the blame bias on how they run their business. "I can see how the blame bias is a problem for people like you and me," said one of the executives in response to our talk. "But my people only care about the money. That's why I have to use the indirect motivators."

The blame bias is a resilient and cunning foe. Not only does it cause us to use indirect motivators, but it makes us justify the choice. We tell ourselves that people *want* the indirect motivators.

Chip Heath, a brilliant organization researcher at Stanford University, tested how much faith we have in indirect motivators.[9] He asked a group of MBA business school students to rank what motivated them at work. Take a crack at it yourself. Rank the reasons you work from the list below:

- For the benefits
- Because the work is worthwhile
- For the praise
- For the money
- To gain skills
- To feel good about myself
- To learn new things
- For the security

The business school students predominantly said they themselves work for direct reasons—to learn new things, gain new skills, and feel good about themselves. Surprisingly, pay didn't even make the top three—they ranked it fourth.

Next, the students were asked to rank order the importance of those same motivators to call center customer service representatives. This created a very different list. The top four reasons were all indirect—pay, security, benefits (economic pressure), and praise (emotional pressure).

Heath then asked the customer service reps themselves to rank order the motives. Lo and behold, they did not rank indirect motives very highly. They too cared about the direct motives.

Figure 12: MBA students thought that they were more motivated by direct motives than customer service representatives were.

■ DIRECT MOTIVES	▨ INDIRECT MOTIVES	
Ranking of what MBAs say motivates themselves	Ranking of what MBAs say motivates service reps	Ranking of what services reps say motivates themselves
1. Learning	1. Pay	1. Skills
2. Skills	2. Security	2. Worthwhile
3. Feel good about yourself	3. Benefits	3. Learning
4. Pay	4. Praise	4. Benefits
5. Worthwhile	5. Feel good about yourself	5. Security
6. Praise	6. Skills	6. Feel good about yourself
7. Benefits	7. Worthwhile	7. Pay
8. Security	8. Learning	8. Praise

The business school students believed they were motivated directly by the work itself, but that service reps were motivated indirectly. If they had assumed that the call center reps' minds worked the same way as theirs did, they would have been more accurate. But the blame bias made them believe otherwise.

Using our culture measurement tool, the total motivation factor, we can see the blame bias happening across our whole economy. We surveyed thousands of employees in large companies across ten industries and calculated their total motivation factors. We also asked these employees to rate why their colleagues work in their jobs, using the same six motive spectrum questions. Then we calculated how much ToMo they perceived their colleagues to have versus themselves.

The results were stunning. Across each industry, employees believed that their colleagues had less total motivation than they did (see Figure 13). And not just a little bit less. On average people believed that their colleagues were 19 points lower on ToMo than they were! That's roughly the equivalent of a Southwest Airlines employee thinking his peers feel as if they are in a competing, lower ToMo airline. It appears the blame bias is everywhere.

THE ANTIDOTE TO BLAME

Can we overcome the blame bias? If so, what happens? The military provides an answer.

Let's say you're a military training officer whose job is to turn combat soldiers into commanders. You meet an incoming group of twenty-five trainees, all of them specially selected for their leadership skills. Still, there's a range of talent within their ranks. Some are exceptional even by the group's high standards. As their trainer, how do you treat them?

Figure 13: People believed that they had greater total motivation than their coworkers.

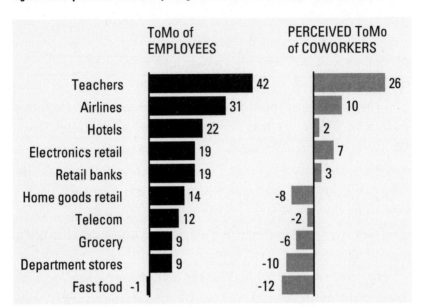

Professor Dov Eden of Tel Aviv University tested this scenario with four training officers and 105 soldiers in the Israel Defense Forces (IDF).[10] The soldiers had been chosen to take an intense fifteen-week combat command course. Each had been selected based on their motivation and skills.

The four officers were told the Command Potential (CP) of their soldiers, a score that was based on the soldiers' previous performance in other courses and tests, as well as their ratings from former commanders.[11] They were told that the CP score was predictive of performance in 95 percent of cases.

Each officer trained a mixed group—a third of their trainees had high CP scores, a third had "regular" CP scores, and a third did not have enough information to create an accurate score. At the end of the course, the trainees took a battery of exams on everything from theoretical knowledge to combat tactics to operating procedures.

They also took a set of practical exams on skills like marksmanship and navigation.

As you might have expected, those with high CP scores outperformed in all areas. Those with unknown scores performed somewhere in the middle. And those with average CP scores performed the worst. The differences were large. High-CP trainees earned the equivalent of A+'s; average-CP trainees earned solid B's.

There is, of course, a catch. The CP scores used to categorize the trainees were completely fake. That's right. The trainees had been assigned a CP score at random. The leaders had been tricked! So how then could the CP score predict performance?

By tricking the officers into believing that some of their students were naturally high performers, the blame bias was eliminated. With no blame bias standing in the way, these leaders naturally became higher ToMo. For example, if high-CP students had a problem learning a military concept like VUCA, the leader didn't blame the learners. It couldn't be their fault because they had such high command potential. Therefore the leader is forced to confront the context rather than the individuals. ToMo increases.

If average-CP students struggle with a concept, it is easier to blame them. When the learners are blamed, the leader naturally gravitates toward indirect motivators, and thus ToMo decreases. With it, performance decreases.

The idea that a leader's expectation can become a self-fulfilling prophecy has been demonstrated in so many experiments that the phenomenon has been given its own name: the Pygmalion effect. The name refers to the Greek myth about a sculptor who fell in love with his creation, the basis for the George Bernard Shaw play *Pygmalion* (which was adapted into the Broadway musical *My Fair Lady*). To briefly recap its plot, Professor Higgins, an expert in elocution, bets that he can transform a cockney working girl into an elegant "lady." Eliza Doolittle, who is the subject of the bet, explains the power of expectation to the gentlemanly Colonel Pickering:

> [T]he difference between a lady and a flower girl is not how she behaves, but how she's treated. I shall always be a flower girl to Professor Higgins, because he always treats me as a flower girl, and always will; but I know I can be a lady to you, because you always treat me as a lady, and always will.[12]

The Pygmalion effect is the flip side of the blame bias. Once blame is eliminated, expectations increase. When expectations increase, a leader more naturally uses the principles of total motivation, which inevitably improve performance.

Professor Eden went one step further. He wondered what would happen if he told a leader that his whole team was excellent, not just a few of its soldiers.[13] Some officers were told that all their trainees were high performers. The others were told nothing.

What happened next? The leaders who believed they had a high-performing team caused *all* of their troops to perform better on theoretical exams (9 percent better) and practical tests (10 percent better on weapons use, 5 percent on physical fitness) judged by impartial observers.

These types of experiments have been conducted in a range of scenarios, from schools to workplaces. The blame bias affects how caregivers treat patients in nursing homes, and how quickly PhD students complete their degrees.[14] Our expectations affect the performance of individuals, and even entire groups.

Unfortunately, it works both ways. While high expectations create high performance, low expectations diminish it.[15] Believing you have underachievers on your team creates underachievers.[16]

One of the most fascinating insights of this work is that we are all more than one kind of leader. We treat people according to how we expect them to perform. A leader who believes in a team member acts in a way that enhances his or her total motivation.

DEBLAMING YOUR LIFE

At this point, you may be thinking: wow, people are really messed up—good thing I'm not. Well . . . blame bias researchers have tested how self-aware we are when it comes to our biases.[17] We tend to believe that other people are more likely to have the blame bias than we are—1.5 times more likely, to be precise. As a leader building a high-performing culture, you must start out by correcting your own blame bias as well as the biases of the people around you. The easiest way is to learn how to give feedback to others.

Take Beth, a call center manager, who had to tell one of her team members, David, that he wasn't paying attention during their huddles. Beth could have handled this feedback in one of a few ways. The first approach is reactionary, emotional, and often not constructive. "David, you need to stop zoning out during our huddles and start contributing," she might say. Such a response is blame-biased and emotionally pressuring.

She could somewhat improve that approach by using a commonly taught method for giving feedback. "David, I noticed during that last huddle that you didn't seem to be paying attention. And that made me feel you're not interested in helping the team. Next time pay more attention." While this approach feels less emotionally charged, it still blames David and it still creates emotional pressure.

Even better, Beth could engage in a blame bias–free way of solving the problem cooperatively. We call this the REAP model of feedback (as in "as you sow, so shall you reap"):

1. **REMEMBER**: Whenever you find yourself blaming an individual for a situation you're confronting, stop yourself and remember

these words: "Assume positive intent." This simple statement should remind you that the person probably means well. It should also remind you of your own blame bias. It may sound silly, but simply saying these words will help you with the next step.

2. **EXPLAIN**: Before even approaching your team member, come up with five scenarios that could explain his behavior—scenarios that do *not* assume a problem with the individual. Could the culture have contributed to the outcome? Could something else entirely be at work? For example, maybe David wasn't paying attention because he was nervous about what he was going to say. Maybe he was still thinking about a nagging issue from a few minutes ago.

3. **ASK**: When you're ready to approach your team member, mention what you observed assuming good intent, but then ask him why. Beth could say to David, "I noticed in that last meeting you seemed to have something on your mind. I'd love to hear about what you were thinking."

4. **PLAN**: Then together, identify the true root cause and develop a plan to remedy it. In this case, David wasn't distracted. After probing, Beth learned that he was having a hard time following her because of her style of communicating. She tends to speak using metaphors and generalizations, and David often fell behind while trying to figure out how to make her suggestions concrete and actionable. Ironically, the right outcome from this feedback discussion wasn't for David to do something differently. It was for Beth.

Beyond better ways to give feedback, some companies have created policies to counter the blame bias. One of Toyota's values, codified in the "Toyota Way," is called *genchi genbutsu*, which translates roughly as "the actual place, the actual part." It reminds managers that they should go to the worksite and assess the actual situation firsthand.[18] Toyota understands that if managers don't see a problem in context, they risk coming up with the wrong solution. Adaptive performance demands objectivity and an open mind.

GOING FORWARD

Once you're aware of the blame bias, you'll see it pop up everywhere in your life. The most powerful personal antidote is to come up with five alternative explanations for the behavior that do not assume a problem with the person. Try it the next time someone cuts you off on your drive to work, or ignores your email.

Next, take time to consider moments when the blame bias has misled your organization. Certain processes—such as performance reviews and compensation decisions—are more vulnerable. We'll address those systems in Part IV. But for now, keep your eyes open, and begin to brainstorm ways your organization can combat one of our most common, fundamental errors.

Frozen or Fluid

Like most of us, you probably hammer out a plan for your day during your morning shower or commute. You prioritize your tasks, thoughtfully blocking out the time you'll need to complete each one. But by ten a.m., some unforeseen wrench is thrown into the works and your plan flies out the window. Somehow or other you muddle through, making up a new plan on the fly. Whether you realize it or not, you're adapting.

A district bank branch manager planned to spend her day coaching colleagues, but received a call informing her that one of her branches had been robbed at gunpoint. She canceled her meetings and headed for the branch to work with the police and her distraught employees. She and her entire team had to adapt.

An Amazon.com executive told us of an angry customer email that CEO Jeff Bezos received and forwarded to him. He quickly pulled together a team of five people and they dropped everything to solve the customer's problem. They adapted.

A Starbucks barista described a day when his coworker fell sick and they ran out of cups for iced coffee. He, his fellow baristas, and their store manager all adapted.

You and your organization live in a chaotic, unpredictable world that changes from moment to moment. If your goal is to build an organization that operates at the highest levels of performance, you need to increase your firm's adaptability at every level, from the executive suite to the front line. No one person can impose adaptability. That's what culture is for.

Here's an analogy for your company and its people: Fill a container with ice; the ice will simply sit there, not adapting to its environment—that's the frozen company. Fill the container with steam and it will quickly escape—that is the chaotic company. Fill the container with water, and it will flow into every nook and cranny— that is the adaptive company. Neither ice nor steam, but water.

Unfortunately, we appear to be living through an ice age.

FROZEN LEMONADE

Even the most educated leaders can freeze their organizations without knowing it. Two economists showed how that can happen when they brought in a group of 379 Harvard Business School students to perform a job for which they should have been overqualified: running a lemonade stand.[1] Although the lemonade stands were virtual, they were part of a business simulation designed to capture the dynamics of a freezing firm.

In the course of twenty rounds, the students could alter their strategies and assess how their changes were affecting profits and customer relations. They could test how their stands performed in different locations, like a stadium or a school. They could test pink lemonade versus green. They could alter the product's lemon and sugar content. They could raise or lower prices. They could also just stay the course, replicating the strategy of a previous manager.

One group of students—let's call them the Indirect CEOs—were put in a classic indirect motive condition. They were told they would earn a portion of the profits they made in each of the twenty rounds of the experiment. It was akin to a salesperson receiving a monthly performance-based bonus.

A second group—let's call them the ToMo CEOs—had a completely different rewards scheme. For the first ten rounds, they would earn nothing. Only during the last ten rounds would they earn a percentage of the profits.

As the simulation progressed, it was clear that the Indirect CEOs were frozen compared to the ToMo CEOs. The ToMo CEOs experimented much more radically than their Indirect counterparts. Eighty-five percent of the ToMo CEOs tested a new location, versus only 48 percent of the Indirect CEOs. As a result, the ToMo CEOs learned much more about their broader business environment than the Indirect CEOs did. By the final round, the ToMo CEOs were earning an average profit of $140. The Indirect CEOs were earning an average profit of $111, a 26 percent difference.

The lemonade stands might have been laboratory simulations, but the same pattern plays out every day in organizations all across the world. When faced with the most important decisions in an organization's trajectory, most leaders freeze the organization rather than maximize its adaptability.

We worked with one very bright senior executive who realized that his business had a major revenue growth problem. Instead of finding new, innovative ways to grow, he spent two years focused on reducing costs. Why? He worked in a system that operated on indirect motives. His job, promotion prospects, and compensation all depended on a short-term target. His indirect motives were high, and there was no countervailing direct motivation in his company's culture. Predictably, he experienced the cancellation effect; even though he knew better, he chose to focus on the easy activity, not the right one.

Every organization comes to a set of crossroads, where it must choose between being fluid or frozen. In many cases, the organization's executives don't even realize that they've made a choice.

You need to see these crossroads coming if you are going to engineer your own high-performing culture. If you've already passed them, you need to know what happened so you can correct your course.

FROZEN BY DESIGN

No organization has ever been born frozen, but in search of clockwork predictability, many leaders inadvertently adopt practices that limit their adaptability. As we have analyzed organizations through the lens of total motivation, we've found that there are four crossroads along the life cycle of a company. At each of these crossroads, they have the choice to remain fluid, balancing adaptive and tactical performance, or to freeze, optimizing tactical performance only:

- *Crossroad 1—The Foundation.* Entrepreneurs face a choice: to focus purely on building a product, or to focus on building a product and a culture. Some focus almost exclusively on the former. They don't take the time to define and nurture the identity of their organization (see Chapter 9, "Identity," for more on identity building).
- *Crossroad 2—The Scale-up.* Once entrepreneurs have found a model that works, they begin to scale. Desperate for talent, many opt for skills and warm bodies over cultural fit. As the organization becomes too large for its founders to be the sole cultural glue, its leaders face another choice. They can cross their fingers and hope that everyone adopts a common culture. Alternatively, they can establish a team of true culture-builders with a mission-critical mandate (more on building this team in Chapter 14, "The Fire Watchers"). Many fall somewhere in the middle. Not knowing the science of total motivation, the magic culture begins to fade.
- *Crossroad 3—Institutionalizing.* At around 150 people, the organization becomes too large for informal human capital

processes (see Chapter 13, "The Hunting Party," for how group size affects culture and performance). Again, leaders have a choice. They can implement indirect motivators and manage the organization bureaucratically as it grows from 150 to 1,500 to 15,000. Alternatively, they can scale the high-ToMo culture they had when they began. Without the tools to systematically implement culture, this is extremely hard to do.

- *Crossroad 4—Renewal.* Eventually, the original growth engine runs out of steam. The organization has either captured its whole market, or competitors have swooped in. Performance begins to suffer. At this point, many leaders ratchet up indirect motivators to squeeze the last drops of blood from the stone. They implement rigid performance management systems, incentives, and adaptability-destroying cost reduction measures, all of them focused on short-term performance (see Chapters 10, "The Playground"; 12, "Compensationism"; and 15, "Performance Calibration" for ToMo-enhancing ways to manage performance). Increasing indirect motives creates a vicious spiral that only makes things worse. The alternative is to invest in adaptive performance, exploring new areas for growth. Again, most organizations choose the former. Those that choose a high-ToMo path of renewal eventually find themselves back at Crossroad 1, as they build their next growth engine.

It's never easy to devote time, energy, and money to something that seems to have a far-off payback. The urgency of everyday challenges takes precedence. Often, leaders don't even realize they've made a choice.

One organization—Medallia—has been an exception to the rule. The fast-growing technology company has chosen adaptive performance at every crossroad it's come to.

It's not easy to build a high-performing culture, even in a small organization. We measured the ToMo of tens of thousands of workers across businesses of different sizes, and found no relationship between ToMo and size. Small companies can have high or low ToMo, just like large companies. Entrepreneurs have to focus on tactical performance; they spend their nights and days under a sword of Damocles, worrying about their fledgling company's survival. It's what Neel did in his first tech start-up, before he understood the science of total motivation and the importance of balancing tactical performance with adaptability.

Medallia, on the other hand, reminds us that it is possible to make the right choices.

MEDALLIA'S CROSSROADS

While it's difficult to measure precisely, some estimate that 90 percent of start-ups fail.[2] Given that failure rate, would you have bet on Medallia?

Medallia is not the type of company that appears on the covers of magazines. While the teams behind Airbnb or Instagram built glamorous consumer-facing products, Medallia creates software that helps companies measure and improve customer experience. While Medallia has a well-stocked kitchen and an open floor plan, its facilities are nowhere near the luxury campuses of companies like Google or Facebook.

By November 2014, Medallia had doubled in size within a year, to over six hundred people. It had raised three rounds of funding from one of the most prestigious venture capital firms. Nine out of ten people who received a job offer from the company accepted it, an impressive win rate in the hypercompetitive world of Silicon Valley.

We interviewed a dozen Medallians, as they call themselves, to find out how the company was beating the odds. Every single one of them credited their cofounders, Borge Hald and Amy Pressman. Hald focused particularly on building great products, and Pressman focused on building a high-performing culture. "What's different here is that culture is not that thing in the side car," one Medallian explained. "Amy and Borge have made it crystal clear . . . that culture is not secondary to our mission. It's the only way to achieve the mission."

It's easy to imagine that great culture builders must be larger-than-life characters—some combination of P. T. Barnum, Walt Disney, Steve Jobs, and Martin Luther King Jr. Yet when we sat down with Pressman, we found that she personified total motivation without any flash or wizardry. Her own ToMo motivated those around her. She was comfortable being vulnerable and sharing stories about her mistakes, reducing emotional pressure. Her laser focus on her company's culture increased the sense of purpose in everyone around her. She constantly sought out new information that would help her thinking evolve, modeling a high sense of play.

Pressman has a constellation of prestigious names on her résumé, including Harvard, Stanford Business School, and the Boston Consulting Group. There's no doubt she's learned a lot about managing tactical performance. But she's also learned the importance of adaptive performance. She's lived in five different countries, where she realized that many things she took as fact were actually culturally determined. She was a Peace Corps volunteer in Honduras, where she had to adjust her original plans to have impact in her host country's context. She was then a legislative aide in the US Senate, where successful politics and adaptability go hand in hand. The mix of these experiences taught her the value of keeping yin and yang in balance.

Pressman and Hald, a former Norwegian Air Force lieutenant with an equally impressive résumé, cofounded Medallia in 2001. Their timing was not ideal. The Internet bubble had just burst; investment dollars were hard to come by. There were few role models for Pressman. Even in 2004, only about 4 percent of venture capital deals went to companies with at least one female cofounder.[3] She was truly a black swan.

But from the very beginning, the two understood what many leaders never do. They could either focus solely on building a product, or strive equally hard to build a great culture. The decision to prioritize culture took courage. A bootstrapped company for its first ten years, Medallia faced steep competition to simply survive while competing against deep-pocketed venture-backed companies. "We were very focused on getting food on the table," Pressman recalled. So "when I talked about culture, people's eyes glazed over."

But they remained true to their vision. When the company was small, Pressman interviewed every single job candidate to assess their cultural fit. As Medallia would soon find out, setting a high cultural bar can have significant costs.

"We interviewed people from great companies, with great educational backgrounds, who weren't cultural fits," said Medallia's head of People and Culture, David Reese. "It was really hard to turn those people down because you *need* to fill [those positions]. You're in pain." The pain only got worse as Medallia's growth accelerated. "There were moments when I know that Amy was interviewing at five a.m." While the cofounders successfully navigated the early days, the cultural fabric stretched thin as the company scaled.

"In 2010, we had two epiphanies in quick succession," Pressman said. "There was one week when we let go of three Ivy League hires. Prior to that, our modus operandi had been: 'hire smart, talented, nonjerk people and they'll do the right thing.' But we realized that many smart, decent, good people were not coachable because they were afraid of not being perfect." The cofounders also realized that this emotional pressure canceled out their team members' sense of ownership. "I still remember one particular quarterly review meeting when a handful of our leaders missed their targets," Pressman said. "Some owned the outcome, while others—the ones who were worried about being perfect—pointed fingers at each other." Pressman and Hald wanted to build a culture that operated like a sports team, where "winning means having the winning record. It does not mean winning 100 percent of the time." They wanted a culture where it was okay to experiment and make mistakes. "Trying to be perfect is counterproductive to actual learning and growing and reaching your full potential," Pressman explained. The drive for perfection was increasing emotional pressure, reducing play, and limiting the organization's ability to adapt. They had reached the second crossroad.

What followed was a period that Pressman describes as a "renaissance," when the organization left its "dark ages." "Past a certain size, we needed more to establish a strong culture so we thought differently about the range of tools at our disposal. [We thought about] organizational structure, training, how you embed the culture into the fiber of everything you do from performance reviews . . . to career paths," Pressman recalled. At this stage Pressman also realized it was no longer tenable to build culture by pulling on the recruiting lever herself. She needed to find a way to expand ownership for recruiting, and she needed new levers.

Pressman had struggled to codify the criteria for the culture interview. She and Hald still wanted their "no jerks" culture, but in reality, they were searching for something more nuanced than just decency. They could have crossed their fingers and hoped to hire people who naturally saw the world their way. But they decided to develop a scalable framework for the culture interview by hiring a psychology doctoral student from Stanford. At this stage in *Primed to Perform*, their conclusion shouldn't surprise you: *why* someone works drives *how well* they work.

"In a normal interview, you serve the ball, the candidate returns it, and the point is over," said one of Medallia's culture interviewers, a member of its customer solutions team. "We will hit it back to you so we can understand why you made the decisions you did." Without fully knowing the science of total motivation, Medallia realized that the difference between average and distinctive performance lay in a person's *whys*.

With this framework built, Medallia established a broader culture interview team (see Chapter 14, "The Fire Watchers," for details on building a culture team). Medallians from across the company were certified to conduct their new culture interview.

But Medallia didn't stop at cultural fit. They hired five more cultural specialists to build out other, more systematic ways to manage their culture. "For our size, we have many more culture people than most companies do," Reese observed, "and fewer classically trained HR people." Today, Medallia has one culture leader for every two hundred fifty people, a data scientist who applies rigorous metrics to culture and performance, and over twenty certified cultural interviewers. Medallia also started to focus on induction, or as they call it, "onboarding."

Their goal is to prime people's *whys* from their very first moment in the company. "We had talked to a lot of other companies about onboarding," Reese said. "They all seemed to focus on getting set up for work. Some had a small session on 'who we are.' Amy and Borge gave us the room to do something transformative, and we ran with it."

Medallia hired an expert in culture building from Zappos to design a weeklong onboarding program that reduced emotional pressure while creating a sense of play. "I thought it would be difficult, but ultimately Amy and Borge chimed in and everyone gave it a shot. Once we got the results we achieved, the entire company was supportive," Reese said. "People asked 'How can we afford to do that while balancing a real need to get new hires working with our clients quickly?'"

Onboarding begins with a welcome letter from Pressman and Hald explaining the company culture: "We are on a journey as individuals and as a company to become our best selves, relentlessly seeking out new ideas, making improvements, and innovating," the letter explains. "Sometimes we experience setbacks. Sometimes we experience them more than sometimes :). When that happens, we pick ourselves up, learn, and get on with the journey. . . . To quote the oft-quoted (Bob) Dylan line: 'he not busy being born is busy dying.'" The letter comes with two gifts: a Fitbit "to 'grow' your health and wellness," and a Kindle, "to 'grow' your mind."

Then, on their very first day on the job, Medallians are asked to do something to make the company a better place. "It establishes this idea that the culture is *your* responsibility," explained one Medallian. Then comes "the real emotional experience. You're asked to be vulnerable." In front of your new colleagues. At work. "At every onboarding I've seen, the class is moved to tears by the end," said one Medallian, echoing what many others had told us as well.

Each person is asked to do something that challenges his or her self-imposed barriers to personal growth. Many choose to confront a long-held fear. One rallied strangers in a park and gave a speech. Another reconnected with an estranged parent. One explained that he suffered from an intense fear of losing his job and not being able to support his family. The group tailored an exercise for him. They dropped him off miles from the office without a wallet, phone, or any valuables. Armed with only an emergency phone number, he had to navigate his way back to Medallia headquarters. "I remember him coming back into the room right before we were about to debrief, and the room just exploded," said a Medallian. "Hearing him recount his experience was just amazing. He came away from it knowing that faced with a challenge he would push through and he'd be okay." The program ends with each new hire reading a paragraph written by his or her hiring manager, describing the special spark that led Medallia to extend a job offer.

Onboarding primes play, but it's not enough to maintain a high–total motivation culture. Leaders are taught to actively combat the blame bias. "It's all too easy for a legal team to develop an adversarial relationship with other departments," explained Medallia's associate general counsel, Aaron Thacker. "Those legal teams come to believe that their role is to be the adults in the room, and their internal chatter tends to revolve around their frustrations of chasing after groups that have a less developed sense of responsibility. We would never, ever talk about our role like that here. At Medallia, we're going to assume good intent. We're going to assume competence. And we're going to work collaboratively to solve problems."

Medallia uses its organization structure to create spaces to play. Medallians form squads of eight to twelve people that meet weekly to share what they've learned. Some squads combine into mega-squads like the forty-person "Chowbacca squad" named after customer solutions director Michelle Chow. This group meets every two weeks to share lessons and celebrate victories, increasing the sense of play and purpose (see Chapter 13, "The Hunting Party," for more). "I want team members to truly get to know each other, learn from each other, push each other to be better, and importantly, not take themselves too seriously," Chow said. "I hope Chowbacca reinforces their sense of belonging, purpose, and pride in their work and accomplishments. We're not just a team, we're a movement!"

Performance reviews are designed to reduce indirect motivation (see Chapter 15, "Performance Calibration"). Medallians conduct self-reflection exercises, and then lead their own review conversations focusing on what they've learned. Feedback is designed to help that person grow, not to establish a year-end grade.

Medallia recently built more formal career ladders to help people understand the skills they need to learn over time (see Chapter 11, "The Land of a Thousand Ladders"). The ladder criteria include tactical skills for each role, as well as cultural and leadership behaviors.

In all of its systems, Medallia seeks to balance tactical and adaptive performance. "Our culture is the Peace Corps meets the Marine

Corps," Pressman explains. "It's this idea that you need to reach people's souls, but you also need to have rigor. You need some tension between chaos and structure."

The impact of Medallia's culture has been tremendous. "Our attrition rate is exceptionally low," Reese said. The 90 percent win rate on offers, mentioned earlier, "is just unheard of in this market," he continued. "If you look at the cost per hire alone, our culture programs more than pay for themselves." And those calculations are just the beginning. "In Silicon Valley, there will be sudden explosions of change," Pressman explained. "To survive in that kind of environment you have to be extremely adaptable. Minor, at-the-margin changes are not going to help you—you need to be able to do a one-eighty." Medallia has created a high-ToMo culture that's able to do just that.

Perhaps most importantly, Medallia recognizes that building a high-ToMo culture is a process of continuous improvement. "A question I get asked a lot is, 'How do we preserve the culture as we grow?'" Reese said. "Amy pushes us to change the conversation to, 'How do we *improve* culture as we grow?'"

THE FOURTH CROSSROAD: RENEWAL OR DEATH SPIRAL

The last of the crossroads, which Medallia has not yet faced, is often the most destructive. Eventually, the original growth engine of a company runs out of steam and performance plateaus. Leaders have a choice. They can double down on the tempting predictability of tactical performance and squeeze a few more drops of blood out of their turnip. Or they can continue to allow for the adaptive performance that can actually right the ship.

Too many companies make the first choice. Rather than confront the need for a new growth engine, they eliminate spending in areas that help them adapt (research and development, spare capacity, brand building), damage customer trust (often through pricing games, or reduced quality), and pressure their own people to focus exclusively on tactical performance.

Bureaucracies are put into place to manage expenses and budgets. Performance targets are implemented to keep output high. Managers are taught to crack the whip. Performance management and compensation systems become more pressuring. Predictably, total motivation drops, and with it, adaptive performance. As adaptive performance disappears, total performance eventually goes with it. Not understanding the link between ToMo and performance, companies try even harder to apply indirect motivators to their people. Thus begins the death spiral. Just when an organization needs to be at its most fluid, it inadvertently freezes itself.

We have seen this unfortunate pattern play out in many companies, and countless empirical studies have confirmed these dynamics. In one, three finance professors asked more than four hundred executives what their company would do when their quarterly earnings targets were at risk.[4] Roughly 80 percent said the company would cut back on long-term spending in areas like R&D or advertising; 55 percent said it would delay starting a new project, "even if this entails a small sacrifice in value"; 40 percent said it would attempt to book revenues this quarter instead of the next, which can worsen the problem down the road. All of these activities reduce the ability to adapt at a time when adaptability should be the number one focus.

Satya Nadella put it brutally, just a few days after he became the CEO of Microsoft: "We all know the mortality of companies is less than human beings."[5] The average time a company remains in the S&P 500 has declined from forty-five years in 1955 to just seventeen years in 2009.[6] The business environment has more VUCA than ever before. The rates of change for technology, business formation, and globalization have all increased. Companies must adapt to survive.

Executives are starting to recognize this fatal pattern. Michael

Dell, founder and CEO of Dell Corporation, took his company private because he believed it was struggling to adapt. "Under a new private company structure, we will have the flexibility to accelerate our strategy and pursue both organic and inorganic investment without the scrutiny, quarterly targets and other limitations of operating as a public company," he said.[7]

After analyzing over a hundred companies, the global consultancy McKinsey & Company concluded that the best growth strategy over a long period of time is to enter new, fast-growing spaces, whether they are new products, new categories, new segments, or new countries.[8] The Fortune 500 company 3M gets this. The maker of everything from sticky notes to thermometers to electronic circuits tracks how much of its revenue comes from products that have been invented in the last five years. They call this metric their New Product Vitality Index, or NPVI. While only 25 percent of their revenue came from new products in 2008, the percentage rose to 33 percent in 2014,[9] and their target for 2017 is 40 percent.[10] They are making adaptability a part of their DNA.

GOING FORWARD

As an ancient Chinese philosopher once said, "a tree that is unbending is easily broken." Variability is an uncontrollable force of nature. Freezing your organization in the face of change is a surefire way to destroy it. Fortunately, even if your organization has taken a wrong turn, it is possible to correct its course.

Before we get there, however, it's worth taking a moment to reflect on which stage of the life cycle your organization is in. What decisions are you making that could freeze your organization? Are you preserving your organization's ability to adapt? At which crossroads could you go astray?

Now that you know the science behind high-performing cultures, it's time to learn how to build them. But first, a brief recap:

- The objective of a high-performance culture is to maximize adaptability.
- Adaptive organizations require adaptive individuals—people with high levels of creativity, problem solving, persistence, and citizenship.
- Individuals adapt when they have high total motivation. The more that people work for the direct motives, and the less that people work for the indirect motives, the more adaptive they will be.
- Great organizations build high-ToMo cultures. They resist their bias to blame individuals. They resist the temptation to freeze. They balance the yin and yang of tactical and adaptive performance.

PART IV

How Can You Build High-ToMo Cultures?

| Even Bad Cultures Can Be Transformed When You
Know the Science and Have the Right Tools

The Torch of Performance

The Total Motivation Factor: By Measuring the Magic, You Can Make the Magic

Imagine if organizations managed their finances like they manage their cultures. They wouldn't have a chief financial officer. Instead, whenever the organization's leaders were worried that they might be running low on money, they'd survey their employees, asking, "What do you all think? Are we running out of money?" Once the survey results came back, they'd hold focus groups. The focus groups would surface three or four ideas and task forces would come together to implement them. Three years later, the organization would survey its employees again, asking, "Are we running low on money?"

Of course, this is ridiculous. Finance is continuously, not episodically, managed. The tools of finance are well known. Double-entry bookkeeping was developed in the twelfth century by Florentine bankers and eventually co-opted by Venetian merchants.[1] For the last eight hundred years we have built on this tradition by creating a complete system of finance. Generally accepted accounting principles (GAAP) provide a common language for all professionals. Accountants are formally certified. Boards of directors are required to audit financials.

But culture, an asset we deem highly valuable, is unmanaged. Who is in charge of a company's culture? What do they measure? What is their common language? How can they tell if their efforts are improving a culture or harming it? How do they know if they are dealing with root causes or symptoms?

W. Edwards Deming pioneered the art of building high-performing business ecosystems; naturally, we're big fans. He is credited with the saying, "In God we trust; all others must bring data."[2] Absent a measurement for culture, it is very difficult to know if a company is becoming more frozen or more fluid. And as organizational theorist Mason Haire once said, "What gets measured gets done."[3]

THE TORCH IN THE DARKNESS

There's an old joke about a drunk man who keeps looking for his lost keys under a streetlight, because that's the only place he can see.[4] For too long, would-be builders of business cultures have been in the same situation. With only an incomplete understanding of culture, they've focused on the parts they can easily measure, like productivity or sales volume (tactical performance), or outcomes like employee satisfaction. Adaptive performance (creativity, grit, problem solving) and maladaptive performance (cheating, lying, running cobra farms) are hidden in the dark.

Organizations need a torch that can light up the whole sidewalk. It should be easy and even fun to use, so that organizations actually use it. We found this torch in the total motivation factor, a measurement that allows you to not only find your "culture keys" but also figure out the right way to use them.

The metric is elegantly simple. It predicts adaptive performance. And because it's created from the six motives, it provides insight into how to improve a culture across jobs, business units, geographies, and demographics.

ON THE SHOULDERS OF GIANTS

As with so many of the insights presented in *Primed to Perform*, we owe a debt of gratitude to the academic community for the total motivation factor.

Its precursor was developed at the University of Rochester by researchers Richard Ryan, Wendy Grolnick, and James Connell. They needed a single metric that combined the six motives of the motive spectrum[5] so they could create statistical models analyzing such questions as whether student motivation or innate personality mattered more to academic performance. Building upon their work, a group of researchers from the University of Ottawa created a similar metric for the workplace.[6]

Their approach was simple. Using a questionnaire, they would measure how much play, purpose, potential, emotional pressure, economic pressure, and inertia a test subject felt for a given activity. To get at motivation, they asked the test subjects *why* they were doing an activity (not how well they were doing the activity or how satisfied they felt about it).

We've conducted many experiments and tests to refine their questions and the arithmetic used to calculate the ToMo factor. With this tool, we can finally shine a light on the keys of culture.

DIAGNOSING TOMO

The legendary consultant James McKinsey, founder of the almost ninety-year-old consulting firm that bears his name, based his initial practice on the insight that financial analysis could lead to better tactical performance. Similarly, deep analysis of ToMo can lead to better adaptive performance.

ToMo analysis has five steps: measure the total motivation factor for your organization; identify issues; prioritize actions; set an aspirational ToMo goal; and develop the business case for investment. We'll take them one at a time.

1. Know Your ToMo

The first step in the diagnostic is to calculate the ToMo for all the people within an organization, and locate the pockets with material differences.

We have developed a number of methods to measure ToMo. Our simplest requires only six questions. Participants state the degree to which they agree with the following six statements, on a scale from 1 (strongly disagree) to 7 (strongly agree). The first five questions all begin with "I continue to work at my current job because . . ."

Take a crack at it yourself, using the questions below or online at www.primedtoperform.com. Rate how much you agree with each statement in the blank "answer" spaces, using a 1 for "strongly disagree" and a 7 for "strongly agree":

QUESTION	ANSWER	× weight =	TOTAL
I continue to work at my current job because the work itself is fun to do		× 10 =	
			+
I continue to work at my current job because I believe this work has an important purpose		× 5 =	
			+
I continue to work at my current job because this type of work will help me to reach my personal goals		× 1.66 =	
			-
I continue to work at my current job because if I didn't, I would disappoint myself or people I care about		× 1.66 =	
			-
I continue to work at my current job because without this job, I would be worried I couldn't meet my financial objectives		× 5 =	
			-
There is no good reason why I continue to work at my current job		× 10 =	
			=

ToMo:

Add the totals for the direct motives (first three) and subtract the totals for the indirect motives (last three)

These statements test the six motives from top to bottom: play, purpose, potential, emotional pressure, economic pressure, and inertia. When we ask the questions in practice, we scramble the order.

The factor is easy to calculate with simple addition and multiplication. Multiply your answers times the weight to its immediate right. Then add your totals for the first three questions and subtract your totals for the last three questions. You can alternatively let our website do the calculation for you.

Because the direct motives increase adaptive performance, they should be added. Because the indirect motives decrease adaptive performance, they should be subtracted. If your culture has less of the direct motives than indirect, it will have a negative ToMo.

The closer the motive is to the work itself, the more powerful that motive is. Hence, the motives have different multiplier weights. Play is more powerful than purpose. Purpose is more powerful than potential.

We determined the weights for the six motives after measuring thousands of employees across different types of companies. These weights make the factor generally predictive of adaptive performance while also creating a scale that ranges from -100 to 100.[7]

Once we calculate the ToMo of each individual in an organization based on their survey responses, we average the scores for the whole company. The result is one number that shows how motivated your team or organization is. The higher the ToMo factor, the stronger the culture.

Anyone can launch their own total motivation survey using these six questions from our website, www.primedtoperform.com. Feel free to do it right now with your own teams.

To get a useful reading, there are a few traps to avoid:

- Use ToMo as a diagnostic tool, not as a report card. There's a reason why we call the metric a "factor" versus a "score." A score is used to judge performance. Emotional pressure will increase and play will decrease. Total motivation for the metric itself decreases, making your people less adaptive (and creating the risk of cobra effects like gaming the survey). A "factor," on the other hand, is an input to be managed along with other factors. A "factor" implies that leaders must understand it and consider new ways to improve it. The metric thus becomes a diagnostic tool to help figure out what cultural changes should be made.

- Don't become dogmatic about the metric. The total motivation factor is meant to be the tool, not the boss. Use it to understand the sentiment of your people, but don't feel like it is carved in stone. Moreover, we have found workplaces in unique industries and in other countries where we needed alternative methodologies to accurately assess ToMo. For example, in some countries admitting to indirect motivators is frowned upon. The process of measurement itself is something that can and should be continuously improved.

- Make sure your employees' responses are anonymous or, at the very least, make an ironclad promise of confidentiality. They should never feel as if they or their managers will be called out or penalized for their responses. Allow them to take the survey in a safe space (perhaps even at home).

- If you wish to demonstrate the value of ToMo by linking it to other performance metrics, you should make sure to include long-term and holistic measures. As we've shown many times, short-term and easy-to-measure performance drivers can be influenced without ToMo. You want to capture performance in a way that includes both tactical and adaptive behaviors. This is why we tend to use measures like customer experience and long-term sales.

2. Test Your Theory

The second step to analyzing ToMo is to use the data that has been collected to begin testing your theories for where total motivation can be improved and through which motives.

Start by thinking of the areas in your organization where adaptive performance is most critical. At the top of the list should be those parts of your organization that interface with customers, impact product quality, require creativity, or are subject to extreme risks. You should also include areas where cheating and other cobra effects could be disastrous.

As discussed earlier, Southwest Airlines has the highest ToMo of any large consumer-oriented organization we've ever measured, but its score shows that even they have room for improvement. Let's examine, for example, the difference between the Southwest employees who are customer-facing versus those who are not. In every "magical" culture we've measured, employees who interact with customers have higher ToMo. This makes sense since customer-facing jobs usually make it easier to feel the purpose of your work.

Southwest's customer-facing personnel have a ToMo that's 9 points higher than its non-customer-facing personnel. Contrast that to three of Southwest's competitors, where employees who interacted with customers had a *lower* ToMo than those who did not. Without knowing more, this suggests that Southwest should consider focusing its culture-building efforts on its non-customer-facing people, like their operations and corporate teams.

When total motivation is quantified, you can study many other ideas you have for improving your organization. Here is just a small sampling of insights we've seen in our research:

- At Southwest, ToMo increases significantly with tenure, a pattern we didn't see in other airlines. This suggests an opportunity to focus on the ToMo of early tenure people.

- At Southwest we saw no material difference in ToMo by race. However, we did see a wide gap in other organizations. In one grocery store chain, for example, we saw a massive 20-point gap between white and black employees. Further analysis showed that black employees felt far less play and potential and far more economic pressure.
- In one bank, we saw that hourly employees and salaried employees had roughly the same ToMo; however, in a competitor bank we saw that hourly employees had an incredible 30-point difference in ToMo versus their salaried counterparts.
- In a multibillion-dollar Middle Eastern company, call center associates had a ToMo factor 31 points lower than store-based associates. Rather than money or lifestyle at the root, we found that the call-center staff had far less play and purpose.
- Of the companies we have measured, Starbucks has the highest ToMo in their industry when compared to other quick-serve restaurants. However, that gap is driven primarily by higher play and lower inertia. Despite having a positive mission, the purpose motive isn't having as large an impact on their ToMo as we expected, suggesting an opportunity to strengthen their culture.

3. Analyze the Keys of Culture

Once you understand where you can improve ToMo and which motives are lagging the most, the next step is to choose the keys that you really need. We wish we could say there was a master key—one initiative that would unlock a company's entire culture. Unfortunately, there isn't.

Great cultures come from many small motivators that are all aligned to increase ToMo. The door to high performance requires many keys. Worse still, not every key works. Yet after testing the impact of many keys across thousands of people, we've narrowed the list down to a set that matter most:

- *Leadership (Chapter 8, "The Fire Starters")*. It is often said that a person's boss makes or breaks his experience. We've discovered that's half right. A leader who practices the specific behaviors that maximize total motivation does add an average of 50 points of ToMo to his or her team. However, it is much easier for a leader to destroy ToMo than to create it. Creating ToMo requires the other keys to work in unison.
- *Identity (Chapter 9, "Identity")*. The strength of an organization's identity, which includes its mission, behavioral code, heritage, and traditions, was the second most powerful of the keys to culture. In general, the difference between a weak identity and a very strong identity is about 65 points of ToMo. However, companies rarely manage their identities in any way. This key is turned all too infrequently.
- *Role design (Chapter 10, "The Playground")*. Designing each and every job to balance tactical and adaptive performance by maximizing ToMo is the most powerful of the keys of culture. The difference between good and bad is a whopping 87 points of ToMo. Like identity, this key is almost never actively managed by an organization. Roles are designed haphazardly, and rarely optimized for adaptive performance. This key remains on the sidewalk.
- *Career paths (Chapter 11, "The Land of a Thousand Ladders")*. Most organizations have "fight to the death" career paths, hoping that the strongest survive. These career paths destroy ToMo and thus adaptive performance. Instead, career ladders where each rung is designed to increase ToMo produce 63 more points of ToMo, and thus better performance.
- *Compensation (Chapter 12, "Compensationism")*. Compensation systems are riddled with inconsistencies that result in ill

will and feelings of unfairness. At the root of these inconsistencies is a lack of clarity of the purpose of the compensation system. Compensation systems that celebrate growth add an average of 48 points of ToMo.

- *Community (Chapter 13, "The Hunting Party")*. Strong communities are an effective way to inspire play and purpose, while also enabling the vulnerability needed to reduce emotional pressure. The difference between strong and weak communities is roughly 60 points of ToMo, making it the fourth most powerful of the keys. Yet like identity and role design, communities are rarely designed intentionally, or in accord with psychological research.
- *Performance management (Chapter 15, "Performance Calibration")*. Many organizations have built performance management systems that commit the cardinal sins of culture building. They either focus entirely on tactical performance at the expense of adaptive performance and/or focus on using emotional or economic pressure to produce results. These systems can end up destroying whole companies. A well-designed performance calibration system, on the other hand, balances yin and yang through total motivation. When in place, these systems can create up to 41 points of ToMo.

Keep in mind, the relationships between these keys and ToMo are not additive—the total motivation factor tops out at 100. Instead, the keys work together. It's easy for any one of these culture elements to limit the power of your culture. Cultures achieve the highest levels of performance when each element is aligned with total motivation.

Also keep in mind that the importance of any one of these keys will likely be different in your organization, and even within each team of your organization. Again, ToMo comes to the rescue.

We analyzed ToMo, its components, and these keys at a business-to-business professional services firm. For this organization, adaptive performance is mission critical. Every project is unique, and new insights and information can bring course corrections mid-project. Here's what we found:

- Low purpose and high emotional pressure and inertia were decreasing ToMo (and thus adaptive performance).
- The keys that were most misaligned were the performance evaluation process, leadership behaviors, and specific elements of role design. Despite popular belief, compensation was not a factor.
- With role design, the core issue was an inability to see the impact of the work, and not having enough time to be adaptive performers. These issues had been misdiagnosed for a while. The organization thought people resented working hard. But in reality, people wanted the time to play, and the ability to see that the hard work made a difference.
- With leaders we saw an overuse of quid pro quo leadership behaviors and not enough behaviors that encouraged curiosity (for play) or role-modeled purpose.

We did a similar analysis on the other side of the world for a completely different set of professionals—teachers in an Asian country. Even though practically all of the teachers surveyed stated they were highly committed to their work, their ToMo score was about 25 percent lower than what we had expected to find. When we looked at the individual motives, we saw that many teachers felt a fairly high degree of purpose, but many also felt a fairly low degree of play.

Then we examined the individual keys to see what might be driving this difference. These were our findings:

- A perceived unfairness with the performance evaluation process drove significant emotional pressure. Emotional pressure often blocks play (as you've seen earlier in this book).

- Play was low during a number of nonteaching tasks that teachers spent a significant amount of time on. This is fundamentally a role design question, and should be addressed using the levers detailed later in Chapter 10, "The Playground."
- Even during teaching activities, there was a major opportunity to increase the sense of play. Low ToMo teachers felt as if they could not participate in developing new ideas to improve performance; they wanted to work more closely with their colleagues to develop new ways of achieving their teaching mission.

Equally interesting, again, is what didn't matter. Formal training, access to tools and materials, and even compensation were not blocking ToMo. Moreover, teachers felt they had a lot of autonomy, yet still they were struggling to feel play in their work.

4. Set an Aspirational ToMo

One organization we worked with, let's call them ABC Inc., was trying hard to build a high-performing culture. They recrafted their mission and formed a culture team. But then they stalled.

They stalled because they didn't have consensus on a common goal. Moreover, their culture team wasn't given the freedom to experiment and so it lacked play. This particular culture also had a very strong emotional pressure motive, further hindering adaptive performance.

To help break their logjam, we met with a group of ABC's executives and showed them a piece of paper. On it was written:

> Our goal is to create a culture that results in a total motivation that is at least 15 points higher than our industry average within five years.

For the remainder of the session, we talked through each of the elements of this simple sentence. What is total motivation? Why a

15-point lead? Why versus the industry average? Why five years? By explaining this simple objective, we were able to create a common definition of winning that gave its culture team the room to play.

We chose a 15-point lead as part of our goal for a practical reason. When we look at ToMo within industries, the magical cultures that we tend to admire typically have a 15-point ToMo advantage over their peers.

- Apple Stores are about 14 points above their peer group average.
- Nordstrom is about 15 points above other department stores.
- Whole Foods is about 14 points above other grocers.
- Starbucks is about 18 points above other fast-food restaurants.
- Southwest Airlines is 14 points above its largest competitors.

At 15 points, the gap is wide enough that your people and your customers clearly and obviously feel the difference.

Organizations in unique industries can set absolute goals, but for many organizations, it makes sense to pick a target relative to the competition. Structural aspects of some professions naturally lead to higher or lower ToMo. Teachers, for example, tend to have higher levels of play and purpose, and thus higher ToMo. The average teacher ToMo is 44, about 25 points higher than the average of people in other industries. Teachers should set their goals for improvement accordingly (see Figure 13 for ToMo by industry).

5. Develop the Plan and Business Case

Setting a goal is only half the battle. The next step is developing a plan and justifying the expense. Every company has limited dollars to invest, and those dollars are fought over by every department and team. Other functions, like marketing and operations, create business cases to justify their expenses. The product team estimates the expected sales and return on investment of a new product. Marketing teams create consumer decision funnels that ideally create profits. In the rare circumstances that a culture team exists, the team struggles to make the connection between spending on culture and economic performance. Without that connection, they lose the fight for investment dollars.

One company we work with spends five times more on human capital than they spend on marketing. Yet they have ten times as many employees optimizing their marketing spend as they have optimizing their culture.

The inherent challenge is that adaptive behaviors are difficult to measure, and maladaptive behaviors are hard to see. How do you justify spending money on things that are so intangible? Yet while adaptive and maladaptive behaviors are hard to measure, ToMo is not. Since we can link ToMo to business outcomes through adaptive performance, we can develop genuine business cases to improve total motivation.

For example, we've measured a number of retailers' total motivation. Figure 14 shows the linkage between the ToMo of their cultures and the quality of their customer experience.[8] To reduce pressure, we took company names off the chart except the top peformers, but it includes a large variety of well-known brands.

Even with this extreme variety of retailers, ToMo still has a strong connection to customer experience. Depending on the organization and its business model, there is a direct economic link between customer experience and profits. Typically, better customer experience leads to higher prices, higher retention of customers, more cross sales, and stronger recommendations to other customers.

And then there's the direct impact on sales. With one of our clients, the difference between a positive-ToMo salesperson and a negative-ToMo salesperson was 28 percent in revenue.

There's also the impact on adaptive behaviors like creativity and problem solving. We analyzed the ToMo of asset managers who make multimillion-dollar investment decisions. The highest performers had the highest ToMo. In their environment, each point of ToMo was worth millions of dollars of economic return from their investments.

Figure 14: ToMo and customer experience in retailers.

Within your own organization, you'll want to maintain and constantly improve a simple calculation: what is the value of one point of ToMo? Each organization will have their own unique inputs, but typically, they should have the following components:

- Increased margin due to improved customer experience, leading to higher prices

- Increased margin from less waste and better cost management
- Increased direct sales revenue through adaptive sales behaviors
- Increased revenue growth (from new products, new segments, or new markets)
- Increased revenue growth (from increased word of mouth)
- Reduced employee acquisition costs
- Reduced employee retention costs
- Reduced cost due to maladaptive behaviors (for example, operational risk, credit risk)
- Reduced volatility due to better dealing with VUCA

By analyzing ToMo in your own organization, and on occasion setting up controlled experiments, you can calculate the ToMo impact for each of the sources of value above. Once you can make that economic connection, you can set investment levels that can be tracked to better performance.

Being able to connect culture to performance is a game-changer. Culture building can be treated as a quantifiable, "hard" discipline, at least as hard as marketing and product development. Business cases and experiments can be created to justify spending money to improve the motivational mindset of your employees.

NIGHT VISION

Now that you understand this new torch, let's see how you can use it to shine light on keys that were once hidden in the dark.

You've just started a new job at a big electronics retailer. You lead hundreds of stores, all across the country. For the last five years, Internet-based stores like Amazon.com and other retailers, namely Apple, have been cleaning your clock. You have the power to make almost any change you want. Where do you begin?

It's tempting to say that you should start by cloning the Apple Stores. Such a strategy wouldn't be crazy. Apple Stores produce more sales per square foot than any other retailer in the United States, including luxury stores like Tiffany.⁹ If you've experienced an Apple Store for yourself, you know they have something special.

Even before we knew about total motivation, we had an inkling that high-performing organizations had something in common. We spent months hovering in airport terminals, retail stores, classrooms, and hospitals, searching for that philosopher's stone of performance. Our consulting practice gave us access to the inner workings of C-suites, where top executives made their most important decisions. All the while, we were carefully observing the people in those cultures, interviewing them whenever we saw outlier performance.

We spent a lot of time at Apple's retail stores and we interviewed many of their employees. They weren't a unique species, born with a rare performance gene (as the blame bias would make us believe). An Apple employee named Justin helped us understand what made the difference. A former soldier, Justin is as no-nonsense as they come. Even our conversations felt mission-oriented. His answers were crisp and to the point. Everything he said could have been punctuated with a "sir" or a "ma'am."

Like many of his colleagues, Justin had worked at another major electronics retailer before he came to Apple. We asked him a lot of questions about each experience, but his most telling answers came when we asked him to describe his best day of work at each of the two stores, starting with Apple's competitor.

"I don't know. I can't really think of a best day," he said. "They were all about the same. I'd come in, work my department, and leave. There weren't any bad days, but none stand out as a best day."

That particular competitor is a well-intentioned, well-run institution. While shadowing a district store manager, we witnessed its strong values and its genuine desire to create a good place to work. It checks all the standard boxes of "good management," but it's not enough, as Justin revealed with his next answer.

"My best day at Apple was more like a best six months," he replied without skipping a beat. His intonation changed completely.

> *One of the shifts I worked was as a support person. I would help people learn how to use their computers. There was this elderly woman, I think in her seventies, who came in to learn how to make a photo album for her grandkids. She had this big desktop Mac that she would have to unload from the trunk of her car and bring into the store so we could help her with her project. After her second session, I realized that she was coming in at the same time and day every week. So for the next six months, at six p.m. each Tuesday, I would wait in the parking lot for her to pull in. When she did, I'd take her computer out, bring it inside, and set it up. I got to know her really well during all this—it's hard not to when you're looking at all her pictures. She was a social worker, something that I also have a passion for. We'd talk about her life, and her work. I was actually sad when we finished her project.*

The point of this story isn't the human connection that it describes, as important as that is. It is all of the culture keys of the Apple Store coming together to enable this interaction to occur. For example:

- The second week when the customer returned, Justin was able to see the customer and intercept her so he could work with her again. This was enabled by the store layout and by flexible policies.
- Justin knew that he could perform adaptively based on how his

leaders role-modeled the behavior themselves and on the month-long onboarding program that taught him how to be an adaptive performer.

- Justin had the flexibility to wait a few minutes each week in the parking lot. His compensation system, performance system, or leaders did not prevent it. That kind of flexibility, the kind that allows you to experiment even in minor ways, builds the play motive.
- Justin's job included a component that allowed him to help customers by using the product to create things that mattered to them, like family photo albums. This inevitably builds the purpose motive.
- Justin did different things on different shifts. The variety fortified his play and potential motives.
- Justin's sales targets never caused him undue emotional or economic pressure; they were low enough that he would clear the target before half a day was over.[10]

The list goes on.

Thanks to the many cultural keys that were sewn into the fabric of the Apple Stores, Justin's customers received the best experience they could possibly get. This builds extreme trust in the brand, which enables a higher price point and ultimately the ability to extend the customer relationship to other product categories. Meanwhile, Justin was performing at his highest levels, maximizing his tactical and adaptive performance. This is the yin and yang of culture and strategy operating to its fullest.

Without a good torch to see how culture affects ToMo, competitors have copied only what they can see at Apple's stores: the wooden tables; the open layout; the blue shirts and lanyards; the Genius Bar. But their clones haven't replicated the invisible factors that count the most.

Figure 15: ToMo and its components measured at Apple Stores and three competitors.

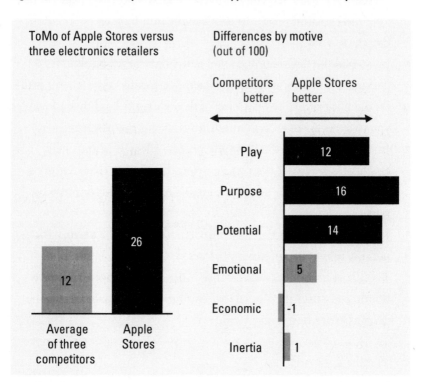

The total motivation factor tells the real story. Apple Stores have a ToMo of 26. Justin's other employer has a ToMo of 14. A 12-point ToMo margin is impressive. Since ToMo is itself made up of the individual motives, we can look at how Apple's stores fare across the whole motive spectrum. For example, you can see in the chart above that the Apple Store's culture produces 12 points more play than its competitors' cultures.

During one of our observation sessions at an Apple Store, we witnessed a customer asking an Apple employee what the difference would be if he bought an iPhone at the Apple Store or a competing store next door. The employee said, "Right now, if you buy it at [the competitor], they will waive the activation fee." A low-ToMo employee might have withheld that information or even lied to the customer (cobra effect). While this individual employee lost a sale, he helped Apple build its reputation for trustworthiness.

The competitor's employees, on the other hand, showed the telltale signs of low total motivation. One associate told us that "constantly shifting priorities" left him demoralized. Conflicts between national and local policies, and "managers [that] expect us to try to align ourselves to both at the same time" caused another to stop caring. "They treat us as though we're completely expendable, which I suppose we are to them," one employee wrote to us. "Frankly I have no idea why I'm still there." This is inertia at its worst.

Measuring ToMo allows us to pinpoint the strengths and weaknesses of an organization's culture. By tracking it over time, we can make sure that it is constantly strengthening, not freezing. By using it in controlled experiments, we can test if our changes are making it better or worse.

In short, ToMo transforms magic into a science. Hogwarts becomes MIT.

GOING FORWARD

Managing culture, like managing your finances, is a never-ending process. But it does have a beginning. To get started, launch a total motivation survey for your people. Feel free to use the survey tool on our website at www.primedtoperform.com. Once you launch the survey, run it on a regular basis, every six to twelve months. By measuring ToMo and making it an ongoing part of the routine of managing your business, you will already begin to make progress.

The Fire Starters

| *The Secrets of High-Performing Leadership*
Have Been Unlocked

Forty-five minutes into a culture meeting at a global finance company, the head of HR spoke up: "Let's address the elephant in the room," he said. "Our CEO is a bad leader." This was unfortunate, but not unusual. It turns out that only one in four leaders inspires total motivation, and even fewer achieve the highest levels. These are the "fire starters," the leaders who ignite total motivation in their teams and across entire organizations.

Too often we think great leaders are born, not made, thanks to some magic combination of innate talent and charisma. Through the total motivation factor, we can objectively and even quantitatively assess the specific behaviors that great leaders use to create high-ToMo cultures and, consequently, the highest levels of performance.

Not only can leadership skills be taught and learned; organizational systems can be put into place that will build leaders at every level. In this chapter, we'll show you how.

FOUR STYLES OF LEADERSHIP
What kind of leader are you? Do you use the indirect motives, focusing on emotional pressure, economic pressure, and inertia? Or do

you use the direct motives to manage your people, focusing on play, purpose, and potential? Perhaps you use both, or neither? Let's look at these four types of leaders.[1]

We call the first group "quid pro quo" leaders. Quid pro quo, as you may know, is Latin for "something for something," and that's how these leaders lead. They believe in giving rewards for good behavior and using punishments or threats to control bad behavior. They command and control. While they usually have good intentions and believe their leadership style is meritocratic, they produce high levels of emotional pressure, economic pressure, and inertia. On average, their people have a ToMo of -1.

The second type is the "hands-off" leader. Hands-off leaders use neither indirect nor direct motivators. They tend to get involved only when there is a problem. Like most people, many hands-off leaders have good intentions. They believe their teams want lots of space. The problem is, they're wrong. Teams perform best when their leaders get involved, building play, purpose, and potential. Many are surprised to learn that hands-off leaders are the second least effective, producing an average ToMo of just 11 in their people.

The third type of leader is the "enthusiast." There isn't a motivator an enthusiast won't try, whether it's indirect or direct. But as we've seen time and time again, direct motives help and indirect motives hurt. A leader who uses both types of motivation has teams with an average ToMo of 14. That's roughly the same ToMo as the leader who is hands-off! The indirect motivators cancel out the direct ones.

The fourth type of leader is the "fire starter." These leaders maximize total motivation by encouraging the direct motives and discouraging the indirect motives. Their teams have an average ToMo of 38. The top 5 percent of leaders—the best of the best—create ToMo levels of 60 or more in their teams.

In an experiment with the Israel Defense Forces (IDF) by Dov

Figure 16: The four styles of leadership as predicted by total motivation.

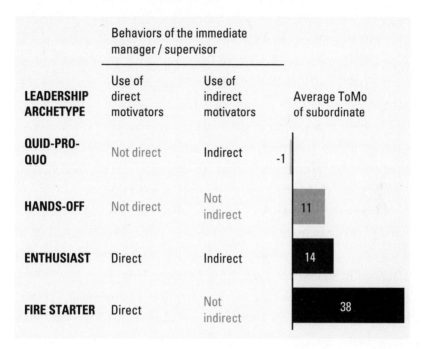

LEADERSHIP ARCHETYPE	Behaviors of the immediate manager / supervisor		Average ToMo of subordinate
	Use of direct motivators	Use of indirect motivators	
QUID-PRO-QUO	Not direct	Indirect	-1
HANDS-OFF	Not direct	Not indirect	11
ENTHUSIAST	Direct	Indirect	14
FIRE STARTER	Direct	Not indirect	38

Eden from Tel Aviv University, Bruce Avolio, now at the University of Washington, and colleagues, a group of officer trainees were taught how to lead through the elements of the motive spectrum.[2] The trainee officers learned to create play by suggesting new ways of working, offering different angles for considering a problem, and helping team members reexamine assumptions. They learned to increase purpose by emphasizing their collective mission and speaking of values. They learned to increase potential through teaching and coaching, focusing on strengths, and treating people as individuals.

The soldiers also learned about some of the dangers of indirect motives. They were taught not to focus on subordinates' mistakes (which can create emotional pressure) and not to offer special rewards for work (which can create economic pressure).

After their training was finished, the soldiers were given infantry troops of their own to lead through basic training. The infantry troops trained by total motivation officers had better outcomes on psychological measures like critical thinking, willingness to put in extra effort, team orientation, and self-confidence than those trained by the IDF's traditional methods. And they scored better on practical tests as well. They performed 5 percent better on a light weapons written exam. They completed the grueling obstacle course an average of two minutes faster than the other troops—a 20 percent improvement.[3] Total motivation leadership affected not just their mindsets but their performance on tests of hard skills.

Complexity scientists have found that the same leadership behaviors that empower individuals enable organizations to adapt to a chaotic, complex world.[4] A study of 105 tech companies found a statistically significant connection between how much a CEO led through the principles of total motivation and company performance up to two years later.[5] The correlation was .54—very high for something as fuzzy as leadership style. Leaders that encourage ToMo create higher performing organizations—you don't have to choose between the two.

THE FIRE STARTERS

Each key within a high-performing culture must keep yin (adaptive performance, culture, ToMo) in balance with yang (tactical performance, strategy, financial obligations). Leaders are no exception. Through the lens of ToMo, we can see exactly how.

We tested dozens of leadership behaviors with thousands of people to see how each affected total motivation, and narrowed the list down to the top fourteen.

Play: Great leaders inspire curiosity and encourage experimentation. Psychologists have shown us how these behaviors create the play motive. Complexity researchers have shown that by "allowing experimentation" and "encouraging novelty," leaders create adaptive performance.[6]

The three leadership behaviors that most drive total motivation through play are listed below. For those interested in the data, we include the correlation between the behavior and total motivation in parenthesis. A highly motivating leader:

- Provides you with time, space, and encouragement to experiment and learn (.50)
- Makes it clear what it means to be performing well (.43)
- Challenges you to solve problems yourself (.41)

Purpose: The blame bias makes us believe that everyone works solely for money. Fire starters help you see and believe in your work's purpose. A highly motivating leader:

- Helps you see that your work is important and meaningful (.55)
- Role models and expects you to live by positive, consistent values and a common sense of purpose (.47)
- Puts the customer's interests first (.44)

Potential: Great leaders help you connect your work to your personal goals and needs. They show you that your investment in your work is also an investment in yourself. A highly motivating leader:

- Actively links the work with your personal goals (.52)
- Helps you to develop and focus your time on your strengths rather than your weaknesses (.45)
- Provides you with more responsibility as your skills grow (.39)

Emotional pressure: To reduce emotional pressure, a great leader reduces the potential for people to feel fear, shame, guilt, or peer pressure. A great fire starter:

- Ensures targets and goals are fair and reasonable (.44)
- Is fair, honest, and transparent (.35)
- Enables friendships at work (.35)

Economic pressure: To reduce economic pressure, fire starters avoid using rewards or punishments to coerce people to work. Instead, he or she:

- Ensures you are evaluated holistically (.35)

Inertia: To avoid building inertia, the strongest leaders remove obstacles from your path and make sure your work will have impact. He or she:

- Makes it easy to get things done and ensures you don't waste effort (.34)

Before you start tattooing leadership behaviors on your forearms, know that you don't have to memorize all of these. Instead, remind yourself that your job is to balance tactical and adaptive performance by maximizing total motivation, and you'll do all the right things.

THE LEADER AND THE BARISTA

Most leadership stories begin with the personality and history of the leader. We believe it's just as important to examine a leader from the perspective of the person being led.

Mike joined his local Starbucks as a barista as a way to pay the bills while he studied anthropology in college. A broad-shouldered guy with a huge beard who enjoys solo hiking and the Discovery Channel, Mike comes off as a grumpy, smart, and principled naturalist—not the type of guy who becomes a Starbucks cheerleader.

"This is only temporary, just to pay the tuition," he told himself on his way to work the first day. His incoming motive was economic pressure. He never thought it could be more.

His first customer ordered a triple grande nonfat latte with caramel drizzle. "What's the point of the nonfat milk if you're squirting caramel all over it?" Mike asked. In his mind, it was a friendly conversation starter. That's not how the customer interpreted it. Mike's sharp, dry sense of humor didn't seem like a good match for the drink line.

That same day, Mike met his manager, Jeff. Fortunately for Mike, the store, and its customers, Jeff is a total motivation leader. On day one, Jeff explained the store's mission to Mike. As Mike put it, "He wants [Starbucks] to be more than a coffee shop. He wants it to be a place where anyone of any culture or any race, high school kids or old people, can come and hang out for a few hours." Jeff had turned the store's mission into Mike's mission.

First, Mike needed to learn how to make people feel at home, a skill that benefited the store and him personally. As an introvert, being social with customers wasn't a natural skill for him. In Mike's first reviews, Jeff encouraged him to experiment with customers until he found a style that clicked. Jeff knew that customer service requires adaptive performance.

Mike practiced different greetings with different smiles and different inflections of his voice. He worked particularly hard to remember the names and favorite drinks of frequent customers, treating it like a game. Eventually, he found a style that worked for him and his customers.

Over the next months he built friendships with many of the store's regulars, and actually enjoyed learning how to provide what he calls "legendary levels of customer service."

Jeff helped create a common purpose that was meaningful and important even to those who weren't naturally good at it. The overarching culture of Starbucks backed him up. He built his store's sense of purpose on top of the Starbucks' mission "to inspire and nurture the human spirit—one person, one cup and one neighborhood at a time." Over time, Mike began to believe that Jeff and the company were authentic. Their mission was reinforced through everyday habits, like calling employees "partners," and through larger investments, like providing employees with health insurance and supporting farmers in seven countries around the world.[7]

Jeff always put the customer's interests first. While the store had sales goals, they were not high stakes. "It was about making you *want* to sell more and providing suggestions on how to get there. At other restaurants, they ask if you want the spicy nuggets before they ask you how you are," Mike said. Mike knew from his leader's behavior that his first job was to create a home for his customers.

Jeff also motivated Mike through potential. He expected Mike to learn far more than how many pumps of syrup go into a Grande Caramel Macchiato (three). Over time, Mike became responsible for more and more of the operations of the shop, from ordering supplies, to managing opening and closing, to implementing new approaches to store cleanliness. He managed each project end-to-end, with the ultimate goal of knowing how to run the whole store. Jeff instilled a sense of ownership in the team. "Any time you wait for your manager to fix a problem is time wasted. You're going to run out of stuff—how do you deal with that? People are going to call in sick—you have to start calling around to find someone or decide to stay yourself. When you leave, you have to make sure that [the store is] still running the same way. A huge benchmark for management is that if you left, the store should be running perfectly," Mike said. By giving Mike the freedom to deal with the VUCA of the store for himself, Jeff created extreme levels of adaptive performance.

Here too Jeff had support from Starbucks' overall philosophy. Have you ever noticed that everyone at Starbucks is dressed the same, without any special outfit for managers? That's so every employee can learn to take the lead. It creates a mindset for store managers that they are coaches, not bureaucrats. Even more subtle: if you flip down the top of the iconic Starbucks green aprons, you will find a hidden message just for store workers:

We create inspired moments in each customer's day.
ANTICIPATE CONNECT PERSONALIZE OWN.

Notice how each of those words describes adaptive performance.

Figure 17: Starbucks is able to generate 18 points more total motivation in its people versus five other fast-food restaurants.

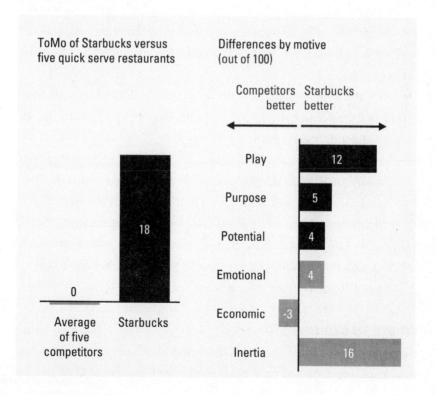

ToMo of Starbucks versus five quick serve restaurants

Differences by motive (out of 100)

Competitors better   Starbucks better

Play 12
Purpose 5
Potential 4
Emotional 4
Economic -3
Inertia 16

18

0

Average of five competitors   Starbucks

Jeff too found a good role model in Starbucks' CEO Howard Schultz, who recently announced a potential-enhancing college scholarship program. As Schultz put it: "You can't just focus on profitability. An enduring great company has to be based on more. . . . Starbucks is a people-based company. . . . Our people create the experience and we have to do everything we can to exceed their expectations."[8] A total motivation culture is integral to Starbucks' core strategy.

This philosophy is paying off in an industry where treating people well is not the norm. Starbucks creates industry-leading total motivation across its more than 180,000 employees in 20,000-plus stores. Starbucks beats its competitors' averages on every dimension of total motivation except economic pressure.

Economically, this gives Starbucks industry-leading employee retention[9] and incredibly high customer loyalty. This builds trust. That trust compels customers to find a Starbucks even when there are cheaper or more convenient alternatives. That trust also enables Starbucks to branch out into new products more easily than its competitors can.

Jeff's decision to make every barista an independent, adaptive problem solver chimes with Schultz's philosophy. As Schultz wrote in his history of Starbucks:

> *Early on I realized that I had to hire people smarter and more qualified than I was in a number of different fields, and I had to let go of a lot of decision-making. I can't tell you how hard that is. But if you've imprinted your values on the people around you, you can dare to trust them to make the right moves.*[10]

WHERE TO BEGIN

Unlike Jeff at Starbucks, most leaders don't have the luxury of being in a relatively high ToMo adaptive culture themselves. They live in a world of tactical performance objectives. A sales leader may have revenue targets. An operations leader may have cost goals. A CEO may have share price targets. We know that these tactical objectives, often managed through indirect motivators, weigh heavily on a leader's mind. Nevertheless, these leaders must still inspire the highest levels of ToMo in their people. Given this natural tension between tactical and adaptive performance, where should a leader begin?

To create balance between yin and yang, rather than treating the fourteen behaviors as a checklist, great fire starters should start by embedding these behaviors and total motivation into every aspect of the rhythm of performance management.

For example, most leaders use goals to manage their team's performance. You may give a sales rep a goal to increase widget sales by five units a day, for example. But think about what this goal assumes. By telling your salesperson to increase sales by five units, you've assumed that he probably knows how but simply doesn't want to. A salesperson could respond to this goal in one of three ways:

- He could work harder to achieve the goal. This isn't an ideal answer because it will take away time spent on adaptive performance. Worse still, it simply isn't sustainable.
- He could create cobra farms to sell more, by exaggerating, lying, or gaming the system. Clearly this isn't ideal either.
- Lastly, he could actually learn how to sell more. This is the adaptive behavior you want, so why not be more direct about it?

Imagine that you have just become the CEO of a cellular telephone company. Your primary objective is to increase the company's market share from 7 percent, a tactical performance objective. Your new chief marketing officer is meeting with you this morning to understand what her goal should be. You have three choices of goal to give her:

- Effort goal: "Do your best." This is what a "hands-off" leader would try.
- Tactical goal: "Increase market share to 21 percent." This is what a quid pro quo leader would try.
- Adaptive goal: "Learn six new strategies for increasing market share." This is what a fire starter would try. Notice this goal does not ask for six new strategies that work. It encourages testing six new strategies regardless of the outcome.

Which one would you choose?

Business school students tackled this simulation, with some receiving a "do your best" effort goal, some a tactical goal (to increase market share to 21 percent), and some an adaptive goal (to learn new approaches).[11] The students could adjust a large number of variables, from the product's pricing to the advertising approach, from research and development to alliance building. For eight rounds of the game, each representing a year, the students developed and refined their strategies. Already, the teams with adaptive goals were performing the best. While the other two groups lost market share (the effort goal group lost 14 percent, the tactical goal group lost 20 percent), the groups with adaptive goals grew market share by 28 percent.

Then, the simulation introduced a shock: deregulation. The regionally restricted market suddenly became open resulting in greater competition. The strategies that had worked for the first half of the game no longer applied.

By the end of the experiment, those with the tactical performance goal performed the worst. Their market share *decreased* by 8 percent. Those who tried to "do their best" performed only slightly better, increasing their market share by 7 percent. Those with the adaptive goals, instructed to learn six new strategies, performed far better. At the end of the simulation their market share had grown 59 percent!

Academic researchers have found that tactical performance goals focus people on just the *appearance* of competence.[12] Adaptive goals focus people on *becoming* competent.[13]

Armed with this understanding of adaptive goals and fire starter behaviors, you should engage in a simple weekly rhythm. Once a week, you should look at your tactical goals and think about how they can be translated into adaptive goals. Informally, you should ensure that all of your people are constantly working toward a set of adaptive goals of their own choosing. Since you already have a perspective on where you need performance to improve, you are helping them set adaptive goals that will matter the most to the team.

For example:

- *Tactical goal*: Increase the number of customers buying two of our products by 5 percent.
- *Adaptive goal*: Find three new ways to describe how two of our products create value together.

- *Tactical goal*: Reduce operating costs within this unit from 80 percent of revenue to 75 percent of revenue.
- *Adaptive goal*: Find three new ways to make our process less complicated.

- *Tactical goal*: Increase customer satisfaction from 75 percent to 80 percent.
- *Adaptive goal*: Find four new ways to proactively address customer complaints on the first call.

Then, on a weekly basis, you should have a team huddle. Gather all the members of your team for a forty-five-minute discussion. The point of this discussion is to answer three questions:

1. What did we learn this week? This question makes you take stock of the week's adaptive goals. It brings to the surface great ideas and allows them to spread across the team. It also allows you to show that even a failed experiment can create value if it adds to the team's knowledge.
2. How did we progress against our purpose this week? This question allows you to have an honest dialogue about the purpose of your work while combating inertia.
3. What do we need to learn next week? This question helps you set the adaptive goals for the following week.

Through this set of questions, you can integrate all fourteen of the fire starter behaviors mentioned earlier into a simple, easy-to-implement routine. By connecting that routine with your tactical goals, you can also ensure that you are balancing the yin and yang of performance. Your team's ToMo increases and with it their performance.

Make sure to have a scribe for this meeting, documenting the three answers. Also make sure to start and end on time. If huddles become unfocused, they become less like play and more like inertia. Lastly, rotate the scribe role, and the huddle leader role, across all your team members so each has a chance to facilitate.

A COMPANY OF FIRE STARTERS

If you surveyed your organization today, you'd likely find that a quarter of your leaders are fire starters. Few will reach their full potential. Most organizations hope that talented leaders will simply emerge; great organizations are more deliberate. They build systems that help all of their people continuously improve their leadership skills. That system requires two primary components: training and feedback.

Training Total Motivation Leaders

> *The company says it is all about ethical behavior and not "gaming" to get sales, but my managers and district managers push gaming and hurting customers as long as we get sales . . . we are constantly being berated for not cheating customers . . . it's sales, sales, sales and more sales.*[14]

The quote above might sound like it comes from *Glengarry Glen Ross,* but it's from an actual branch manager of a bank.

While your local bank may be a fairly sterile place to visit, managing it can be incredibly stressful. Layoffs have become common, as customers use branches less and less frequently. Performance pressure can be high. While much of the work is disbursing cash and accepting deposits, large shares of revenue come from selling credit cards, mortgages, and loans. These are tough sells since it is hard to differentiate your products from that of your competitors.

Branch employees need a range of qualities. They need creativity and problem solving to match products to customers' needs. They need grit to handle the constant stream of rejection. They need ethics to turn down customers who don't qualify for loans.

Three researchers wanted to find out if leadership training for branch managers would make a difference to sales.[15] They randomly selected managers from a top bank and gave each of them one day of leadership training on the principles behind total motivation, plus four "booster" sessions on how to motivate their teams.

After these sessions, credit card sales rose 20 percent more for the directly motivated teams versus a control group. Their personal loan sales were 47 percent higher. A similar study across one hundred

Austrian bank branches confirmed the result, showing a statistically significant relationship between high-ToMo leadership and performance.[16] Leadership training using total motivation is surprisingly effective.

Your first step should be to design and test your own training sessions. For small companies, they can be as simple as convening discussion groups and instituting peer-to-peer coaching. The discussions should focus on how team leaders can bring more play, purpose, and potential into daily routines, meetings, and performance check-ins, using examples from successful leaders in the organization. Peer-to-peer coaching can be as simple as brainstorming with a peer on how to increase total motivation in your team.

While some larger companies have leadership training programs in place, few focus on the psychological drivers of performance. Integrate total motivation into your curriculum through formal courses, online training, and discussions with high-performing leaders.

Remember, the process of learning should itself increase total motivation; the training sessions should be infused with play, purpose, and potential, and they should be conducted in low-risk, nonevaluative settings to reduce emotional pressure. Once your people understand total motivation, the next step is to help them see the progress they make in their leadership skills. The best way to do this is through feedback systems that enable continuous improvement.

Feedback for Continuous Improvement

In its early days, Google famously tried to eliminate managers. Founders Larry Page and Sergey Brin wanted to replicate the collegial culture of their Stanford graduate program. But as the company began to grow at an exponential rate, they realized they couldn't keep up with all the questions coming their way.[17] To figure out how to lead people in the right way, they reinvented yet another field—human resources.

Google tasked its "People Operations" team to make all of its decisions using data and analytics. A third of the team is composed of strategists and a third hold advanced technical degrees in fields like psychology and statistics.[18] Each team member's laptop proudly showcases a sticker that reads: "I have charts and graphs to back me up. So f*** off."[19] Few organizations bring this kind of fact-based rigor to their HR processes.

People Operations decided to use their world-class analytical rigor to find out if leaders mattered, and if so, what makes a good leader. As Laszlo Bock, the head of People Operations, put it, "Part of the challenge with leadership is that it's very driven by gut instinct in most cases—and even worse, everyone thinks they're really good at it. The reality is that very few people are."[20]

Though they didn't use the language of total motivation, Google found that its best leaders inspire play (for example, by empowering their teams), purpose (by setting a clear vision), and potential (by helping team members with their career goals and being a good coach).[21]

Once Google shared the results of its analysis with the organization, it set out to design training courses that focused on particular skills, such as how to define a vision and bring it to life through compelling stories. High-performing managers led panel discussions in which engineers could ask other engineers about how they manage their teams. Managers from around the world joined them online.

But learning new skills requires testing those skills in the real world and seeing how they work. You need to know if your leadership skills are actually improving. So twice a year Googlers fill out a survey to provide anonymous feedback to their managers.

Importantly, the surveys are launched separately and independently from performance evaluations to avoid creating indirect motivation.

Google's training and feedback systems have shown results. From 2010 to 2012, the median leadership score for the company rose from 83 percent to 88 percent. The biggest impact, according to Harvard professor David Garvin, has been on low performers. One vice president in sales, for example, had good reviews from his manager but "terrible" scores from his team. He sat down with a colleague in People Operations and came up with a plan to change. After just two survey cycles, his rating had risen from 46 to 86 percent. "I came here as a senior sales guy," the VP reflected, "but now I feel like a general manager."

GOING FORWARD

Building a world-class culture starts with you. Begin your own continuous improvement cycle, selecting one leadership behavior to work on every two weeks. Find a friend going through the same journey and share ideas. Huddle regularly with your team and help them develop play, purpose, and potential. To create change at an organizational level, develop trainings and feedback cycles that fit your organization's culture and routines.

Improving leadership skills is a surprisingly effective and low-cost way to begin to change the culture of your organization. But while a fire starter can ignite motivation, she can't keep it going alone.

A high-performance culture is strongly influenced by its organizational identity—its objectives, standards of behavior, and heritage.

Identity

A researcher places a marble between the handles of a spring-loaded handgrip and tells you to hold it there for as long as possible. The moment your hand weakens, the marble will drop and the experiment will come to an end. A minute into the exercise, your forearm is burning.

The experiment, conducted by researchers from New York University and Tel Aviv University, was focused on understanding the effects of identity on perseverance.[1] After the subjects set a baseline for their performance, they were divided into two groups. Let's call them the "tactical" group and the "identity" group.

The tactical group was asked, in a seemingly unrelated survey, "How do I maintain good personal relationships?" Their answers generated a related series of four more questions. For example:

1. How do you maintain good personal relationships? They could have answered, *"By spending time with my friends every week."*
2. How do you spend time with your friends every week? *"I spend time with my friends by going to dinner with them."*
3. How do you go to dinner with your friends? *"I check in with them on Mondays and we pick a day to get together."*

4. How do you check in with them on Mondays? *I put a reminder in my calendar for every Monday at noon.*

The identity group went through the same exercise, except instead of being asked *how* they maintained personal relationships, they were asked *why* they maintained them. For example:

1. Why do you maintain good personal relationships? *Because I really value having friends.*
2. Why do you value having friends? *Because friends make me happy.*
3. Why do friends make you happy? *Because it feels good to have people to share your life with.*
4. Why does it feel good to have people to share your life with? *Because I'm the kind of person that cares for people.*

By the fourth question, this group was reflecting on who they were at their cores—the values, behaviors, and aspirations that made up their identity.

So how did the performance of the two groups compare? Surprisingly, the resilience of the tactical group decreased. They held the handgrip five seconds shorter on average than their baseline. If the average person holds a handgrip for about a minute, this represents an 8 percent decrease in their self-control.[2] The identity group, on the other hand, got more resilient. They held the handgrip a whopping eleven seconds longer (roughly an 18 percent increase) than their personal baselines. Just as interesting, both sets of participants reported no change in their mood even while their resilience was changing.

Reflecting on your identity—who you are and what you stand for—increases purpose and often play. Your organization also has an identity: a reason for existing, a set of values and behaviors that guide its decisions, heritage, and traditions. When we measured the strength of an organization's identity and compared that to its total motivation, we found a 65-point swing in ToMo between people who worked for an organization with a strong identity and those who worked for an organization with a weak identity. This made identity the second strongest of the keys to culture, following only role design (discussed in Chapter 10, "The Playground").

Let's take a look at why an organization's identity is so important, and how it's formed, starting with a story about a company that makes software.

IT'S ALL IN THE "WHY"

If you've walked through a major airport over the last few years, odds are that you've seen a sales kiosk for a company called Rosetta Stone. Located in Virginia, Rosetta Stone makes and sells software that teaches languages. What are your impressions of this company?

A few years ago, we were sitting in a New York coffee shop, talking about how languages adapt despite the absence of a central control system. A man sitting next to us leaned over. "I didn't mean to eavesdrop, but I couldn't help but overhear your conversation," he said. "I work at Rosetta Stone where I help preserve endangered languages." He went on to explain the company's efforts to preserve languages from the Navajos in the Four Corners region of the American southwest to the Inuit tribe in Newfoundland, Canada.

So deep was Rosetta Stone's love of languages that it maintained a pro bono program to save dying languages. Using its own software and tools, with little hope of making money, it made sure that there would always be a record of these endangered tongues.

Now what do you think of Rosetta Stone? Again, if you're like most people, understanding why it exists—glimpsing an identity that goes beyond selling software and making money—reshapes your impression of the company. Actions speak louder than words.

This phenomenon is surprisingly ancient. In the fourth century B.C., Aristotle was teaching the art of rhetoric to his pupils at Plato's Academy. In his teachings, he describes three methods of persuasion, which he called *logos*, *pathos*, and *ethos*.

Logos is persuasion through logic. Given our love of data, we like to believe that logic trumps all, but unfortunately, it is often a fairly weak form of persuasion.[3]

Pathos is persuasion through emotion. You see it in action when politicians use patriotism or fear to win your vote, or when advertisements use provocative images to sell products.[4]

Ethos is persuasion through identity. A speaker's history, ideals, and actions persuade you. Her beliefs, experiences, and character make her trustworthy. It's why we want to understand the personal stories of our politicians. It's why we want to know the credentials of our doctors, and the values of our schoolteachers. As Aristotle puts it:

> *Of the modes of persuasion furnished by the spoken word there are three kinds. The first kind depends on the personal character of the speaker; the second on putting the audience into a certain frame of mind; the third on the proof, or apparent proof, provided by the words of the speech itself. Persuasion is achieved by the speaker's personal character when the speech is so spoken as to make us think him credible . . . his character may almost be called the most effective means of persuasion he possesses.[5]*

In the case of Rosetta Stone, just a glimpse of its identity creates a strong positive impression. Imagine what a broad, well-designed identity could do. Unfortunately, the opposite is also true. Without a compelling and convincing identity, cultures become weak and organizations become less adaptive. Performance weakens as customers lose trust.

A venerable international bank had a string of scandals, including accusations of money laundering, rate fixing, manipulating commodities markets, and fraud. An investigative commission attributed these scandals to a lack of identity. "We believe that the business practices for which [the financial institution] has rightly been criticized were shaped predominantly by its cultures, which rested on uncertain foundations," it concluded. "There was no sense of common purpose in a group that had grown and diversified significantly in less than two decades."[6]

Customers are also affected by the character of a company. A recent study conducted by McKinsey & Company found that the biggest driver of satisfaction for bank customers wasn't its products, prices, or ability to resolve problems, but whether it inspired trust.[7]

Similarly, marketing expert Simon Sinek (watch his incredible TED talk for more of his insights) points out that the best brands in the world "Start with Why." Understanding why a person or organization operates—understanding identity—builds the highest levels of brand loyalty.[8]

All that said, it's not easy for organizations to build and manage their identities. An identity comes alive through your objectives, behavioral code, heritage, and traditions. When these are designed and aligned to increase total motivation, they help create high-performing, adaptive cultures.

YOUR OBJECTIVE

Your objective is the anchor of your organization's identity. It should explain your "why" to your people and your customers.

Your objective clearly drives the purpose motive, but it also drives the play motive. When people are clear on the objective, they can accomplish a task without needing micromanagement, enabling them to experiment and adapt (a behavior that increases ToMo by roughly 70 points, and the primary component of good role design).

The military has a long tradition of using objectives to give people flexibility in how they work. Called "commander's intent," it requires every soldier to understand the intent of a mission, so that if the plan fails, soldiers can improvise. As one former US Army officer explained it to us, the concept of commander's intent is "the lifeblood of how we operate. . . . Without it, you can't expect people on the ground to make decisions for themselves." If the intent of your mission is to demolish a target at all costs versus to maintain good relations with the local people, soldiers will improvise in very different ways when plans go awry.

Major Jim Storr of the British Army explains how a leader should operate when using commander's intent:

> *Superiors should state a minimum of control measures, so as not to constrain subordinates' freedom of action. This grants the subordinate considerable latitude. In an environment of trust and initiative, such latitude also speeds the production, dissemination and comprehension of orders, thus increasing tempo. Mission Command is intended to avoid the production of long and detailed orders, and to allow initiative and the seizure of fleeting opportunities. It can only work where both parties trust each other to act appropriately.*[9]

Some of the greatest leaders in military history have depended on commander's intent. One stunning early example occurred in 1805, off the coast of Spain, in a battle with the highest of stakes. Napoleon had assembled a fleet of forty ships to invade England. With only thirty-three ships of his own, Great Britain's Admiral Lord Nelson was literally fighting for his country's freedom.[10]

Traditionally, opposing navies formed two parallel lines and opened fire. There were good reasons for such a nonadaptive strategy. First, the giant wooden galleons had side-facing canons. By keeping their ships in a straight line, navies could avoid the risk of friendly fire while concentrating on their strength.

The second reason is more subtle. During the heat of battle, the commander of the fleet—its admiral—would ride on the flagship. From this flagship, he would issue commands to his captains using signal flags. To receive these commands, the whole fleet would need to have line of sight to the flagship or the ability to quickly relay commands to one another. Again, the simple answer was to line up the ships.

The two-line strategy rarely resulted in decisive victories; most battles ended when one side retreated. In a battle of strength versus strength, Nelson stood little chance when his opponent had over 21 percent more ships and almost 24 percent more canons. Even if he could prevail in this matchup, Nelson didn't want Napoleon's navy to retreat and recoup for another day. In his own words, he wanted to "make the business decisive."[11]

Instead of pitting tactical performance against tactical performance, Nelson realized that he could win by better balancing tactical and adaptive performance.

The tactical portion of the British Navy's plan was simple, although completely unconventional. Instead of forming one parallel line of ships for strength, Nelson's plan required his ships to approach the enemy head-on in two perpendicular lines. Their goal was to divide the enemy's line into three pieces as quickly as possible all while taking on a hail of enemy fire that they could not return. Nelson himself would lead the charge and direct his own ship to take out the enemy's flagship. Nelson believed that his enemy was so focused on tactical performance that without a clear line of sight to their leader, they would crumble.

Once the tactical portion of the plan was completed, then came the adaptive portion. Nelson told each of his captains that they had discretion on which targets to choose and how to attack them.

Nelson described this philosophy in his Trafalgar Memorandum[12] (a theory of impact, as you will see in Chapter 10, "The Playground") that clearly expressed every part of his intent.

- *First, he describes the VUCA inherent in battle:* "Thinking it almost impossible to bring a Fleet . . . into a Line of Battle in variable winds, thick weather, and other circumstances which must occur, without such a loss of time that the opportunity would probably be lost."
- *He goes on to describe why perfect planning is impossible:* "Something must be left to chance; nothing is sure in a Sea Fight beyond all others. Shot will carry away the masts and yards of friends as well as foes."
- *To win, Nelson writes, we need to be adaptive:* "But, in case Signals can neither be seen or perfectly understood, no Captain can do very wrong if he places his Ship alongside that of an Enemy."

By clearly laying out his intentions, he was able to trust his men to make their own best judgments in the smoke of battle. Nelson trusted the adaptive performance of his captains so much that he wouldn't need to issue orders during the battle. This was fortunate for the British since Nelson died from a gunshot wound shortly after crippling the enemy's flagship. The only commands he issued to his fleet during the battle were at its onset: "Prepare to anchor after the close of day," "Engage the enemy more closely," and "England expects that every man will do his duty."[13]

In this battle of adaptive versus tactical performance, adaptability won the day. Napoleon's navy didn't know what hit them. Despite their superior numbers, they lost twenty-two ships while the British lost none. Moreover, it is estimated that French casualties outnumbered British casualties more than three to one.[14] Nelson not only saved England from invasion, but established the "decisive supremacy of Great Britain's sea power."[15]

Nelson didn't wake up that October morning in 1805 with a grand strategy. He had been preparing his men to improvise throughout his whole career. He spent hours dining with each of his many captains, sharing his own ideas and listening to theirs. As one contemporary described it, "He would fully develop them to his own ideas of the different and best models of Attack . . . they could [as a result] ascertain with precision what were the ideas and intentions of their commander without the aid of further instructions."[16]

The concept of commander's intent grew more critical throughout the 1800s, as armies of 200,000 or more needed to work together toward a common objective. No one commander could possibly make all the necessary decisions. Many of today's executives, with hundreds or hundreds of thousands of employees around the world, can relate. But when the objective is clear, your people can take initiative, experiment, and innovate. You can have hundreds or thousands of smart, coordinated decision makers.

Having a clear objective, however, is only part of the battle. As we saw with Rosetta Stone, that objective must also be compelling. Leadership and values experts from Cornell University examined how a company's objective influences people's employment decisions. They asked over eight thousand people to rate jobs that included indirect factors like pay and promotions, but also direct factors like fairness, concern for others, honesty, and work ethic. When they computed how much each factor mattered, the ability to help others outranked both pay and promotion opportunities. Only fairness ranked higher.[17]

Professor Adam Grant has extensively studied how objectives with a "prosocial purpose" increase motivation and performance. When we feel like we're helping others and the world, we bring our best to the table.[18] An objective that is plainly and obviously helpful to others is the easiest way to drive the purpose motive. This holds true across cultures. In a survey of people across thirteen nations, from Singapore to the United States to Brazil, people rank benevolence—acting kindly toward others—as the most important human value. (Note: the second most important value was self-direction—essentially the play motive).[19] When an organization's objective intersects with its employees' and customers' values, the purpose motive ignites.

The objective of your overall organization should also be tailored to each business unit and team. Begin by answering two simple questions:

1. Is our objective clear?
2. Is the reason for that objective compelling?

Once you have your objective, you'll need a behavioral code: the expectations for the ways that people will achieve their objective.

THE BEHAVIORAL CODE

Many organizations have lists of values like "honesty" and "integrity." Unfortunately, these restatements of basic human values aren't enough. While we often blame the values of an individual for misbehavior, few people believe they're acting unethically in the heat of the moment. Moreover, reasonable people can disagree on what "respect" or "excellence" looks like in practice. Instead, companies need a behavior code that details *how* people should make decisions, especially in thorny situations.

A code exists so that your employees can adapt, making complicated decisions without having to check in with leaders all the time. It is the set of playground rules—once you know the rules, you are free to play. A behavioral code is complete when you can leave your people to make their own decisions for the company and trust that those decisions will be made appropriately. The code should cover such topics as:

1. *Problem solving*: How do you expect people to solve problems? You want your behavioral code to correct for the blame bias and other common decision making biases (for example, confirmation bias, coordination neglect, short-termism, narrow aperture).
2. *Prioritization*: How should people prioritize competing objectives, for example adaptive activities (like learning or experimentation) versus performance activities (like sales)? What should be prioritized—better experience for customers, or a near-term sales target?
3. *Conflict*: How should people deal with issues and decisions that fall in the "gray area" between obviously right and obviously wrong? How should they deal with conflicting opinions? When is consensus required and when are people able to make their own decisions?
4. *Motivation*: How do you expect your leaders to lead and motivate? How do you expect your people to build and maintain a system of culture and motivation?
5. *Heritage*: Which symbols, practices, or rituals are sacred, never to be eliminated or ignored?

At McKinsey & Company, all new consultants learn that they must "Uphold the obligation to dissent," meaning that they must speak up if they disagree, no matter how junior they are, and that they must listen when others do the same. Another component of the code is to "Use our global network to deliver the best of the firm to all clients." One of the most astounding things to newcomers at the Firm (as employees call it) is that they can email anyone in the organization to ask for help and help will be provided.[20]

Keller Williams is one of the fastest-growing real estate firms you've probably never heard of. During the housing crisis in 2009, while many other firms shrank, Keller Williams grew. The organization gives a lot of credit for its success to its behavioral code, which helps its seventeen thousand agents work for the right motives.[21] The BOLD Laws, as the code is called, are formally taught in a course called BOLD, which stands for Business Objective: Life by Design.[22] They're also used frequently in the day-to-day work of many Keller Williams teams. One former agent, Jordan, described the laws that most resonated with him.[23] A former marine, he was initially skeptical of the enthusiasm with which his colleagues celebrated the code, but he was soon hooked on phrases like:

- *"Don't listen to your drunk monkey."*[24] The monkey is the voice that distracts you with thoughts of lunch and baseball games, as well as the voice that "sits on your shoulder and tells you not to do things because you're too scared," Jordan explained. It's the voice that says you're going to embarrass yourself, the voice of emotional pressure. Imagining that voice as a drunk monkey enables BOLD users to laugh and push it aside.
- *"Motion = emotion."* You can't hold off on starting a task until you feel energized. "Movement itself will change how you feel," Jordan said. If you're avoiding making your morning phone calls because of emotional pressure, don't wait until the pressure goes away to start. Once you start calling, the pressure will begin to fade, and you'll rediscover the play and purpose of your work. The law helps Jordan get through the unexpected twists in his day. "In real estate, you're hit with these emotional blows throughout the day, whether it be a house not appraising or a deal falling through. Constant movement makes everything ok—it reminds you that you can run your life."

- *"It's not about selling real estate; it's about following a schedule."* Keller Williams believes that if you control your inputs
  (your schedule), the outputs (sales) will follow. This saying
  encourages people not to worry about outcomes they can't
  control, but to trust the process. Jordan blocks out his day
  with specific prescheduled tasks, following the complementary
  BOLD law: "If it is not on your schedule, it doesn't exist."
  Yet he recognizes that he needs time to adapt—he has a prescheduled time blocked for unexpected tasks. He doesn't have
  to worry about balancing tactical and adaptive performance:
  he's carved out time for both.
- *"Living a life by design, not by default."* Perhaps most importantly, the laws encourage users to start with their ideal life, and
  work backwards. Don't let inertia take control. Instead, actively
  manage your own ToMo.

"When you're taking the course and learning these BOLD laws
for the first time, they're eye opening, even though they're really just
common sense," Jordan explained. They prompt Keller Williams
members to think critically about how they prioritize, and apply a
new level of discipline to their routine. "They are the avenues that
point you in the right direction," Jordan explained, a shortcut to
high performance.

Steve Jobs understood the importance of the behavioral code
too. Among his final priorities was codifying and teaching the practices that led to Apple's success. The company recruited top business
school professors from places like Harvard University to research
how Apple made its most critical decisions.[25] It hired the dean of the
Yale School of Management to build a program to teach the code to
employees, and Apple University was born. Few photographs of the
university have surfaced, and information about it is closely held,
but the *New York Times* found three employees who were willing

to share some details of the program.[26] Employees study pivotal moments in Apple's history, like the decision to make the iPod and iTunes software work with Windows. Steve Jobs was opposed to Windows compatibility, but his team overcame his objections, leading to the success of Apple's music player and, as the *Times* reports, paving the way for the iPhone. A course entitled "What Makes Apple Apple" compares a Google TV remote with seventy-eight buttons to a slim, three-button Apple TV controller. A course on "The Best Things" reminds employees to surround themselves with top talent and materials.

If you're like most organizations, you don't have a behavioral code. If that's the case, we suggest you use this simple exercise to write one. Begin by finding examples of difficult adaptive decisions that your organization has made in the past, including some that were made well and some that were made poorly. In small groups, talk through each of the good decisions and ask yourselves how that decision was made, and what behaviors led to it. Once you have your code, test it against the decisions that were made poorly. Would these principles have prevented the situations that ended badly?

YOUR HERITAGE

"I think I saw the descendants of the original Cailler cows," a Nestlé management trainee we interviewed told us. "I couldn't help but feel pride in my company."

The speaker, who we'll call Davi, had just visited one of the company's first chocolate factories, located in a picturesque gorge in the Swiss Alps. The factory was founded by François-Louis Cailler, who spent four years in Italy studying the art of chocolate making before setting up his own farm and factory in the early 1800s. His creativity and determination led to a breakthrough a few years later: the invention of chocolate so milky smooth that it could be molded into slabs. The chocolate bar was born and humanity rejoiced.[27]

Nestlé employees fly into Switzerland from all over the world for training, where they study business cases related to all the components of the company, from marketing to research and development. The Cailler factory includes a museum celebrating the history of chocolate; test kitchens underline the company's ongoing commitment to innovation. "We saw the chocolate being made, and tasted it directly off the line. We saw the city where Nestlé was born. Experiences like that define your identity in relationship to the company," Davi told us.

It's not enough to have a clear and compelling reason for being, or a behavioral code that everyone lives by. You have to make your identity credible and omnipresent. You can't prove that you're funny by telling people how funny you are. You have to tell them a joke that makes them laugh. The same is true about your identity. You cannot tell people that your identity is genuine—they have to feel it.

Walking the walk affects how behaviors pass from one person to the next. Researchers from Northwestern University recruited a group of third, fourth, and fifth graders to see how this works.[28] The students participated in a miniature bowling game, during which they earned gift certificates redeemable for money. Some of the children, who we'll call the "charity group," heard a research assistant claim, "If I win any money today, I am going to give some to poor children." Another group of children, the "greed group," heard a research assistant say he would keep his winnings for himself.

When the charity group saw a researcher practice what he preached—both encouraging charity and giving away his winnings—64 percent of the children donated their winnings to charity too. When the researchers preached charity but practiced greed, only 47 percent of the children gave away their earnings. Startlingly, when the researcher preached greed but practiced charity, practice trumped preaching and 63 percent of the children gave away their earnings. Actions speak louder than words.

Objectives and behavioral codes are not enough. Your people must see them in action. One way to do this is to preserve and share your heritage—the real examples of how your organization has lived up to its identity even in tough times.

CEO Gary Lubner understands the importance of heritage. His company has turned something that many might think of as mundane—fixing broken car windshields—into something noble. Belron, the world's largest vehicle glass repair and replacement company, operates in thirty-four countries and employs more than 25,000 people, employees that Lubner regards as "everyday heroes."

The company's story began over a hundred years ago, when Lubner's grandfather pushed a wheelbarrow filled with glass through the streets of Johannesburg, South Africa. Lubner's parents expanded the family business, focusing on car windshields but always putting service first. When a young couple's car broke down one Friday and couldn't be fixed until Monday, his parents lent them their own car so they could get through the weekend.[29] This story is told over and over again at Belron; every executive knows it by heart. It reminds the workforce of their company's ethos, and as a result, the tradition continues.

For example, a man who operated a home-ironing business walked into a Belron branch in Portugal. Branch manager Joana Cotas saw the worry on his face when her team couldn't fix his van in time for his afternoon delivery run and no cars were available for rent. Following in the footsteps of the Lubner family, she loaned him her own personal car. Joana was profiled on Belron's "heroes website," where she was named a 2013 "Belron Everyday Hero."

Alain Bélanger, another Hero, created a cold chamber to make sure windshield wipers from a new supplier would stand up to Canadian winters. Using his own personal time, he also created an online system for evaluations, reducing administrative work. Davide Bonini in Italy developed a Remote Customer Advisor kiosk to connect customers in small branches with experts across the country. Osman Hanbarci in Turkey digitized the company's insurance system. A file now closes in 60 percent of the time and subcontractors forward 30 percent more jobs.

Lubner, the CEO, personally delivers the Belron Exceptional Customer Service Award to a select number of employees every six months, whether those employees are in China or Brazil. Dave Meller, Belron's head of People and Leadership, told us these stories with pride. "They're the heartbeat of the organization," he said.

TRADITIONS

If heritage is backward looking, traditions are meant to be carried forward. Traditions are the shared experiences that define who you are as an organization. As you'll see, they literally and figuratively put your people in synch, allowing them to practice what you preach.

The New Zealand Rugby Team, the All Blacks, is the winningest national team in the world. Not bad for a country of only 4.5 million people (roughly half the population of New York City). The principles of total motivation show up in their rugby program in unusual ways. Before each match, the team performs the Haka, a traditional Maori dance for warriors who are going into battle. Dancing may not sound macho, but when their competitors see the All Blacks performing the Haka, they quake.

As intimidating as the Haka is to watch, anthropologists suggest it may serve another purpose—to remind a tribe of its identity. It certainly does that for the All Blacks.

The very act of moving in synch is surprisingly powerful. A group of researchers put a group of test subjects in rocking chairs.[30] For ninety seconds, half of them rocked in synchronicity with a partner, while the other half rocked freestyle.

Afterward, pairs of test subjects jointly held a wooden labyrinth containing a steel ball, and worked together to steer it down a specific path. The pairs that had synchronized their rocking were 17 percent faster at this simple problem-solving exercise than the others.

Rituals go far beyond synchronized movement. Researchers in New Zealand tested to see how generous people were after completing various types of rituals. Some rituals were physical, involving various forms of singing and dance. Other rituals were spiritual, focusing on priming identity and shared values. These included a Christian service, Buddhist chanting, or Hindu devotional singing. Groups that had performed physical rituals were 8 percent more generous than the control group. Groups that had gone through a spiritual ritual were 24 percent more generous.[31] High levels of citizenship—when members of an organization generously help one another—is critical to adaptability.

Organizations can also use traditions to strengthen their shared identity and values. Medallia, the software company we discussed earlier, sends every new hire through an induction program that becomes a common bond for every Medallian.

Belron holds a biannual event in which the top technicians from around the world, winners of their national competitions, compete for the global "Best of Belron" title. The international event takes place at an exhibition center in a major European city. The scene looks like a cross between a car show and a championship athletic game. There's TV coverage and trophies, stage smoke and banners featuring blown-up pictures of the competitors. With hundreds of colleagues, suppliers, and partners looking on, the winners of the country-level competitions compete to repair windscreens, replace rear windows, and communicate with "customers" better than anyone else. It's a celebration of Belron's daily work, built to inspire its technicians to be the best they can be.

New hires at Gentle Giant, a Boston-based moving company, prove their mettle by racing up the steps of Harvard stadium while president and CEO Larry O'Toole, who calls Gentle Giant a "people development" company, cheers them on. A "respectable" performance is climbing all the stairs throughout all thirty-seven sections of the stadium in less than thirty minutes. The best can climb them in less than twenty. The race prepares employees—or "Giants," as the company calls them—for moving people into new homes and apartments, some up many flights of stairs. While it's the "ultimate test of fitness and determination," it's also a celebration of the company's "pride in making the hardest work look effortless." Like Belron's, Gentle Giant's tradition is especially powerful because it celebrates the core of its business.[32]

Remember, someone has to start a tradition—it's never too late to begin.

THE IMPACT OF IDENTITY

Constantly improving isn't easy in a decade in which new technologies are forever upending how people communicate, shop, and even live. It can be hard enough to get the basics right. The same might have been said in the 1950s. A new medium, television, took the country by storm. While 10 percent of households had TVs at the beginning of the decade, 90 percent did by the end.[33] Cars enabled people to move out of the cities, and a new mode of shopping, the supermarket, emerged. Suburban living completely changed many people's day-to-day lives.

Four business pioneers of the 1950s showed us that adaptability and a strong identity go together. They weren't born with this understanding. They figured it out together, over their lunches in the elegant dining room of the University Club of New York.

On one side of the table sat David Ogilvy, a college dropout and erstwhile cook and door-to-door salesman who founded the advertising agency Ogilvy & Mather. Next came Marvin Bower, the managing partner of McKinsey & Company, who coined the term "management consultant" while growing the Firm from eighteen people to a world-spanning "CEO factory." They were joined by Gus Levy, a self-made man who would become the head of Goldman Sachs. Last but not least came Leonard Spacek, who held the accounting firm Arthur Andersen together after its founder's death and grew it to the largest professional services company of its time.

By many accounts, these men built the most iconic cultures of their day. Professional services firms had typically been small, led by just a few partners. When partners retired, their firms died. These four wanted to build true institutions that would outlive any individual. It wasn't easy.

One topic these four icons returned to over and over again, according to Ken Roman, Ogilvy's protégé and the eventual CEO of Ogilvy & Mather, was the importance of culture and identity. "We didn't use the word 'culture' back then to describe what we were doing," Roman told us, as he recalled the growth of the Firm. "Ogilvy built a unity of purpose."[34]

David Ogilvy was famous for his creative antics—he preferred showing to telling (through presentations called "magic lanterns"). Attendees at one high-level meeting walked in to find Russian nesting dolls in front of their seats. They opened the first doll and then the smaller doll inside it, and on and on until they found a tiny note:

> *If you hire people who are smaller than you are, we shall become a company of dwarfs. If you hire people who are bigger than you are, we shall become a company of giants.*[35]

Roman told us how that lesson guided Ogilvy executives through hiring decisions for decades to come. Ogilvy became so successful that in one seven-year run the Firm didn't lose a single competition for a new client.

Spacek faced a different set of challenges. He didn't inherit a single firm, but a loose collection of partners. He needed to unify Andersen and to do so he relied on tradition.[36] The heavy wooden doors at the entrance to its main training center matched the ones that had stood outside Arthur Andersen's own office. Dozens of flags representing all the countries its trainees came from hung in the lobby. New hires, known as "green beans," recited the founder's motto, "Think straight, talk straight," and Andersen's "four cornerstones": "provide good service to the client"; "produce quality audits"; "manage staff well"; and "produce profits for the firm."

Spacek defined a clear goal for the company: to operate according to the highest levels of ethics.[37] In one instance, he accused the mighty Bethlehem Steel of overstating its profits by 60 percent. On another occasion, he berated the Securities and Exchange Commission for not pursuing companies with low-quality accounting. "The man on the street," Spacek wrote, "has the right to assume that he can accept as accurate the fundamental end results shown by the financial statements in annual reports."[38]

This onetime strength of Andersen makes the company's eventual devolution in the wake of the Enron scandal all the more poignant. You can't "set and forget" your identity. It requires constant work.

Marvin Bower joined McKinsey & Company in 1933, seven years after the founding of the Firm.[39] He believed that a leader alone could not build a firm's identity: it must be embodied in the behavior of each and every employee. "The total impression that our Firm makes depends on two principal factors," he wrote in a famous internal memo in 1953.

1. "The collective personal impressions made by each of us as individuals," and

2. "The Firm's objectives, major policies, and working approaches which guide (or should guide) each individual in what he does, writes, and says in carrying on Firm activities."

The memo goes on to articulate a very precise behavioral code, detailing the kind of work that McKinsey would and wouldn't do, and the principles with which the Firm would develop new clients.

Bower practiced what he preached. He once refused to work for Howard Hughes because he didn't believe the problem he had been asked to solve was the most pressing one facing the business. Bower fired a highly profitable partner because he was doing too much low-impact work for his client.[40] Consultants were even given a strict dress policy. After one meeting in which the client spent the whole time looking at a consultant's ankles, Bower sent a memo banning argyle socks. Stories like this became lore, creating a rich and powerful heritage.

As Ron Daniel, a protégé of Marvin Bower who rose to lead McKinsey & Company, told us, "Bower deeply believed that perpetuating the Firm mattered much more than economic gain."[41]

Gus Levy's core belief was that the greatest talent can come from anywhere. Levy's personal narrative echoed this belief. *Forbes* called him a "pragmatic, unpretentious character" who was "always explicit, matter-of-fact, and to the point with everyone at Goldman Sachs."[42]

The son of a wooden crate manufacturer, Levy was born in 1910 and raised in New Orleans. Levy's father passed away when he was sixteen. At eighteen, unable to afford college, he moved to New York,[43] where he lived in the 92nd Street Y (and owed them two dollars when he moved out). (Eventually, he would become the president of the parent organization and a major benefactor, more than erasing his debt.)[44] Soon he began working as a runner for brokerage firms while attending college classes at night.

Eventually, Levy found his way to Goldman Sachs, where he rose to become its lead partner. Never straying from his self-made roots, he established a tradition echoing this core value. Lisa Endlich, an author and former vice president at Goldman Sachs, writes:

> *Although the firm had a long-established practice of hiring M.B.A.s, Levy, a man without a degree, had his own system for staff recruitment. Early in the morning, before the markets opened, he would invite high school seniors into the office to play bridge or poker with him. He would play whichever game each visitor knew best, watching how his opponent's mind worked. Did he remember which cards had been played? Could he judge risk? Under pressure, could he keep his wits about him? These were the skills he sought. Successful trading, Levy believed, rested on ability as well as steely nerves, integrity, and luck. For years many of the firm's best traders had no higher education, but had passed Levy's entrance exam.*[45]

Building an identity requires courage. It isn't easy to fire a profitable partner for his values, like Bower did, or to denounce a company for overstating its profits, like Spacek. Ogilvy's and Levy's grand gestures might have made them look foolish in some people's eyes. Yet the greatest culture builders realize the importance of building an identity in ways both big and small.

GOING FORWARD

The French writer and aviator Antoine de Saint-Exupéry once wrote, "If you want to build a ship, don't drum up people to collect wood and don't assign them tasks and work, but rather teach them to long for the endless immensity of the sea." Identity turns jobs into callings. It unites your team with a common objective, behavioral code, heritage, and traditions. It provides a common purpose, and the ability to play. It feeds a total motivation culture. If your organization's identity is not clear, compelling, consistent, and credible, take some time to answer a few important questions:

- What objective unites and inspires my organization, business unit, and team?
- What behavioral code empowers people to make decisions and solve problems in a consistent, values-based way?
- What pieces of heritage will help celebrate and maintain our unique identity? Which new traditions should be seeded for tomorrow?

As Shakespeare once wrote, and the National Archives Building in Washington, D.C., memorialized in stone, "What is past is prologue."

The Playground

| **The Most Overlooked Key to Culture Is Also the Most Powerful**

ONE SIZE FITS ALL

The most powerful and the most overlooked source of total motivation is the design of a person's role within an organization. Often, jobs are designed entirely around tactical performance. We have a strategy. We turn that strategy into a process. We then write a job description to execute that process. Rarely, however, do we craft a role that inspires total motivation and adaptive performance. Poorly designed roles can make it almost impossible to create a high-performing culture.

The practice of role crafting began over a hundred years ago, when Frederick Winslow Taylor became famous for his efficiency studies. You may have heard of "Taylorism," the religion many companies follow when it comes to designing jobs.

Taylor was supposed to go to Harvard, but he believed the future was at the front lines of industry, not in academia. He rejected his wealthy family's ambitions for him and became a "lowly" machine shop apprentice instead.[1] According to biographer Robert Kanigel, Taylor spent what could have been his college years "shuttling between the manicured hedges of his family's home and the hot, cussing, dirty world of the shop floor."

Taylor began his apprenticeship in a shop that was disorganized, slow, and inefficient. He thought they could do better. So armed with a stopwatch, he set about discovering the "one best way" to perform each task. Nothing escaped his attention. At one point he even examined the science of shoveling. He determined that the average man shovels most productively when lifting 21.5 pounds. Yet different materials, like coal or soil, have different densities. Taylor required that shovels be made in different shapes and sizes, so that a "shovelful" always weighed the same.

Taylor became a bona fide celebrity in his time, an "industrial messiah." He popularized the idea that the design of a job could be studied and improved, building the field of "scientific management."

Unfortunately, no one is the "average man," or woman for that matter. Taylor's belief in "one best way" to do every job meant that he froze the way men worked. Workers were punished for deviating (or in other words, adapting).[2] While he believed higher productivity would lead to higher wages, bringing prosperity to all and reducing class hatred, his methods led to revolt. Unions declared that he was "out to destroy the workingman's health and rob him of his manhood," and that he reduced "skilled mechanics to common laborers" and men to "mere mechanical instruments." A strike at a government arsenal in Watertown, Massachusetts, led to a congressional investigation into his approach.

We owe credit to Taylor, who taught us to treat job design as a science. Yet he also showed us the danger of believing that there is only one way to do a job. What's needed is a total motivation approach to role crafting.

TAYLOR-MADE VERSUS TAILOR-MADE

More than half a century after Taylor's death, in the 1970s, Travelers insurance employed a hundred people in a job that seemed like it had one best way: keypunching.[3] Computers were still in their infancy; instead of using disks or USB drives, they read information off stiff paper cards with holes punched in them. Hundreds of (mostly) women spent their days turning written documents into punch cards.

But Travelers had a problem. The keypunchers worked painfully slowly. Deadlines were missed and error rates were high. Absenteeism was rife, especially around holidays. Supervisors spent all their time dealing with crises, complaints, apathy, and even "outright hostility."

Many organizations have hundreds of workers in repetitive low-paid jobs. Often, efforts to address motivation run along the lines of recruiting "better" people, or redesigning their compensation plans. It's rare for an organization to ask whether the design of the job itself is the problem, yet that's just what Travelers did.

Keypunching required seven steps:

- Step 1: Receive documents from one of Travelers' business units (the internal "customer")
- Step 2: Review the documents to make sure there are no obvious errors
- Step 3: Send flawed documents back to the customer
- Step 4: Divide the correct documents among the keypunchers, prioritizing those that are urgent
- Step 5: Punch the cards
- Step 6: Proofread the punched cards for errors, correcting those that are wrong
- Step 7: Report back to the customer

Many companies still follow Taylorism: to maximize tactical performance, they give each task to a specialist, who can become really good at it. That's exactly how the Travelers keypunchers worked. Documents were received and proofread by an "assignment clerk." A supervisor sent those with errors back to the customers. Keypunchers then received batches of work in one-hour chunks. A different group of "verifiers" proofread and corrected the work.

The approach is logical—if we were building machines to do this work, we'd design one for each step of the process. There would be "one best way." The trouble is, people aren't machines; they are capable of adaptive performance and equally capable of becoming demotivated.

Following a new theory of role crafting that had been developed by J. Richard Hackman, then a professor at Yale, and his doctoral student Greg R. Oldham, who later became a professor himself,[4] Travelers was able to overcome its blame bias. It took a risk and gave a group of ninety-eight grumpy, unproductive, sometimes hostile keypunchers more responsibility, more contact with customers, and less supervision. Another group of keypunchers in another location continued to operate in the old way, to act as a control group.

In the redesigned model, each keypuncher became the point person for a specific department. The keypuncher owned all the interactions with that customer, from receiving the documents to proofreading the final product. She could set her own schedule and daily work plan. Travelers also started giving each keypuncher her own weekly error reports, rather than handing them to her supervisor. In the new world, each keypuncher knew exactly how well she was performing without someone having to tell her. As you have no doubt realized, these role-crafting tactics are classic ways to create the play and purpose motives.

Sure enough, new behaviors emerged. The keypunchers developed relationships with the departments they served. They became experts in the types of errors their customers frequently made. They could now proactively correct them. In short, their new roles enabled adaptive performance.

Just from changing the design of the job, error rates dropped 35 percent compared to the control group. Absenteeism dropped 24 percent (while the control group had a 29 percent *increase*). The women were happier in their jobs, with a 17 percent higher satisfaction score. And productivity jumped 40 percent. By the end, only 60 people were required to do the work of 98 people before the experiment. Some of the former keypunchers were even promoted to work for their internal customer, something that had never happened before.

Travelers saved a lot of money from higher productivity, lower absenteeism, and the elimination of controls they had previously needed to monitor performance. The supervisor no longer spent his days putting out fires. Instead, he too became more adaptive, working on projects that would help the keypunchers be even more successful.

The new job broke all of Taylor's rules. Instead of one "efficient" way to keypunch, there were now many slightly different versions, each adapted for a different customer and keypuncher. Instead of redesigning the hiring process, Travelers had redesigned the jobs. They didn't change the player. They changed the game.

While keypunching is a thing of the past, a lot of jobs are still structured in the same way. Millions of people get a small piece of work, with strict instructions on how to complete it. A few hours later, the work is whisked away, with no opportunity for the employee to learn if it met the customer's needs. Unless you can see the connection between your work and its impact, you cannot adapt.

While few of us have heard of role crafting, there is a large body of research on the subject.[5] The academic literature overwhelmingly confirms the importance of good job design. A meta-analysis of hundreds of studies found that job design characteristics explained 34 percent of the variance in subjective performance, 38 percent in perceived stress, 55 percent in job satisfaction, 65 percent in feeling overloaded, and 87 percent in job involvement. Our own research on thousands of workers has shown that the design of a job is the biggest factor in total motivation, more than leadership, performance management systems, or compensation systems. Another study found that people in jobs where there are "few possibilities to learn new things" (in other words, few opportunities to play), were more likely to be hospitalized for heart attacks.[6] Human beings have evolved to learn and adapt; everything from our productivity to our health depends on it.

THE PERFORMANCE CYCLE

Designing a job for *tactical* performance is relatively straightforward. We know how to turn a strategy into a process, and that process into a job description. It is much harder to design a job that supports adaptive performance and total motivation. Yet while the tactical portions of every job are completely different (a nurse's job is completely different from a computer programmer's), the process of adaptive performance is the same for every job. Every job has to enable an ongoing, five-step performance cycle that starts with a theory of impact:

- *Step 1: Theory of impact*: Does your role give you the ability to understand cause and effect? Can you see how your actions drive performance?
- *Step 2: Inspiration*: Does your role inspire your curiosity and help you come up with new ideas for improving your performance?
- *Step 3: Prioritization and planning*: Does your job give you the time and tools to figure out which of your ideas are tortoises and which are hares?
- *Step 4: Performing*: Does your role include space for a playground where adaptive performance is the norm?

- *Step 5: Reflection*: Does your job give you the time, tools, and ability to see if your actions actually lead to the impact you expected?

1. IMPACT THEORY

To become a high performer capable of both tactical and adaptive performance, your job must enable you to understand how your work creates impact. Better still, it should give you the ability to continually improve that theory. Consider how a salesperson's theory of impact can improve as he learns and grows through his career:

- *Theory 1*: I create sales by learning my talking points and using them with my customers.
- *Theory 2*: I create sales by finding the right talking points for the right customer segment, and pointing out how cost effective our product is.
- *Theory 3*: I create sales by first understanding who my customers are and what would create impact for them. Then, if our company can help, I find ways for customers to experience the product for themselves and understand what our company stands for. Then I help improve future sales by sharing customer feedback with our research and development team.

You can see that the theory of impact can grow in sophistication as a worker learns more. *Primed to Perform* itself was originally conceived as our own theory of impact for what we do.

In his book *The Hard Thing About Hard Things*, the entrepreneur and venture capitalist Ben Horowitz recalled how frustrated he became with his product managers when he was director of product management at Netscape.[7] So he wrote "Good Product Manager/ Bad Product Manager," a short document that he used to share his expectations with his team. The document was his impact theory. "I was shocked by what happened next," he wrote. "Product managers whom I had almost written off as hopeless became effective. Pretty soon I was managing the highest-performing team in the company."

Every role benefits from a theory of impact that frames where a person needs tactical performance versus where she needs adaptive performance. That clarity inspires play and purpose. The best-case scenario is when the role itself enables an employee to figure out her own theory of impact.

Because the Travelers' keypunchers gained ownership over the entire process of delivering impact to a customer, they were able to figure out their theory of impact. Over time, they could self-identify how to improve their performance.

On a Toyota assembly line, it is impractical to give a single worker ownership over the entire process of building a car. However, Toyota rotates factory workers from position to position so they can see how the car is built. This inevitably makes it easier for them to learn how to improve the function of any one part of the line. Without understanding the value of adaptive performance, one would be tempted to do the opposite. A worker would be kept on the same position on the assembly line so they could become an "expert" in their area. Yet without seeing the whole process, they wouldn't have a high enough vantage point to solve for the VUCA in their role.

Lionel Vasquez works as a Beer Specialist for the Northridge, California, Whole Foods Market store.[8] His job is not to stock the beer shelves or assemble displays sent by headquarters. He talks with customers about their preferences, decides what types of beer to stock, gets to know representatives at breweries, especially at the hard-to-get brands, and studies what sells. By seeing the entire chain of activity for his work, he can form a detailed theory of impact. This helps him experiment as much as if he owned a small business. "Getting to hand that bottle of hard-to-find beer to a customer who has been looking for it for weeks and making their day is probably the best part of my job," he said.

In all these cases, there is a common underlying factor. The role was designed so that the employee could see enough of the chain of activities to connect action and outcome, cause and effect. Their vantage point was high enough to see how VUCA caused performance problems, and how their actions could solve for that VUCA.

2. INSPIRATION

Well-designed roles spark curiosity and play. They enable you to find your own ideas to improve performance. Training programs help, but ideally, your job is designed so that you can come up with new ideas while you're doing the work itself.

On a Toyota assembly line, workers can see real-time data on the performance of the whole line. They can immediately self-diagnose problems and consider ways to improve them.

Apple uses its workplace to encourage engineers to "serendipitously" interact with one another, ideally sparking new ideas with each conversation.

Whole Foods clerks have the time to talk to customers, visit competitors, and meet local producers to find new ideas. Whole Foods also supplies their store personnel with extreme amounts of data.[9] If you cannot predict how your people will solve for VUCA, how can you predict what data they will need?

Ideas stimulate curiosity. Curiosity fuels play. When you have a theory of impact, and new ideas to explore, the performance cycle starts rolling.

3. PRIORITIZATION AND PLANNING

It is common to think that prioritization is about deciding which ideas should be done now versus later. That's only half the story. Great prioritization requires you to also figure out which of your ideas are tortoises, and which are hares. Tortoises are ideas that require broad consensus before they are tried. Hares are ideas that can be tested quickly, even if they may fail.

Gore & Associates, the maker of Gore-Tex fabric, has a principle called the waterline. They teach their people that the company is like a ship at sea. If they are playing with live ammunition above the waterline and accidentally blow a hole in the ship, it isn't a disaster. However, if they blow a hole below the waterline, the ship sinks. They go out of their way to make sure people understand when they are above and when they are below the waterline.

The Ritz-Carlton has very high standards on how to treat guests. But they found an elegant way to ensure their people can separate the hares from the tortoises. Every employee, from housekeepers to bartenders, has a budget for helping guests. One waiter in Dubai overheard a man talking to his wheelchair-bound wife about how nice it would be if they could spend time together on the beach. The waiter used his budget to build a wooden walkway so the couple could eat their dinner on the beach.[10] The waiter not only had permission to play, he could see the results of his experiment and know that it made a difference for his customers.

In many organizations employees do not know where the waterline is in their roles. As a result, they can't execute on any of their ideas. Good role design clarifies where the waterline is and constantly works to make it lower.

4. PERFORMING

When coauthor Neel learned to drive, his father would take him out on the roads and highways of New York City in their four-door family sedan. On the roads, he knew that he had to follow the rules. On occasion, they would pull into an empty parking lot where there were no rules. They could play—seeing how hard the car could take corners, or how fast it could break. This is the playground, where learning happens fast. In this simple story, it is obvious where the playground begins and ends, but in most jobs, it isn't so obvious.

Organizations spend far too much time telling employees what they *can't* do. At the extreme, employees must follow scripts and strict protocols in every aspect of their job, all designed to maximize tactical performance. Employees feel as if there is no playground where they can try new ideas and change how they work.

While every job is subject to nonnegotiable policies and strategies, a well-crafted role should also have a place where it's normal to experiment and learn. We call this zone "the playground."

To build a playground, you should first consider where the job needs adaptability to achieve the highest levels of performance. Where is VUCA the greatest? The playground may be in the area where your competitors are most active, where quality is most important, where requirements change most frequently, or where the customer needs distinctive treatment.

At a Toyota assembly line, there is significant VUCA causing manufacturing defects. The line workers' playground is in identifying ways to improve their process or tools, or solving quality problems at the source. Toyota goes through great lengths to build this playground right into the job itself. For example, above each station at the assembly line hangs the famous andon cord. If an employee has an idea for an improvement, he can pull the cord, and a manager comes to his station to act on the idea.

At Starbucks, how a barista makes your triple-grande soy latte must be the same from store to store. That's the zone of tactical performance. However, how they deal with each unique customer, or how they address the problems that inevitably arise, is the playground where they can experiment with better ways of working.

Agile software developers face significant VUCA from constantly changing business requirements, new technologies, and even bugs.

The whole process of developing a feature or product can become a playground (as you will see later in the chapter).

Whole Foods strategy of sourcing the best organic goods from local producers has extremely high VUCA. From season to season, the best producers or even customer tastes can change. The process that store clerks follow to select merchandise is their playground.

The playground isn't about Ping-Pong tables. It is about giving people clarity that when doing certain parts of their job, they have wide degrees of freedom to experiment, and even fail, as long as they learn from it.

For a long time, we thought that giving people autonomy was critical to a high-performing culture. Many have focused on giving people freedom to work *when* they want (flex time), and *where* they want (flex space). We found that neither of these freedoms are material to driving adaptive performance.

From our own testing, we learned that flexibility in *how* people work, rather than where or when they work, is the key. People who had freedom in how they worked had an average of 40 more ToMo points than those who didn't. Where and when hardly moved the needle on ToMo.

5. REFLECTION

An experiment isn't an experiment unless you can see the outcome. Purpose is more meaningful when you can see the impact for yourself. Jobs need to be designed so you can reflect on your work. The period of reflection must help you see clearly whether your actions achieved the impact that you expected.

Our intrepid keypunchers, for example, got to read their own quality and productivity reports, and saw firsthand the impact their work had on their customers. By seeing the outcome with their own eyes, they had higher total motivation and, thus, adaptive performance increased.[11]

On a Toyota assembly line, when a worker has an idea for an improvement, managers try to test the idea as fast as possible, often within a day. Workers can immediately see the outcomes of their adaptive performance. Toyota describes this behavior with the word *hansei*, which means to reflect on what can be done better.

At a Whole Foods Market store, the stocking clerks who make decisions about what products to put on the shelves in their aisle have the data to see how effective their decisions were. Better still, they are able to interact with the people who buy these products to see the human impact.

Aside from driving play, reflection serves a big role in driving purpose. We had just finished giving a presentation on total motivation to a group of European business leaders when Fabrice Enderlin, Executive Vice President Talent & Company Reputation at UCB, a biopharmaceutical company, came up to us and shared a story about how he'd helped revive the purpose motive for his whole company through a form of reflection. "In my job, in twenty-five years in the pharmaceutical industry, at three different companies, I'd met thousands of physicians," he said. "I'd met all the big players in the industry. I'd spent many hours with our regulators. Yet I'd never seen a patient. Not once. I'd never heard stories of real people who benefit from our work."

"Since more than ten years now, at UCB, patients are at the heart of everything we do" Enderlin said. "We started by bringing patients to an entire three-day executive leadership off-site. During a breakout session, members of the marketing group were arguing about whether they should call the people who used their products 'clients' or 'patients' or 'customers.' One of the visitors raised his hand and said, 'Please, we don't care what you call us. Just hurry up with a solution that will cure the disease or help us live with it.' Presence of patients has now become the norm within company meetings."

Bringing patients into the everyday work of UCB's employees had a powerful effect on engagement. Over a few years, the percentage of employees who said they were proud to be at UCB increased to around 80 percent. "Our true north is clear," Enderlin said. "It is the patient."

Reflection leads right back to the first step. What people learn from reflecting should enhance their theory of impact. The cycle begins anew. Every single job should have this cycle designed right into the job itself. Better still, the job should take great care to make this cycle as short as practical.

Since the ToMo factor provides a single numerical view of the strength of a culture, we can use it to analyze how a role is designed. By correlating different role design levers to ToMo, we can see which ones are most important. After analyzing the ToMo of thousands of workers across many different types of jobs, this is what we found:

- A job designed to enable experimentation increases ToMo by about 68 points
- A job designed to enable learning through variety increases ToMo by about 68 points as well
- A job designed to make you feel a sense of purpose increases ToMo by about 64 points
- A job designed so that you do not work alone increases ToMo by about 36 points

THE SPY SHOP

One man who spoke to us on the condition of anonymity provided us with a perfect example of role crafting.

John Doe had the kind of top-secret job that belongs in a movie. He worked in his country's intelligence unit, tracking geopolitical developments around the world to prevent terrorist attacks and global disasters. Considering how high the stakes were, he expected everyone in the organization to be extremely motivated. He was wrong.

On his very first day on the job, John learned that he had to manage a group of ten technicians. Their job was to sit in a back room monitoring the agency's technological systems for eight hours a day. Occasionally, something would malfunction and one of the technicians would fix it. The work was routine, and usually boring.

John's predecessor wished him luck. The technicians faked illnesses, he said. They worked strictly nine to five, while everyone else worked late into the night. They barely completed their assigned tasks. In many ways, they sounded like modern-day keypunchers.

John's predecessor suggested that he fire them en masse and put in for a better crew. But John saw through the blame bias and decided to redesign the technicians' jobs. He didn't know about total motivation at the time, but his intuition led him to the kind of answer that the science recommends.

John's first step was to end the eight-hour shifts. Those "babysitting jobs," he said, "were boring and provided nowhere to grow." The shifts also signaled to the technicians that after eight hours, they could relax. Instead, he gave the technicians two four-hour shifts to maintain the systems, spaced throughout the day. In between their maintenance shifts, John expected the technicians to do *more* work. He gave them special projects that ranged from fixing bugs to creating a tool that improved collaboration with other agencies. The projects allowed the technicians to do what they found most fun: redesign computer systems, experiment, and solve problems. For the first time, they had a playground.

The technicians hadn't really felt like they'd made much of a contribution to the organization. If one system was down, how much difference did it really make? They'd use another system for a while.

John wanted the technicians to be able to develop their own theories of impact, generate their own ideas for improvement, and reflect on whether their ideas worked. He moved them from their back room to the mission control room, where live threats were being tracked, phone calls requesting urgent information were coming in, and real-time decisions were being made. He took the technicians on trips to the customer, an agency that developed strategy based on the intelligence they gathered, and asked the customer to start sharing feedback on the impact their data was having. Finally, he started sending weekly emails to everyone in the organization, including the top boss, in which he described the impact the technicians' projects were having.

John wanted the technicians to feel that their jobs were worthwhile for them personally. The special projects allowed them to build skills that would be valuable throughout their entire careers. While in the past the technicians' supervisor was someone from the elite staff, John promoted one of the technicians to run the group. All of this drove potential. John reduced emotional pressure too, by pairing each technician with a mentor who made sure to make the technician feel supported and encouraged.

As the technicians began to enjoy their work and see its impact, they stopped malingering and started putting in longer days. The indirect motivation tactics the boss had used in the past, from screaming at them to giving them poor performance reviews, were no longer necessary. Friction between the technicians and the rest of the group became a thing of the past.

John knew his changes were making a difference when late one afternoon he overheard a colleague inviting a technician to watch some TV with him. "No," the technician answered, "I need to finish this project. It's important." And he was right. Many of the projects were useful. Some were game changing. One technician fixed a legacy system that had stopped working, opening up a whole new source of information.

THE YEAR OF LIVING DANGEROUSLY

Fortunately for John, he needed to focus only on redesigning the jobs of his team. But sometimes an entire organization needs to be remade.

Back in 1999, Salesforce.com was a start-up that believed that providing software as a service would allow them to win in an industry of giants.[12] Speed and agility were key: they updated their software four times a year, while many competitors could update only once in the same time.[13] They grew quickly.

But just seven years after its founding, the company began to freeze. In 2006, it released only one software update. Massive outages disrupted customers' ability to access their accounts. A leading engineer quit after giving a doomsday speech about where the organization was heading. The blame game began.

At the time, Salesforce.com's software development business was organized like an assembly line. One group of people met with customers to understand their needs. Another group created the blueprints for what the software should look like. Still another group wrote the code, yet another checked it, and still another documented it. Coordinating across departments was a pain. Last-minute changes created disasters.

Steve Greene, a product manager at the time, saw his colleagues begin to turn on one another. But Greene avoided the blame bias. "The model was broken, not the people," Greene told us. "We needed to fix the model, not push harder on people to make fewer mistakes and do a better job."

Salesforce.com had tried freezing the product design so no one could make last-minute changes. They had tried requiring everyone to predict what they could accomplish in the next six months and holding them accountable for it. Neither worked, Greene said. The software industry moved too quickly for them to freeze designs, and no one could know what challenges they would face until they got into the weeds. Strategies that destroy adaptive performance in the name of tactical performance eventually fail. Even in software engineering, VUCA is extreme.

So Greene did something incredibly bold for a person who had been at the company for only a year. Along with his colleague Chris Fry, he approached Parker Harris, one of Salesforce.com's cofounders, and proposed that the company redesign each and every one of its jobs by implementing the Agile approach to software development.

The Agile approach was born in 2001 when seventeen software engineers met at the Snowbird ski lodge in Utah. They were frustrated because they felt their profession as a whole was loosing its adaptive performance. Process was replacing judgment to ill effect. Together they posted online the "Agile Manifesto," along with an image of engineers huddled around a glowing whiteboard.[14] The picture looks like one you might find in a high school history book of the founding fathers writing the Declaration of Independence. A revolutionary new form of job design had been declared for software engineers: henceforth, software would be built through self-organizing teams. Projects would be "built around motivated individuals. Give them the environment and support they need, and trust them to get the job done."[15] They had redesigned their own jobs to maximize total motivation and adaptive performance.

Greene's idea was that they test the new approach at Salesforce.com with a small, isolated group. He thought his idea was a tortoise. He didn't think they should risk breaking the company by rolling it out all at once. But Harris believed the company was already broken and wanted a "big bang." He wanted a hare.

Within three months, the entire engineering department was in Agile teams.[16] Over the next eighteen months, they refined the process.

The assembly-line model was dismantled and a playground was built. Instead of having product managers pass their work off to separate groups of engineers, people worked in teams of about ten that included product managers, designers, engineers, quality assurance people, and everyone else who was needed to move a piece of software from concept to finished product. The team usually sat in the same room and spent a lot of time together, on the principle, also stated in the manifesto, that face-to-face conversation is the best form of communication. This end-to-end view of the work allowed them all to form constantly iterating impact theories of their jobs and projects.

Teams worked in "sprints" lasting two to six weeks. At the beginning of a sprint, the team decided what feature to build and created a work plan. Everyone on the team had immense opportunities to play, by deciding what to build, how to build it, and how to run the process. At the end of the sprint, the team had a completely finished feature that was ready to be "shipped" to the customer. Projects were no longer left sitting on the shelf while engineers finished up other jobs. As a result, the team could immediately see the impact of its work. The duration of the sprints allowed them to reflect frequently, quickening the speed of their performance cycle from what was once many months long.

The Agile model increases total motivation for software developers. Play and purpose increase because team members can create a theory of impact for their work and can make real-time adjustments. A product manager, for example, can see how her actions affect teammates working on the product's design or engineering and adapt based on their feedback. The whole team gains feedback from the customer every few weeks. At the end of each sprint, the team conducts two reviews or reflections: one of the product created and one of the process they used to make it. Even the process of working together is constantly being refined.

Indirect motivators decline because there is no formal manager. One person is assigned to make sure the team follows the Agile rules and to remove hurdles from its path. Inertia declines, not only because someone is removing obstacles, but because it's far easier for a team of ten to get things done than an organization of hundreds or thousands.

Greene refers to the transition as his "Year of Living Dangerously."[17] For a long time, it wasn't clear that the changes would work. Employee surveys raised complaints: "It seems that we spend more time talking about [Agile] . . . than we spend time talking and working on Salesforce.com," one comment read.[18] "The lingo is ridiculous," read another.

The teams fought most against the fifteen-minute meetings that Agile teams are supposed to hold every day so that everyone can share their progress. "Many asked, 'Couldn't we just do this by email?'" Greene remembered. But as people grew into their new roles, "the daily meetings ended up becoming probably the most popular part of the methodology," Greene said. "It allows you a sense of ownership" and aligns the team around common goals. "Everyone always knows what's happening and when they have a problem or an obstacle, it gets fixed right away."

By the end of 2007, the results spoke for themselves. The average time it took to release new features improved by 61 percent.[19] The company could once again meet its delivery deadlines. Ninety-four percent of employees said they would recommend Agile to others. Getting that many people to agree on anything is an impressive feat, and those results aren't even unusual. Agile has taken Silicon Valley by storm and companies that implement it are increasing their productivity by 200 to 400 percent.[20]

Sometimes it's not enough to change the way one person works. You have to change how everyone works together.

GOING FORWARD

From roles as diverse as management consultants, computer programmers, baristas, grocery store clerks, and auto-line workers, thoughtfully shaping each job is the single biggest way you can increase total motivation and adaptive performance. Doing so requires you to embed the performance cycle into the job itself. We'll leave you with a simplified checklist just to get you started:

Theory of impact:
❑ Does the role allow you to see enough of the end-to-end experience to enable you to fully connect cause and effect for VUCA and your own adaptive performance?

Inspiration:
❑ Does the role give you ways to source new ideas and be inspired by different ways of doing the work?

Prioritization and planning:
❑ Does your job give you enough insight to figure out which ideas should be tried quickly (hares), versus which should be driven through consensus (tortoises)?

Performing:
❑ Does the role clearly delineate where tactical performance is required and where adaptive performance is required?
❑ Is the zone of adaptive performance—the playground—designed to solve for the VUCA of the role?

Reflection:
❑ Does the role give you time to reflect?
❑ Does the role give you clarity into your performance and impact?

These simple questions, if answered honestly for the jobs you're creating, will help you create roles that inspire ToMo, and thus the highest levels of performance. Taylorism has had its day. We now know that people perform their best when they work in their own best way.

The Land of a Thousand Ladders

| *Your People Can Either Fight Each Other to Survive or Fight Their Competitors to Win; Your Culture Drives the Choice*

It is easy to assume that money is the most powerful indirect motivator in an organization. But what about the prestige that comes with career advancement? What about the pressure and fear that comes from not being advanced? When you're up for a promotion, or in danger of being fired, you experience the highest levels of emotional and economic pressure.

In the world before ToMo, some people suggested that this pressure was a good thing. They argued that career paths should be designed like tournaments, in which people competed for promotions.[1] The larger the prize at the end of the tournament, like the CEO's salary, the harder people would fight to win. But as pressure and indirect motives increase, people start to compete against one another rather than the true competition. Total motivation is destroyed and cobra effects become the norm.

Another outcome of the typical promotion system is the Peter Principle—the idea that if the prize for good work is a promotion, everyone will rise up the ranks until they reach the point where they're no longer good at their jobs.[2] A genius engineer becomes a manager, for example, because that is the reward for top performers.

She may find that she has moved from a job she loved to one she dislikes and isn't very good at. Taken to its limit, the Peter Principle concludes that entire companies are eventually managed by people who are unfit for their jobs.

Instead of a fight-to-the-death tournament, high-ToMo cultures require different ways of recognizing and advancing people. Rather than funneling all your people up one pathway, you should create a land of a thousand ladders.

WORK SMARTER, NOT HARDER

Strange things happen to us when we're all gunning for the same prize.

Anat Bracha, a senior economist at the Federal Reserve Bank of Boston, noticed a troubling trend while she was working on her PhD at Yale, and later when she was an assistant professor at Tel Aviv University.[3] Competition to publish papers and win tenure was fierce. Many academics worked hard. But she wondered if they were working on the topics that really mattered. "Many people think about effort in a one-dimensional way," Bracha explained to us. "They think more effort equals better outcome." But is all effort created equal?

"For example, in academia, there are two types of papers you can write as a graduate student," Bracha said. "You can tackle a new idea that brings the profession forward, by identifying a new problem or coming up with a new way of thinking. But this is difficult. It requires creativity, and it's risky. On the other hand, you can write a paper that has a much higher chance of getting published by improving or correcting an existing piece of knowledge. The first path can lead to true breakthroughs. But, if your idea doesn't result in significant findings, your journey to become a professor could be over." Was the competition for tenure causing the best people to take the easy path?

Bracha and a colleague set up an experiment at Harvard University's Decision Science Laboratory.[4] Their goal was to see if tournaments changed people's appetite to do more complex work or to stick with low-risk and low-reward tasks.

Harvard students entered the decision lab, sat down in front of a computer, and were offered a choice between two tasks.

In one task, students were asked to figure out the missing number in a sequence. For example, what should the first number be in the sequence below?

_____ 9 30 51

You'd have to figure out that the difference between each pair of numbers in the sequence is 21. If you subtract 21 from 9, you get -12.

The other task, which Bracha called the filing task, was much more basic. Students were told to categorize numbers as odd or even. For example, is the number below odd or even?

73

Not much work to do here, the number is odd.

The students were paid more for solving sequences than filing numbers. They lost money for wrong answers. They were rewarded for doing some of both tasks to mimic the real world. After all, success in most things requires both some problem solving and some tactical work. They had to earn as much money as possible in ten minutes.

Bracha and her colleague found that students spent about 64 percent of their time on the sequences, and the rest of their time on filing. They earned $34 on average. Not bad for ten minutes of work.

Of course, there was a twist. Another group of students did the same exercise, but as part of a tournament in which they had to beat another student. The winner would walk away with $60. The loser would get only $10.

Both sets of students should behave the same way—after all, they're both trying to earn as much as possible. Both sets even have the same $35 "expected earnings"—a term used to describe the average payout of a situation. But the tournament changed their behavior.

The students in the competition group spent 13 percent less time on the sequences, even though it was the more lucrative of the two activities. As Bracha put it, when feeling competitive pressure, the students "worked harder, not smarter." They took less intellectual risk. They did the busy work.

Even stranger, Bracha found that the students who were best at solving the sequences were more likely to avoid sequences during the competition, compared with similar students in the tournament condition.

You might have seen this in the workplace. When the stakes are high, like when two people are competing for a promotion, people may prioritize the low-risk, easy work that makes them look busy and deprioritize the activities that require problem solving or creativity. They become afraid of risk. They prioritize tactical over adaptive performance.

Total motivation predicts this outcome. The tournament is designed to change your motive. Instead of doing the work for play, purpose, or potential, you're now doing the work for a big reward (economic pressure) or to avoid feeling like a loser (emotional pressure). The people most capable of doing the work may feel the greatest emotional pressure, reducing their total motivation even more. Of course all of this leads to worse adaptive performance.

Competition affects us at the neurological level, as a group of researchers learned when they scanned the brains of people who agreed with statements like "I cannot stand being defeated by opponents" (a form of emotional pressure) and "Success is getting fame and high-ranking positions" (a form of economic pressure).[5] The researchers found that these indirect motives were processed in a different part of the brain than direct motives.

The direct motives were processed in the same part of the brain that makes educated guesses about how your behavior might affect a situation and then learns from what really happens. Neurologically, the direct motives and adaptive performance are one and the same.[6]

Competitiveness, on the other hand, was associated with a part of the brain that enables us to handle "distressing emotions." This sheds some light on why we can hold both the indirect and the direct motives at the same time. It also begins to explain how the indirect motives can lead to distraction and cancellation effects. Our mind is literally in two places at the same time (and one of those places isn't very pleasant).

Therein lies the conundrum: competitive career ladders make us spend our time thinking about how to get promoted instead of how to do great work. Yet at the same time, we need to give people opportunities to grow and take on more responsibility. How can we create opportunities without damaging total motivation?

The answer: by giving each person his or her own individualized career ladder.

THE THOUSAND LADDERS

Four guiding principles will help you as you figure out how to create an ideal set of ladders for your organization:

- *BYOL—bring your own ladder*: Your organization needs experts not only in management, but also in content knowledge and customer relationships. So why not encourage expertise and make it a competitive advantage. Rather than one path for all your people, your organization should enable people to design their own career ladders.
- *Aspiration points*: Make sure that each ladder ends in an "aspiration point." The managerial ladder typically culminates in a CEO position. What should knowledge and customer-centric people aspire toward?
- *Define the rungs*: Crisply define the skills and values required for each step up. This enables people to understand where they are today and what they need to learn to progress. It ensures

that your organization accelerates people's careers fairly. More-over, the rungs are the primary mechanism to adjust compensation. Rather than pay-for-performance, the system requires a person to learn-to-earn.

- *Reward with ToMo*: Finally, as people progress from one rung of the ladder to the next, make sure they get increasing opportunities for play, purpose, and potential. We call this rewarding with ToMo.

BYOL (Bring Your Own Ladder)

When we hear that someone is "climbing the corporate ladder," we assume he or she is becoming a manager, and then a senior manager, and so on. But there are many valuable career paths that don't require supervising other people.

One of the first fields to formalize expert career ladders was an organization where promotions almost always meant commanding more people: the military. In the early days of the British Navy, noblemen commanded ships, even though many didn't actually know how to sail.[7]

Experienced sailors, who would manage the operations of the ship, became highly valued, often more so than experienced officers. To encourage seasoned sailors without breaking custom, these sailors would receive the Royal Warrant. Eventually, the navy created the position of warrant officer, held by professional sailors with deep knowledge of fields like navigation and artillery. Modern-day "warrant officers" in the United States continue this tradition of expertise in areas like repairing and flying fighter planes, running supply chains, or managing human resources. These are people whom the most senior commanders will turn to with questions like "Can we fly in these conditions?" or "How can I feed and support ten thousand men in the middle of this war zone?"

Warrant officers have their own highly specialized training sessions.

They even have their own review and rating systems, separate from the normal command pipeline. As one officer told us, it gives them the ability to say what they truly think to their commanders, based on their technical knowledge rather than on their need to please the boss.

Specialized career ladders have more recently emerged in the education world to meet a challenge of the teaching profession. Teachers usually join the profession because they love working with students, but their promotion path to principal and then district administrator takes them out of the classroom. There are few ways that veteran teachers can share their expertise with others.

The Pittsburgh public school district has been pioneering one of them. In 2010, seventy teachers, principals, and district and union officials gathered together to find a better way to reward and recognize their teachers. They created a career ladder program.[8] Teachers who were ready for more responsibility could apply to several newly created positions. In one role, expert teachers would teach and coach their colleagues. In another, veterans would spend some of their time helping an entire school improve its learning environment and culture. "We had some amazing educators, and we wished they had exposure to more children because they had such a tremendous impact on the students they served," explained a former leader of talent at the district. "A lot of the teachers that wanted to increase their impact really loved working with kids, and didn't want to leave the classroom for administrative roles." They could now pursue alternative career paths to share their knowledge while continuing to develop their own skills.

While every organization will have its own unique ladders, we've seen three basic templates that provide useful starting points:

The managerial ladder. A managerial promotion should not be a reward given to the top performer. It should be a path pursued by those who find play in learning how to manage and coach. People on this ladder should become knowledgeable about total motivation. They should learn to understand their decision-making biases. They should master business problem solving and strategy setting and become experienced in launching and executing continuous improvement projects. It should be an apprenticeship to gain mastery rather than a tournament to amass wealth or power.

The expert ladder. These employees should be mastering a technical skill or other area of knowledge required for the success of their company. For the military, it may be supply chain or human capital management. For Pittsburgh's schools, it is the art of teaching, learning, and culture building. At each rung of the ladder, people should have more opportunities to expand their expertise. Moreover, as experts move up the ladder, they should not just be learning, but developing new knowledge and sharing it within their company and even the broader world.

The customer ladder. These employees should be mastering the science and art of working with customers. In a high-ToMo company, the distinction between sales and service should appear meaningless, so people on this track need to understand both. They should develop a deep understanding of the mission and value proposition of the company, while advancing their skills in customer interaction and marketing.

Ladders don't make themselves. As you put them together, you'll need to figure out how each rung can help an employee grow in a meaningful way, while also adding value to the company.

If your organization is large, you'll need to estimate how many people you have and need at each stage of each ladder. But perhaps, most importantly, you'll need to build respect for the two ladders that are not so common today—the expert and customer paths. The easiest way to change the attitude toward these ladders is to create legendary aspiration points.

The Aspiration Point

Each ladder must be worth climbing. We call the top of each ladder the "aspiration point." The managerial ladder usually rewards with pay and prestige (indirect motives), and often with increased ability to play and see the impact of your work (direct motives). While the aspiration point of the managerial ladder is easy to see—the CEO position for general managers, for example, or CFO for those on a finance track—the aspiration points of other ladders may require a little more imagination.

IBM created one of the early expert career ladders back in the 1960s, when it realized it was wasting its most brilliant minds. IBM had been taking its top scientists—the ones who were leading break-throughs in the lab—and "rewarding" them with management positions that took them away from the science they loved. They were living the Peter Principle on a global scale. Dr. Gardiner Tucker, a director of research at IBM in the 1960s, realized that they needed to find a way for the "wild ducks" of innovation to "survive and thrive," and not be caught up in bureaucracy.[9]

IBM's answer was to create the "Fellow." They chose the name as a nod to the way universities honor their top scholars. Today, Tucker still envisions the Fellow as a person who "embodies a place with pioneering vision in an ever-expanding field."[10]

The Fellows program made it clear that for IBM a career in research is as prestigious, if not more prestigious, than a career in management. Many consider it more prestigious to be a Fellow than to be the CEO. In fifty years, IBM has created 246 Fellows. Five have earned Nobel Prizes.[11] The Fellows helped create the systems that put the first man on the moon; the first microscope that made atoms visible; and Watson, the computer that beat human champions in both chess and the game show *Jeopardy*.[12]

Chandu Visweswariah remembers walking into the cafeteria of IBM Research in Yorktown Heights, New York, in his mid-twenties.[13] He had just received his PhD from Carnegie-Mellon and was interviewing for a job. In the cafeteria, he saw the wall of IBM Fellows. "I was looking at the inventors of Fortran, the tunneling microscope, the disk drive . . . all these legends and I thought, 'Wow, they worked here. It just blew my mind,'" Visweswariah said. "That display had quite an impact on my desire to join IBM."[14] Twenty-five years later, Visweswariah is still at IBM, doing work that has led to more than sixty-five patents. He leads IBM in reimagining the boundaries of chip design, and became a Fellow himself in 2013.

The Fellows program not only inspires recruits and employees, but also shapes the way IBM moves great ideas through its massive organization. Tucker envisioned the Fellows as "gadflies" or "catalysts," people who could "stimulate ideas in others, and help colleagues overcome bottlenecks."[15] Fellows were the people who could call the corporate office and get the CEO on the line.

IBM's Fellow program worked: for twenty-one straight years, IBM has filed more patents annually than any other company. As an aspiration point, it is legendary: imagine if your organization's career ladders produced Nobel laureates. Finally, more than one person can reach the aspiration point. Fellows don't battle their colleagues to become Fellows. They each pursue their own fields of research, climbing their own individual ladders, battling not for power but for knowledge.

Define the Rungs

Once you've defined your career ladders and aspiration points, you need to think about the rungs of the ladder. What skills and experiences do people need at each level? Defining the rungs helps your employees understand what's expected of them. It allows them to prioritize their learning and development and ensures that promotions are fair. It also drives how much each person is paid.

For a prime example, we turn to an unlikely place: the YES Prep Public Schools in Houston, Texas. On April 29, 2014, all thirteen YES Prep schools were empty. Over a hundred buses and many more cars had transported 10,000 students, parents, faculty members, and staff to the Toyota Center, the arena where the Houston Rockets play. Over 450 seniors, most from low-income backgrounds, had signed "letters of intent" signaling their commitment to attend college. At the stadium, they announced to a cheering crowd which university they would attend in the fall. Ninety-nine percent of them had been accepted to four-year colleges.

YES Prep's first dreams weren't nearly as big. The organization started in 1995. Its early classes were held in a collection of trailers in a parking lot.[16] Eventually, the organization raised enough money to construct a real building. The leadership team sat down to review architectural plans for a campus that would rival the beauty of the city's best private schools. And then they stopped. "We had to decide who we would be as an organization," Jen Hines, one of the original teachers, and eventual chief operating officer, told us. "We had to ask ourselves, why would we invest that amount of money for one building for one set of kids?" The team scratched the fancy building, and spent the money on expanding the program to reach more students. That decision has defined YES's identity ever since.

As it grew from one to thirteen schools, YES realized it needed a more systematic approach to developing teachers and a consistent definition of what "good teaching" meant. Hines wrote the first draft of YES's performance management system while she was on maternity leave. Teams of teachers and administrators have revised it since.

The system hinges on YES Prep's career ladder. Teachers progress from the "novice" rung until they hit advanced and master levels. Compensation increases as they move up the ladder. A rubric defines performance expectations for teachers at each stage of the ladder. The very first category of that rubric is culture. "It's the foundation for any learning you're going to do," Hines explained.

The culture section includes a number of criteria, but the very first is student motivation. As Hines explained, teachers should inspire an intrinsic love of learning in their students. Despite the national focus on test scores, YES Prep believes that direct motives inspire performance.

The other sections of the rubric focus on continual learning, contribution to the community, and the demonstration of school values. Adaptability is expected and celebrated. Master teachers never stop evaluating and reevaluating the school's mission and programs. They constantly suggest constructive ideas for improvement.

The rubric succeeds on many levels. It's holistic; it considers values and behaviors, not just outcomes like test scores. It defines expectations while still leaving room for play. "I knew I wanted to inspire a love of reading, but how I chose to do that was up to me," explained Jamie Elfenbein, a former YES Prep sixth-grade literacy specialist. She would choose the reading assignments that most resonated with her students, for example, or adjust the mix of group versus individual activities based on student needs, increasing their ToMo along the way.

First-year teachers at YES Prep are paired with instructional coaches to be "your cheerleader, your support, your mirror, your guide," in COO Hines's description, "but not your evaluator." They help new teachers understand the rubric and plan their learning goals.

YES Prep's approach has earned them the right to be an official certifier of new teachers in Texas. Students consistently beat Texas averages on standardized tests, and 74 percent of its graduates are either enrolled in college or have earned their degree(s). YES Prep appears on *US News & World Report*'s list of the nation's top one hundred high schools, and it is recognized as one of the best places to work by the *Houston Business Journal.*[17]

Clear expectations enable consistent, fair performance reviews for employees, and they create common experiences and standards for customers. We studied people in organizations with and without the hallmarks of good career ladders. We measured how much higher the ToMo factor was for people with well-developed career ladders. Keep in mind, the difference between great cultures and their nearest competitors is typically 15 points of ToMo.

- Career ladders with high (versus low) clarity on what good performance looks like at each rung increase ToMo by 33 points.
- Career ladders that have holistic expectations at each rung, acknowledging both tactical and adaptive performance, increase ToMo by about 28 points.
- Workers who can self-identify whether or not they meet the criteria for good performance (without a manager having to tell them) typically have higher ToMo by 29 points.

The individual rungs are also the primary mechanism to drive compensation gains for people in a high-ToMo culture, so it is important to get them right (more in Chapter 12, "Compensationism").

Borrowing from a phrase we heard at Zappos, we call this concept "learn-to-earn." Zappos eschews traditional forms of pay-for-performance that often result in cobra farms. Instead, they inspire their people to grow their skills, elevating their compensation as they do so.

Each rung must create more organizational value than the previous rung. The rubrics that define each rung must specifically address how additional value is created. As a person progresses along an expert track, for example, they will teach others to tap into their knowledge, creating more value for the company.

Reward with ToMo

Companies can support their employees' career ladders even if there are few or no formal opportunities for promotion. Small companies, especially those whose leaders stay in their roles for decades, may have to "reward with ToMo" by providing employees with more opportunities for play, purpose, and potential even if their titles don't change.

At IBM, and at many universities, scientists receive more resources in the form of lab space, research assistants, and access to critical tools as their careers progress. Some organizations increase play and purpose through travel or educational budgets, enabling employees to participate in industry conferences or learn new skills as they move up the ladder. Others give people the opportunity to showcase their knowledge internally and externally through workshops, speeches, recruiting events, or other activities.

The Federal Reserve, where Bracha conducted her research into the effects of competition, enables its economists to conduct original research, publish in influential journals, and share their research results at academic conferences. They have access to computing facilities and data sets, support from research assistants, and access to speakers and workshops that facilitate and encourage the exchange of ideas.[18]

Robin Hood, a poverty-fighting foundation in New York City, hasn't promoted a managing director since it started more than twenty-five years ago, but it pays with total motivation. Eric Weingartner became managing director of its "survival" program in 2008. Weingartner typically invests in existing organizations that help New Yorkers on the brink. But after some time, he felt like he'd mastered this role. He began looking for more provocative ways to make a difference in the field, and continue his own growth and development. He found one in 2012, when he learned about federal judge Robert Katzmann's efforts to transform the justice system's treatment of immigrants.

Katzmann and other judges ranked almost half of the lawyers who appeared before them to argue immigrants' cases as "inadequate" or "grossly inadequate."[19] Weingartner suggested that Robin Hood and Katzmann partner to launch a new organization, modeled on the Peace Corps, which would recruit graduates of top law schools like Harvard, NYU, and Columbia and team them with talented undergrads who spoke languages from Haitian Creole to Bahasa Indonesia.

In 2014, with funding and support from Robin Hood, the Immigrant Justice Corps was born. It began in New York City with twenty-five fellows, but within three years it hopes to handle as many as fifteen thousand cases a year in New York and other cities around the country. "My job description wasn't to create a whole new reality for our country's immigrants," Weingartner told us from his office in Union Square. "But Robin Hood—which usually invests in existing nonprofits rather than founding new ones—supported me. The more experience I gain, the more opportunities I've had to imagine my own future. Robin Hood has allowed its staff to take risks that can change the nonprofit and policy landscape."

Even as Weingartner expanded his own horizons, he encouraged and supported younger Robin Hood employees' careers by enabling them to conduct research projects and speak at conferences. To build an organization with the highest levels of performance, every rung of the career ladder should provide opportunities for total motivation.

GOING FORWARD

Many organizations have built management fast tracks. But when they provide career ladders for every role, they set the expectation that everyone will be constantly learning, growing, and increasing their contributions to the company. Not only will your people be happier, their performance will increase as they become experts in the areas that matter to your organization. Because your people are gaining material skills, you can promote from within without falling prey to the Peter Principle.

Take a moment to consider whether there are paths for your managerial, knowledge, and customer experts. Are the end points of those ladders deeply aspirational? Does each rung on the ladder increase total motivation? If you're a small organization, your team may need to brainstorm the answers to those questions. If your organization is large, human capital managers trained in total motivation can help you design consistent ladders across the company. These ladders will then become the frame for your performance management system and compensation plans. All three need to be aligned to create the highest-performing cultures.

Compensationism

| *The Most Misunderstood Key to Culture*

When helping organizations build high-performing cultures, no topic raises passions like pay. Many leaders believe in a religion called Compensationism, which decrees that performance-based pay is the key to motivation. Performance-based pay not only drives people to be their best, the mantra goes, but also ensures fairness and meritocracy.

A simplistic view of total motivation would suggest that the opposite is the case. Surely performance-based pay causes the indirect motives to increase, and thus reduces ToMo.

The reality is more nuanced. Like all motivators, pay-for-performance is neither inherently good nor inherently bad. Depending upon the circumstances, it can be either, both, or neither. The key to building a high-ToMo organization is knowing when pay-for-performance works and when it doesn't.

CLEAR AS (AUTO) GLASS

In 1994, the Safelite corporation, a company that manufactures and installs auto glass, came under new management. Its new leaders decided to change the way people were being paid. While installers had previously received a flat hourly wage, they'd now be paid according to how productive they were. The more windshields someone installed, for example, the more he would earn. Stanford Business School professor Edward Lazear tracked how the change affected three thousand employees.[1]

Average worker output increased 44 percent, seemingly a resounding success for Compensationism. Isn't this incontrovertible proof that the theory of total motivation is wrong? If we look at the details, we can see that by designing its incentives to increase play and purpose without increasing economic pressure, Safelite actually increased total motivation.

Through updated technology, employees could track how many windshields they installed. Now when they made changes in their work, they could see what impact the changes had on their productivity. Receiving feedback from your work typically increases play and purpose and decreases inertia, as we saw in Chapter 10, "The Playground," on role crafting.

More importantly, Safelite designed the change so that it would not increase economic pressure. Autoworkers were guaranteed a minimum hourly wage no matter how many units they installed. Ninety percent of employees earned *more* money after the change, even though many of them didn't install enough units to earn more than the guarantee. Employees did not need to fear the new system. It had an upside, but very little downside.

While half of the improvement came from more motivated employees, the other big chunk of improvement came because Safelite was better able to recruit talented individuals from its competitors. Safelite's average pay was now 10 percent higher than the industry. While money is a poor motivator, it can be an effective activator, overcoming someone's inertia. It can be the reason you take a job or switch from a low-ToMo company.

The system also avoided one of the common pitfalls of pay-for-performance: the sacrifice of quality (adaptive performance) for quantity (tactical performance). Safelite had a few advantages.

First, when it comes to windshields, major quality problems surface quickly; windshields crack or leak soon after they're installed. Second, the company had a world-class computer system for 1994. When a windshield broke, they could tell who installed it. At first, they thought that social shame and peer pressure would be enough to minimize bad work. Yet quality really improved when Safelite required the same person who caused the error to fix it. As Lazear summarized it, Safelite's compensation system worked because "Output is easily measured, quality problems are readily detected, and blame is assignable." In other words, adaptive performance was not threatened by the compensation system.

Finally, the new payment scheme worked because the interests of the customer and employee were aligned: both had an interest in speed. Such an incentive system may not work so well if a customer wants a salesman to patiently walk her through the pros and cons of a new product, or if she'd like her doctor to take his time explaining potential treatment options.

Safelite's compensation plan worked. But as we'll see throughout this chapter, some nearly identical compensation schemes backfired.

DRIVEN TO DISTRACTION

Despite his six-figure education loans, Andrew turned down a number of high-paying corporate jobs to throw in his lot with a software start-up that had pulled in $75 million in venture capital. The press called it the type of company you should bet your career on, and Andrew did.

Andrew is an electrical engineer turned marketer with multiple patents to his name, two prestigious degrees, and experience at one of the most reputable tech companies in Silicon Valley. Despite his track record of overachievement, his new company still thought he and his peers needed to be motivated by quarterly bonuses.

At the beginning of each quarter, Andrew wrote up a set of goals and refined them with his boss. If he met those goals over the next twelve weeks, he'd get $2,500. It wasn't a huge percent of his salary, but it was still significant.

Two weeks into the quarter, a customer emergency arose, requiring all hands on deck. Andrew's original plan to conduct customer interviews went out the window. A few weeks later, Andrew got the chance to forge a partnership with a company that would help promote the start-up's products. To do so, he deprioritized the case study that had been his other major goal. His work on the emergency and the partnership created significant value, but he didn't earn his bonus. "I have to continually make trade-offs between doing what's best for the company and what will earn me my bonus," Andrew said. "The right thing to do for the company changes every week and every day—not every quarter."

We asked Andrew why he didn't update his goals with his boss. "I could do that once or twice," he said. "But I need to be flexible all the time. I'd rather not get my bonus than be constantly renegotiating it. I want to focus on the work—the bonus is already enough of a distraction."

That trade-off earned its own catchphrase: "This quarter I'm working for the equity, not the [bonus]." A sense of unfairness crept into compensation conversations. At the end of each quarter, a flurry of activity occurred as people "checked the boxes" on goals that were no longer important. Even more demotivating, sometimes a goal couldn't be completed because of something completely out of the individual's control. The management team wanted an extra two weeks to consider a website redesign, for example, and so Andrew missed his goal of launching a new webpage within the quarter.

Andrew's compensation system created the distraction effect. For a company that needs the degree of adaptability that Andrew's does, this can be a real problem.

Compensationism can not only distract people from the work at hand, it can also cancel out behaviors you need (the cancellation effect), and create side effects that are even worse than the problem you were trying to solve (the cobra effect).

COMPENSATION AND CANCELLATION

As mentioned in Chapter 3, "Rethinking Performance," a review of 128 academic studies[2] found that performance-based rewards tend to cancel out the natural sense of play, reducing persistence. And sometimes they cancel out even more.

A major commercial bank wanted to incentivize high performance and attract top talent to its small business loan division. Under the old system, loan officers received a flat salary. Under the new system, officers would get bonuses for approving more loans and making decisions faster. In the spirit of fairness, they were also given a bonus for approving larger loans since they made the bank more money. Researchers from the Federal Reserve Bank of Chicago tracked what happened.[3]

The new program looked like a spectacular success. Approval rates went up by 47 percent. Compensationism works!

But over time the bank realized it had made a mistake. The number of bad loans increased by 24 percent. The bonuses had gotten the loan officers to work faster (tactical performance), but they canceled out the problem-solving skills that led to wise decisions (adaptive performance). They also canceled out citizenship—acting in the best interest of the company.

The program didn't even attract top talent—the reverse occurred, as more and more employees left the bank. Our interviews with loan officers revealed how important their working environment is. Many consider their work a highly skilled craft and want the time to make decisions they can be proud of. Many express dismay at having to compromise their values to meet high quotas. And many feel uneasy about treating customers with small loans as less important than big accounts.

THE COBRA EFFECT

While the cancellation effect can be harmful, most concerning of all is when a compensation system creates cobra effects.

In 1992, the chairman of Sears, Roebuck & Company announced the end of sales commissions and goals for the company's auto-repair workers.[4] Undercover investigators had visited Sears' repair shops and been recommended unnecessary services 89 percent of the time. Further investigation demonstrated what we now know quite well. The employees weren't bad people. Instead, a system that created economic pressure using sales goals that threatened employee commissions and hours led to a predictable cobra effect. To Sears' credit, they realized this and put an end to the practice.

Unintended consequences occur in all kinds of industries. As Chapter 6, "Frozen or Fluid," discussed, the majority of executives said their companies would forgo value-creating activities to meet quarterly goals.[5] As we saw in Chapter 3, "Rethinking Performance," a majority of salespeople surveyed at a US multinational admitted that they would engage in some form of noncustomer-centric or noncompany-centric behavior to achieve their sales goals.[6]

Even teachers aren't immune to the cobra effect. In 2010, third-grade teacher Jackie Parks agreed to wear a wire to help state investigators explore their suspicions of cheating at public schools in Atlanta, Georgia. Parks reported gathering in her principal's office after exams to erase and revise incorrect answers.[7] According to Parks, the cheating had been going on for years. By the time the dust settled, the state investigation implicated 178 teachers and principals, across 44 schools.[8]

The blame bias would suggest that the alleged offenders are simply bad people, but that's not the case. State investigator Richard Hyde listened to hours of taped conversations to uncover the depth of the cheating. "I heard [the educators who cheated] in unguarded moments. You listen, they're good people. Their tone was of men and women who cared about kids," Hyde said. He described another source as "a really fine person . . . another single mom under terrible pressure."[9]

Once again we see a cobra effect that will inevitably come from a system that lowers total motivation. While explaining their behavior, the teachers cited significant emotional pressure from their bosses. They feared losing funding for their students. They felt economic pressure because they believed they could lose their bonuses or their jobs.[10]

Atlanta was not alone. Cheating scandals have been uncovered across the country, from Los Angeles to El Paso to Chicago.[11] Several newspapers have conducted statistical analyses of strangely large gains in student test scores. *The Atlanta Journal-Constitution* found that 196 school districts across the country had suspicious results. At some, "the odds were greater than a billion to one that scores improved without some intervention, such as cheating."[12] A *USA Today* analysis found 1,610 statistically rare gains on state tests in six states and the District of Columbia (for example, a whole fifth-grade class in one school would have a suspiciously large improvement from the previous year).[13] Paying for performance can create the cobra effect, even in teachers.

Experiments have shown that paying teachers for performance is no silver bullet. An experiment in Nashville paid teachers bonuses of $5,000, $10,000, or $15,000, based on how their students performed on tests. The merit pay had no significant effect on student achievement or on teachers' teaching practices.[14] An experiment to pay New York City teachers $3,000 bonuses if their schools met a target also showed no improvement in student performance.[15] "If anything, the evidence suggests that teacher incentives may decrease student achievement, especially in larger schools," wrote Harvard professor Roland Fryer. Paying for performance is not the quick fix we hope for.

By now, these outcomes are familiar to you. You could have predicted them using the lenses of adaptive performance and total motivation. Teaching at the highest levels of the craft is an adaptive occupation. The best teachers are constantly figuring out how to adapt their approach to the needs of each and every student. A low-ToMo teacher who is feeling distraction and cancellation will inevitably be worse at his or her craft.

The desire to pay teachers for performance is rooted in the desire to create a meritocracy, assure accountability, and retain talent. But there are other ways to do this. As discussed in Chapter 11, "The Land of a Thousand Ladders," YES Prep Public Schools has created a career ladder for teachers, called the Teacher Continuum, in which teacher pay increases as they learn new skills. Critically, they consider both tactical skills, like how well students learn the material, and adaptive performance, like a teacher's ability to adjust the culture of her classroom to meet individual students' needs.

"YES Prep does not believe that our teachers will suddenly work harder for the promise of earning a higher annual bonus," YES Prep states.[16] "However, public education is one of the only remaining industries where salary is determined by years worked not value-added, and we think it's time that changed. The goal in implementing the Continuum is to reward great teachers and create teacher-leadership pathways where our most effective teachers can continue to grow without leaving the place where they are making the greatest impact—the classroom."

WHEN SHOULD YOU PAY FOR PERFORMANCE?

As these examples show, pay-for-performance is complicated. Sometimes it increases and sometimes it dramatically decreases total motivation.

We've discerned an interesting pattern in our own research. In most cases, having a sales commission decreases the total motivation of the employee. However, if the employee deeply believes that his company does the right thing for its customers, the sales commission slightly *increases* ToMo. In other words, an incentive scheme like sales commissions could have a positive or negative affect on the total motivation of your people, depending on how the rest of the culture makes them feel.

Given all this, how do you know what kind of compensation system is right for your organization? Is your company more like Safelight, where a pay-for-performance system worked? Or will it make things worse, as it did for the loan officers?

When helping organizations make these decisions, we analyze their situation using nine questions. These questions attempt to do two things. First, they measure how valuable adaptive behaviors are in the situation. The more critical adaptive behaviors are, the less effective a pay-for-performance scheme is likely to be. Second, they measure the likelihood that pay-for-performance will reduce total motivation. If your people have high levels of ToMo, the negative effects of pay-for-performance are less likely to hurt them.

Our nine questions are below. The more times you answer no, the more damaging pay-for-performance and goal-based bonuses are likely to be.

I. ARE ADAPTIVE BEHAVIORS IMPORTANT?

1. *Is the job routine, with very little VUCA?* As we saw in Chapter 3, "Rethinking Performance," paying people for performance can work when there is no need for adaptive performance, like punching keys in a computer lab.[17] But once the job includes VUCA, it requires adaptive behaviors like creativity, problem solving, resilience, and citizenship. Beware your blame bias when answering this question. In our experience, most jobs benefit from adaptive performance.

2. *Do your people face no conflicts of interest?* Conflicts of interest create opportunities for cobra farms. If your people are constantly making trade-offs between tactical performance (producing more widgets), adaptive performance (helping a colleague), and maladaptive performance (sabotaging a colleague), indirect motives can push them in the wrong direction. If they don't have to make trade-off decisions, there's less room to do harm.

3. *Is your company insulated from the financial and reputational risks that come from an individual's distraction, cancellation, or cobra effects?* In some industries, the magnitude of risk caused by distraction, cancellation, and cobra effects can be enormous. In many industries, the maladaptive behavior of a single individual can damage consumer trust in an entire organization. Moreover, social media can magnify and spread even the smallest mistakes. The more risk the job entails, the more damage pay-for-performance can do.

4. *Is teamwork unimportant to drive the highest levels of performance?* If your organization benefits from colleagues helping or learning from one another, a pay-for-performance system may ultimately decrease performance.

II. WILL YOUR COMPENSATION SYSTEM REDUCE TOTAL MOTIVATION?

5. *Can you fairly measure important behaviors, especially adaptive behaviors?* When adaptive behaviors are both important and hard to measure, it's unlikely that pay-for-performance systems will be fair. Some achievements may be the result of team efforts, and can't be disaggregated to the individual. Sometimes success depends on luck, rather than effort or skill. Again, beware your blame bias when answering this question.

6. *Can you determine the value of the behaviors you care about?* You can figure out how much to pay someone per widget, but

you may struggle to put a value on more complex contributions. You also may not know how valuable a behavior is until months or years have gone by.

7. *Are your people resistant to emotional pressure, economic pressure, and inertia?* Some situations are more susceptible to indirect motivations than others. If the job market is tight, people may feel more economic pressure. If status and pride rest on a bonus, indirect motives will be hard to avoid. If people live paycheck to paycheck, a bonus may be critical.

8. *Is ToMo naturally high in your company?* Your identity could be so strong that it's impossible to turn a missionary into a mercenary. If so, your people are more likely to view variable compensation as a way to track their progress than as an external force pressuring their behavior.

9. *Is it easy to align incentives between your customers, your employees, and your company?* If your customers expect service and your compensation plan encourages your employees to close a sale quickly, for example, then the pay-for-performance system can be damaging.

If after asking yourself these questions you still believe that pay-for-performance is the right strategy for you, we recommend that you tread carefully and conduct long-term experiments to make sure your compensation system does not create negative side effects. You will need to assess both tactical and adaptive behavior, which may require some creativity and expense. In the end, you may find that an investment in culture building yields higher performance dividends than pay-for-performance.

There are alternatives to performance-based pay that are worth considering. As described in Chapter 11, "The Land of a Thousand Ladders," pay can be differentiated based on a more granular and holistic view of the value the person adds to the organization ("learn-to-earn"). This is done through the design of the rungs on the career ladder, which allows you to link compensation with skills and overall impact. Profit sharing (whether at the team, group, or organization level) is also a form of variable compensation, and is more likely to increase ToMo (and provide a cash-flow buffer for the organization during bad times).

TAKING THE PLUNGE

Some organizations have begun to reject the religion of Compensationism, implementing some of these alternatives instead. In 2010, the Lear Corporation, a Fortune 500 company that manufactures aircraft and automotive parts, stopped linking compensation to performance reviews for all 115,000 of its employees.[18]

According to its HR chief Tom DiDonato, performance reviews linked to compensation created a "blame-oriented culture." "They're self-defeating and demoralizing for all concerned," he said in a *Harvard Business Review* blog post, whether you're a low performer, high performer, or manager. Lear replaced annual performance reviews with quarterly discussions between each employee and supervisor. The conversations focused on gaining new skills and mitigating weaknesses. The conversations had "no connection to decisions on pay. None." They even ended annual individual raises. Salaries change according to local market conditions.

It was a big risk, but DiDonato believed that "the way to drive high performance is through honest feedback that employees and managers *really hear*. Think back to the last performance reviews you received and conducted," DiDonato explained. "Does anyone really hear anything except whether they've met their goals and are eligible for their full bonuses? Does anyone feel free to say anything about the boss's shortcomings? . . . By taking away concerns about money and status, we've freed employees to relax and hear what their managers have to say, and vice versa." Lear believes the "prospect of promotion" is usually reward enough. The only exceptions are for those who have accomplished some extraordinary technical feat, to whom Lear gives special stock awards.

A few other big companies have realized that traditional compensation systems can cause more harm than good. The software company SAS has grown to $3 billion in revenue without using stock options or sales commissions. Cofounder and CEO Jim Goodnight believes that "sales commissions do not encourage an orientation toward taking care of the customer and building long-term relationships." The company ranked fourth on *Fortune*'s Best Places to Work list in 2015.[19]

Small companies are experimenting too. Fog Creek, the software company behind products like Trello, spent a decade struggling to figure out a sales commission system that, as Chief Operating Officer Rich Armstrong put it, "rewarded the exact thing they wanted to reward."[20] The company had high turnover in the department: it had to hire new people for all four of its sales representative positions every year from 2008 to 2011.

Inspired by the work of total motivation researchers, the company decided to end commissions in 2011. What a difference it made. As one salesperson reflected, "It's removed the 'me, me, me' mentality. Now I want to share information with everyone on the team, and everyone is willing to pitch in because it doesn't hurt me to help my colleagues."[21] Stress and "quibbling" declined. Cooperation increased between departments. Fog Creek moved forward with record sales.

GOING FORWARD

We wish that Compensationism was a "silver bullet"; it would be so much easier if you could make your people behave exactly as you wanted them to with just the right carrot or stick. But it doesn't work that way.

Compensation has a powerful impact on an organization's culture. It can help people track their growth and their contributions. But it can also distract them from the work itself, and cancel out their best behaviors. It is the quickest way to increase the population of cobras.

The Hunting Party

At First You Shape Your Organizations;
Thereafter, They Shape You[1]

Every time you create a team or division in your organization, you're making a big cultural decision, whether you're aware of it or not. You probably already consider business needs, like how many people are needed to handle the work. You probably consider interpersonal needs, like who will work well with whom. You may consider how many people a manager can "control." But few of us consider how teams and divisions can create communities that increase total motivation and performance.

MANY HANDS MAKE HEAVY WORK

The year is 1882, and you are a foreman on a farm. You have fourteen strong men working for you, and you need some of them to grab a rope that will pull a plow. The rope is long enough that you could have all the men pull it. How many should you assign to the task?

The intuitive answer is to put all of them on it. After all, many hands make light work. But by this point in *Primed to Perform*, you know that there's no simple answer when it comes to human performance.

In 1913, to answer this question, Max Ringelmann, a French agricultural engineer, conducted what many believe was the first re- corded social psychology experiment.[2] He carefully measured how much force people exerted when they pulled a rope alone, and when they pulled it with up to thirteen additional people. He conducted additional studies in the lab and in the field and summarized all these results together.[3]

His results were mind-boggling. Applying his findings back to the rope experiment, Ringelmann found that when a person was added to the rope, everyone pulled with *less* strength. When two people were on the line, they each pulled with 93 percent of the force of a person working alone. Three people each pulled with 85 percent of the force, and so on. By the time eight people joined the rope, they were each pulling with half the force of a single person. As a result, a team of eight pulled the rope with no more total force than a team of seven.

The Ringelmann Effect is another name for the dreaded free- rider problem. Free riders are people who try to hide in a crowd and let others do the work.

Organizations fear free riders as if they are cockroaches. To fight the infestation, they organize their people to hunt them down.

If your kitchen were infested with bugs, you would have a few options. You could hire ten people to stand guard and squash them whenever they appear. Or you could have those ten people give your kitchen a thorough cleaning and keep it spotless thereafter. Strangely, the blame bias causes us to choose the former in our organizations. Lest one of the cockroach guards turn out to be a free rider him- self, we hire a manager to oversee them as well! Most companies use the phrase "span of control" to describe how many people a leader can adequately monitor. As you have seen by now, the cost of this unending bug hunt is the adaptability and performance of your organization.

Psychologists have done hundreds of experiments since Ringelmann's day to understand the psychology of the free rider. A summary of seventy-eight free-rider experiments published in the *Journal of Personality and Social Psychology* validated Ringelmann's finding—that increasing the size of a group causes a decrease in individual effort.[4] But the study went a step further and examined the structural elements of cultures that cause free-rider behavior.

As it turns out, the three most powerful causes of free-rider behavior could have been predicted by total motivation. Free-rider behavior was greatest when the person felt the activity itself had little intrinsic meaning or value. Free-rider behavior was also high when the person's individual contribution could not be determined. These two findings substantiate the view that role design is still the most powerful cultural key (see Chapter 10, "The Playground"). The third most significant driver of free-rider behavior was whether the person simply knew the other people—an early step to building community.

A strong community solves for many motives. A strong community reduces emotional pressure. When you're working in a strong community, it feels safe to be vulnerable. Because you feel safe, your play and purpose are not canceled out by anxiety. A strong community reduces economic pressure by making you feel less afraid of punishment. A strong community increases your sense of purpose because the identity of the group is naturally stronger. Because you and coworkers feel safer to share new perspectives and ideas, a strong community inspires the kind of curiosity that drives play. In our studies of tens of thousands of workers, we found that people in a strong community had 60 more ToMo points than people in a weak community.

But how can an organization ensure that its communities are cohesive and strong? Like many aspects of ToMo, the answers to this question can be found in the fundamental nature of human beings. After all, we are born to perform.

MARKETPLACES AND SOCIETIES

Two types of communities have especially high adaptability: the marketplace and the society. But only one of the two will work for your organization.

A capitalist economy, for example, is a highly adaptive marketplace. Darwinian forces encourage winners and destroy losers. In the same way that termites use pheromone chemical trails to attract resources to an opportunity, marketplaces use money. These monetary signals cause new ideas and insights to spread across the system.

When a new technology is invented or a new market opens, entrepreneurs flood to the gold rush. When something is no longer of value, it is allowed to die, enabling resources to shift to areas of higher value. As we've described earlier, the extreme adaptability of a marketplace ensures that there's milk and bread at every corner bodega in Manhattan, despite the unpredictable nature of the food-supply chain.

At this point, you may be tempted to organize your own people like a marketplace. That's what most of the companies we work with have done. In such a marketplace, each person would overtly or tacitly compete with the person next to him for survival. Performance management systems that rank people or rate them on a forced distribution curve are implemented. Strong incentive compensation schemes are put into place. When people are performing at the bottom of the curve, they are fired, and new people are brought into the tournament.

The logic here is that if a marketplace works for our economy at large, then it should work just as well for a team or organization. But the conclusion rests on four faulty assumptions:

Assumption 1: Organizations don't need citizenship to scale adaptive behaviors. In a marketplace, monetary signals are used to scale new ideas. If you see a competitor try something that works, it is easy to copy them.

But if one person in your company does their job particularly well, it is easy for them to hide their "secret sauce." Without citizenship, they will not share.

Assumption 2: Cooperation and consistency among players in the organization is not needed. It is very difficult to create consistency, cooperation, or citizenship of any kind across players in the marketplace at large—in fact, that's precisely its point. Think about how difficult it is for competitors to agree on standards, like Betamax versus VHS, or the cords you need to buy to charge laptop computers. But consistency is critical for tactical performance in an organization. And adaptive performance can't occur without cooperation and citizenship.

Assumption 3: Organizations don't need participants to improve shared resources. In a marketplace, shared resources (like the environment) are managed through transactions, just like everything else. Participants won't improve these resources without compensation. And they have a strong incentive to be a free rider whenever possible. But organizations can't deliver their value proposition to their customers unless they are constantly improving their shared resources like their tools, technologies, and processes.

Assumption 4: Organizations don't carry the costs of cobra effects. If one company in a marketplace cheats and is eventually caught, it faces the consequences. The rest of the marketplace does not (usually) bear those costs. But the brand and culture of an organization are common goods that any single person can harm, sometimes irreparably. When misconduct occurred inside Barings Bank or Arthur Andersen, it was enough to bring down the Firm.

Organizations require a different model for community building: the society. In a society, ToMo drives behavior, not monetary signals or Darwinian forces. Identity, performance management, compensation design, and leadership behaviors are all pieces of the puzzle. But there is one more cultural key that we have yet to describe: the overall structure that brings all those parts into harmony.

Every company is different. Each unit in each company is different. Like the rest of the culture keys, there is no one silver bullet. As you design your organization, you'll need to study the different types of societies that people naturally form and adapt from them as necessary.

BUILDING A SOCIETY

As you can see all around you, humans naturally build marketplaces and societies. Our families operate as societies. Tightly knit communities operate as societies. So do friend circles. To understand how to structure your organization, you'll need to understand how nature has already solved this problem.

Anthropologist and evolutionary psychologist Robin Dunbar, the head of the impressively named Social and Evolutionary Neuroscience Research Group in the Department of Experimental Psychology at Oxford University, has studied the patterns of primate societies, attempting to unearth their hidden structures.

When you see a group of primates in the wild, they are surprisingly human-like. They play together. They experiment. They care about fairness. They form cliques that groom one another. Dunbar discovered a fascinating pattern about the structure of primate communities.[5] First, he found that there was a natural limit to how large cohesive societies can be. Take note because his finding should make you think differently about your organization.

He carefully tabulated the average size of the societies of thirty-eight different types of primate.[6] For each of these animals he also tabulated the sizes of their brains, particularly the neocortex. His hypothesis was that community building is mentally taxing. You have to remember faces, biographical details, names, stories, etc. Shouldn't there be some connection between brain size and group size?

Lo and behold, there is an incredibly strong connection.

Dunbar found that the number of animals in a primate community was proportional to the size of a specific part of their brains, the neocortex. The neocortex, or "new brain," plays a role in memory, learning, and conscious thought.[7] It is where humans process language.

Dunbar then used his formula to predict the maximum size of a human community. The result, famously known as Dunbar's Number, is approximately 150 people. As Dunbar wrote, "Put simply, our minds are not designed to allow us to have more than a very limited number of people in our social world. The emotional and psychological investments that a close relationship requires are considerable, and the emotional capital we have available is limited."[8]

Dunbar and others have analyzed group sizes for a variety of

Figure 18: Dunbar's analysis of brain size and group size across primates.[9]

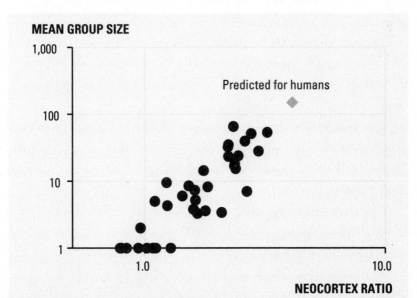

naturally formed human groups. Dunbar's Number, it seems, has been hiding in plain sight:

- The mean size of modern hunterer-gatherer societies (like the Inuit in Canada or the Warlpiri in Australia) was calculated to be 148.4 people.[10]
- The average size of the smallest independent military unit (the "company") ranges from 80 to 300 people, averaging about 160.[11]
- An analysis of 1.7 million people on Twitter shows a maximum level of social connectivity within circles of 100 to 200 people.[12]
- A sampling of how many Christmas cards people sent in an experiment showed an average of about 125 people in a Christmas card network.[13]
- Our own preliminary analysis of total motivation by organization size showed a slight ToMo increase for organizations around 200 people. We didn't study this comprehensively, however, and further research will be required.[14]

Dunbar referred to groups of 150 people as "villages." While this was already an insightful finding, Dunbar wasn't done. He found three more common group sizes, representing different levels of emotional connectivity.

One level below the village, people form more deeply connected groups of about fifty that share resources and protect one another. Dunbar called this group the "band." It's easiest to create a sharing community at this size.

One level below the band, people form natural groups of about fifteen. This is the level at which people work closely together toward specific common goals. We call this the "hunting party."[15]

At the lowest level, people have a handful of very close friends, what we call "confidants." Confidant cliques tend to be around five people. This is the level of deepest trust, and it is where, if managed appropriately, adaptive performance can be the highest.

All four of these structures are required for natural societies to form. The culture engineers of your organization will need to use each of these structures to maximize adaptive performance (see Chapter 14, "The Fire Watchers").

You can see this pattern in the organization of the communities that belong to the Church of Jesus Christ of Latter-day Saints, or the Mormons. Typically, a congregation, or "ward," is the size of a village, with several hundred people. The Cambridge, Massachusetts, church, which attracts larger numbers of students, creates multiple wards of college students, graduate students, and adults, so that none get too large. Other locations create wards based on languages, from Spanish to Chinese.

Since it can still be easy to get lost in a ward, some subdivide into smaller groups of about fifty, the size of a band. One ward, for example, has a band of fifty men, and another of fifty women. Every Sunday, the congregation meets not just as a village, but also in smaller one-hour breakouts as bands. "That's the level at which the most discussion and sharing occur," one church member told us. "It's when we share lessons about parenting, successful marriages, navigating change. The discussions create really strong bonds." Finally, each person is assigned about two confidants. "This is to make sure that everyone has a friend—someone to watch out for them. If I'm sick and need help getting medication, this is the person I'd call. If I'm moving, or struggling to figure out my finances, I know this person will help."

The reason that we tend to form four types of groups is still a mystery. One, however, seems to be scarcity of time. Dunbar has shown that if you don't interact meaningfully with someone within four months, your feeling of emotional closeness will quickly degrade. Confidant relationships require a much greater investment of time than relationships at the village level.

Assuming that you only have about twenty-eight hours a week (four per day) that you can devote to meaningful social interactions, you can spend only about forty-five minutes per month (or about six minutes per week) with each person in your village. Unfortunately, if you spread those forty-five minutes out evenly, you won't be close to anyone. You won't have confidants, and you won't be close enough to the members of your hunting party to carry out complex work. Some very rough math suggests that to make the time limits work, each group requires a different amount of your time:

- Each village member: an average of ten minutes per month
- Each band member: an average of thirty minutes per month
- Each hunting party member: an average of an hour and a half per month
- Each confidant: an average of four and a half hours per month

Organizations should actively work to facilitate the creation of villages, bands, hunting parties, and confidants. The first step is to eliminate the phrase "span of control" from managers' vocabularies. While this is often the governing framework for organizing a company, it sets the wrong tone. It assumes that teams should be designed to be controlled, and that leaders exist to monitor their teams. Instead, you should be concerned with "spans of adaptability."

THE VILLAGE

Though villages, bands, hunting parties, and confidants form by themselves in nature, they do not spring up automatically in organizations. Some companies build groups that are too large. Others use so many indirect motivators that self-protection, jealousy, insecurity, and feelings of injustice trump community.

Organizations must intentionally construct villages. The good news is that it's not hard to do. People naturally want to affiliate, as demonstrated in a series of experiments conducted by researchers from Stanford University and the University of Waterloo.[16]

The experiment was set up a lot like a first day at a new job. The subject entered the experimental room and was given an ID tag, which was either red or blue and had a unique number on it. The researchers primed some subjects to believe they were working alone and others to believe they were part of a team.

People primed to believe they were alone were addressed by the number on their ID tag. For example, they'd say "you are 24601." People primed to believe they were on a team were told either "You are a red" or "You are a blue." They were then given the names of the other people in their group—people whom they would never actually work with.

Then members of both groups were set to work, individually, on a math problem that was impossible to solve. Individuals that were primed to feel like part of a team spent more than twice as long on the problem as those who had been primed to feel like an individual. Simply being told that they belonged to a group caused their resilience to double even though they never worked with their team.

Imagine the power of an entire culture that's designed to build a society.

To do so, you need to break your company into villages that are each around 150 people in size. Each village should have a name, an objective, a heritage, traditions, and perhaps a more personalized version of the behavioral code that governs your entire organization. Villages help break down hierarchies; they create opportunities to form relationships across levels.

Instead of just giving people an employee number, prefix it with a code that signifies their village. Track membership to a village on your company's intranet. Show who is an alum of each village. Though people may change villages over time, daily reminders will help them feel a sense of belonging.

If a village grows too large, you'll eventually want to split it into two. At best, your people will have about ten minutes to spend with each of the members of the village in a given month. Consider how you can best use that time to build community. For instance, members of your village may all eat or work together in a way that facilitates idea exchange. An operations center we worked with in Scotland, for example, had an end-of-week huddle for the whole village in which they shared stories from the week, including ones from their ever-escalating prank war.

THE BAND

One level below the village is the band. While a common social fabric can stretch across a village, people feel the greatest sense of safety and are most likely to share resources in a band of about fifty. In organizations, a band is the ideal size for sharing knowledge and scaling up the creativity of individual play.

Researchers and scientists often call bands "communities of practice." One of the most revered and studied communities of practice was the PARC (Palo Alto Research Center) lab at Xerox. This group of brilliant engineers and scientists invented the computer mouse, the graphical user interface for computers, and laser printers. (For a variety of other cultural reasons that led to low adaptability, Xerox was unable to market many of their innovations.) John Seely Brown, until 2002 the chief scientist of PARC, described band members as "peers in the execution of real work. What holds them together is a common sense of purpose and a real need to know what each other knows."[17]

Here are a few simple questions and ideas to help you think through how to form bands in your company:

- Is there a natural grouping where the knowledge that comes from play should be pooled and exchanged? The group could form around a topic, or a specific objective.

- How can you help each band form a common identity, based on trust and caring?
- How does the band build credibility?
- How do you encourage the band to include apprenticeship in its behavioral code?
- What routines and resources are needed for the band to share knowledge effectively?
- How will the band learn together?

THE HUNTING PARTY

Part of Amazon.com's behavioral code is the "two-pizza rule": if a project team can't be fed by two pizzas, it's too big.[18] The rule exemplifies Bezos's belief that real work should be managed by the smallest teams possible. It is also a perfect illustration of a hunting party.

Sports teams are an apt analogy for hunting parties. Most team sports that require players to coordinate closely with one another have somewhere between five (e.g., basketball) and fifteen players per team (e.g., rugby, hurling). The average seems to be around eleven players on the field (e.g., soccer, American football).

The relationship between the performance of a hunting party and its cohesiveness is highly reciprocal. Bonding leads to high performance and high performance leads to bonding. While some jobs may be solitary (like receptionist or salesperson), each person can still spend some of her time in a hunting party with an objective to improve some component of the organization.

Your processes and routines should allow for a hunting party to spend at least half an hour per week together.

THE CONFIDANTS

A group of doctors tracked over a thousand patients who had suffered heart attacks to see what, if anything, helped them avoid another attack or complications a year later.[19] Their results were surprising.

Emotional depression did not predict further heart problems, but whether or not the patient had a close confidant did. Twenty-six percent of those without confidants had further heart problems, compared to 14 percent for those with close friends.

Remarkably, even very small degrees of interpersonal caring can improve performance outcomes. Researchers at Stanford proved this with a clever experiment.[20] Test subjects were asked to draw a map with a few conditions. First, all of the countries on the map needed to be contiguous (sharing common borders), and each had to be shaded a color. Second, no two adjacent countries could have the same color. Third, the map must require five colors, no fewer.

This problem is actually impossible to solve. In 1977, mathematicians proved that you only need four colors for this particular mapping problem—the first major mathematical theorem to be proven by computers.[21]

During the exercise, each of the test subjects received a tip written on a piece of paper. Here is where the experiment gets interesting. For half of the test subjects, the piece of paper had only the tip and the name of the test subject. Let's call this the "neutral tip" group. The other half of the test subjects received a paper that also included the name of the person that the tip came from. This is the "friendly tip" group. You can see the blank tip sheets used in the actual experiment in Figure 19.

Could this incredibly small show of community and friendship be enough to change the persistence and problem-solving ability of these test subjects? You bet it was.

The test subjects who received tips from an identifiable person spent 48 percent longer on the unsolvable task (17 minutes versus 11.5 minutes). Moreover, a computerized mental reflex test used to measure fatigue showed that those who'd received the friendly tip were 40 percent less drained than those who hadn't. The group that received the friendly tips also attempted about 20 percent more test

Figure 19: The very simple differences between the two tip sheets.

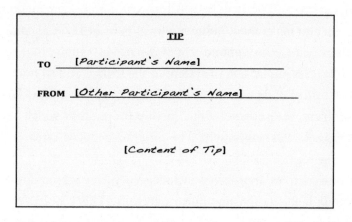

maps (after controlling for the time spent) than the unfriendly tip group. They were more creative and had more persistence, all because of a simple reminder of social support.

As important as the impact of friendships on performance is, the sad reality is that many people still lack confidants. According to our own research, only 56 percent of the workforce feel they have confidants at work. Another study conducted by academic researchers found that a quarter of C-level senior executives, such as CEOs and CFOs, had incredibly low connectedness scores, suggesting that they had no confidants at all.[22]

Organizations can do quite a lot to help their people find confidants at work. The easiest is to institute a voluntary mentorship program and make mentorship a part of your behavioral code. The Hillsborough County public school district in Tampa, Florida, the eighth-largest public school system in the United States, found that almost a third of its new teachers left after their first year. To solve the problem, they created a mentorship program in which veteran teachers help the newcomers. The program reduced attrition from 28 to 5 percent.[23]

More complex approaches include structuring jobs and teams so that confidant relationships form naturally. This requires the creation of smaller subteams of no more than five or so people. These teams are typically leaderless and have to work closely together for extended periods of time.

A COMPANY OF CITIZENS[24]

Think about the world of your organization. If it is like most companies, each individual employee treats just a few close confidants as society members. The rest of their work world is structured like a marketplace. Competitive performance management ensures that the law of tooth and claw governs their relationships with their peers. The company interacts with customers, suppliers, and competitors, using a marketplace model as well.

In the ideal scenario, the high-performing culture flips this model at almost every level, using the principles of total motivation. The only people you should be competing against are your organization's competition.

To build this type of high-ToMo society, you will need to think proactively about your organizational structure. Imagine, for example, the organization of a customer service call center for an online retailer:

1. At the lowest level are leaderless groups of five people. These group members coach and support one another. The goal is to form confidants.

2. One level up, three groups of confidants become a hunting party of fifteen. An official coach helps the party accomplish a clear, common objective.

3. Three hunting parties form a band. They likely have similar objectives, and can share knowledge with one another. Typically, the leadership of these bands is informal.

4. Finally, ten hunting parties form a village of one hundred fifty that has its own leader (who will directly coach about ten people). This village creates a common sense of community and identity for the whole group.

A few companies purposefully manage their society. Among them is W. L. Gore & Associates, the maker of Gore-Tex fabric, which, unusually, was built from the ground up on the principles of total motivation. Play is a part of its DNA; in fact, the company's motto is "Make Money and Have Fun."[25]

Gore & Associates was founded in 1958, after Bill Gore had come to believe that his employer, DuPont, was undervaluing the potential of Teflon, the ultra-slick chemical used to make "nonstick" pans. Inspired by an idea from his son Bob, then a sophomore at the University of Delaware, Gore realized that Teflon could also be used as a superior insulator for wires. He and his wife and thought-partner, Vieve, risked it all to start their business. "If we mortgaged our house and took $4,000 from savings, we could make a go of it for two years," recalls Gore.[26] Two years later, when they were on the verge of calling it quits, their first major order came in for $100,000 and the company took off.

Ten years after its founding, the company had another big

breakthrough when Bob, now a partner in the company, was experimenting with Teflon in an attempt to create a new kind of pipe tape. He pulled a polymer rod out of a hot oven and stretched it by hand to see what would happen. The result was a fiber that blocked water while letting air through—what would become the basis of Gore-Tex.[27]

A student of management theory, Gore senior had been deeply influenced by the works of Douglas McGregor. McGregor published a best-selling book in 1960, *The Human Side of Enterprise*, which offered an alternative to the management dogma of the day. Theory X, according to McGregor, assumes that people will avoid work unless forced. McGregor proposed Theory Y instead, that people actually *want* to perform. This theory was one of the early dominos that led to the work of Edward Deci and Richard Ryan, and the total motivation framework.[28]

Though Dunbar's Number was yet to be discovered, Gore intuitively understood how communities were formed. According to the Darden School of Business at the University of Virginia,

> Gore believed a precipitous drop in cooperation appeared as the group size became large enough so that everyone no longer "knew" everyone else. He believed that, at a certain point, individuals heard "we decided" become "they decided." Gore felt this precipitous drop in cooperation was difficult to forestall in groups larger than about 150 people.[29]

With rare exceptions, Gore organized his people into groups smaller than two hundred. As groups approach this size, Gore split them into smaller groups with a common objective. Gore calls this the "amoeba organization."[30] When teams bubble off of other groups, they remain small and nimble while maintaining the behavioral code of the parent.

Gore also understood the value of hunting parties. While at DuPont, he had been part of a team that was focused on finding uses for Teflon (which is what ultimately led to his own company). "The task force was exciting, challenging, and loads of fun. Besides, we worked like Trojans. I began to wonder why entire companies couldn't be run the same way," Gore recalled.[31]

Bill Gore's own company has no bosses, no job titles, no "employees," and no organizational chart. Project teams—its version of hunting parties—are formed organically as people have ideas. Through the power of play and purpose, they have to convince their colleagues to support them.

Fast Company magazine reports on the organic innovation that occurs at Gore.[32] Typically, employees are encouraged to spend up to 10 percent of their time playing. While engineer Dave Myers's main project was inventing plastic heart implants, he spent his playtime creating better cables for bicycle gears. He later used his playtime to recruit a colleague from the dental floss group to help him improve guitar strings. They recruited another half-dozen people to pursue the project in addition to their regular commitments.

Gore even builds confidants into its system. Every new hire is given a "sponsor" to help him or her acclimate to the new culture, which can be jarring for those from indirect-motive organizations. Electrical engineer Jim Grigsby remembers that his sponsor encouraged him to spend his first few days just meeting other people.[33]

But Bill Gore realized that organizing people into teams isn't enough to create a high–total motivation culture. He simultaneously built an identity with an incredibly strong tradition and behavioral code.

He believed that words are important. If there was a Gore dictionary, it would include entries like:[34]

- Sponsors, not bosses
- Leaders, not managers

- Personal commitments, not job titles
- Guidelines, not rules
- Investments, not expenses
- Associates, not employees

Gore's behavioral code is equally compelling. It speaks of ensuring fairness to one another, which of course is key to the reduction of emotional and economic pressure. It calls for the freedom to allow "associates to grow in knowledge, skills, and scope of responsibility," effectively writing "Play" into the code. It calls for commitment, encouraging people to choose what they do rather than be forced to do something.[35]

Finally, and perhaps most interestingly, is the "waterline principle," which we read about earlier, in Chapter 9, "Identity." "The waterline principle means that it's ok to make a decision that might punch a hole in the boat as long as the hole is above the waterline so that it won't potentially sink the ship," Steve Shuster of Gore's enterprise communication team explained.[36] "But, if the decision might create a hole below the waterline which might cause the ship to sink, then associates are encouraged to consult with their team so that a collaborative decision can be made."

Gore's culture has led the company to tremendous success. It has reported profits every year since its founding. With recently reported revenues of $3.2 billion, it is one of the top 150 largest privately owned companies in the United States. "The voluntary turnover rate at Gore was around 5 percent—one-third the average rate in its industry (durable goods) and one-fifth that for private firms of similar size," according to research done by Babson College.[37] "Pound for pound, the most innovative company in America is W. L. Gore & Associates," concluded a *Fast Company* magazine analysis.

GOING FORWARD

Take a moment to reflect. Does your organization behave more like a marketplace, or a society? Where could your organization form natural villages, with a common purpose, and bands, that can share common learning? Are your hunting parties lean enough to get things done? Does every person have the opportunity to form confidant relationships with their peers?

While Gore built play and total motivation into its culture and organization structure from the get-go, most companies have a long legacy of indirect motivators to overcome. In the next chapter, we'll show you how to begin the work of transformation.

The Fire Watchers

| *Every Flame Needs Fanning*

The founder and former CEO of Southwest Airlines, Herb Kelleher, understands the value of culture. While we've measured the total motivation of many large companies, no large firm has had a higher ToMo than Southwest. That's no accident. As Kelleher wrote,[1]

> *Before people knew how to make fire, there was a fire watcher. Cave dwellers may have found a tree hit by lightning and brought fire back to the cave. Somebody had to make sure it kept going because if it went out, there was no telling when another tree would be hit by lightning. And so, the fire watcher was the most important person in the tribe. I said to our culture committee, "You are our fire watchers, who make sure the fire does not go out. I think you're our most important committee at Southwest Airlines."*

Now that you've seen some of the more important elements of the culture system, let's explore the role of the fire watcher.

CULTURE AS ECOSYSTEM

Having now seen many of the keys of culture, you may be tempted to believe that building a highly adaptive culture is simply a matter of checking boxes on a tactical list of things to do. Unfortunately, cultures are like living, breathing ecosystems. Building them requires more than checking boxes.

Harvard Business School professor Ethan S. Bernstein studied adaptability on an assembly line at a company he code-named "Precision."[2] Based in Southern China, Precision was the second-largest manufacturer of cell phones in the world at the time.

Adaptive performance was central to Precision's strategy. Cell phone technology evolves, rapidly requiring new manufacturing techniques. Manufacturing processes are subject to variability as well. Building a single phone involves the perfect coordination of roughly a million components, a hundred assembly tools, and seventy-two people. Parts arrive with defects. Tools break. People have bad days. No engineer can perfectly design a line this complicated.

Precision's need for adaptive performance goes beyond the typical demands of VUCA. Competition for contracts is so tough that the company often agreed to deals that would turn a profit only if their efficiency improved after they started manufacturing.

As a result, Precision borrowed from the Toyota production playbook, and invested in building an adaptive factory. Precision "implemented sophisticated systems and processes to ensure cross-line transparency for learning and continuous improvement," according to the researchers.

Each of Precision's assembly lines produced 2,400 identical devices every shift. There were sixteen lines, each set up in accordance with the "visual" approach made popular by Toyota. A "clear line of sight" was established "across factory floors, each football fields long, so that learning could be quickly captured, distributed, and replicated by managers," Bernstein related. Their designers thought those lines of sight would maximize adaptive performance. As Bernstein would learn, they did exactly the opposite.

To conduct his research on adaptive performance, Bernstein recruited five Chinese-born undergrads and secretly embedded them at Precision. Their coworkers had no idea who they were. They lived in the factory dorms, went through the standard introductory training, and worked on the production lines. And they discovered something that neither company-supplied data nor interviews would have revealed.

When their supervisors were watching, the line workers followed the guidelines that had been imposed on them. Deviation was not tolerated. Supervisors likely believed that the engineers had already optimized each line to find the best ways of working. Who were they to second-guess them? Because they didn't adapt, the factory was frozen.

Still, the instinct to adapt is hard to extinguish. When their superiors were away, the operators used their own optimized techniques. The embeds were surreptitiously introduced to "'better ways' of accomplishing tasks, a 'ton of little tricks' which 'kept production going' or enabled 'faster, easier, and/or safer production,'" wrote Bernstein, quoting the operators.

Due to the blame bias, we might assume that the employees broke the rules to benefit themselves at the expense of the company. But Bernstein noted that the operators were working to make production faster and safer, without any sacrifice of quality. They weren't even paid for the improvements. They made a flat rate per shift, regardless of how many phones they made.

Bernstein was puzzled. While the employees constantly innovated when management was away, the suggestion box remained empty. Bernstein's embeds probed to figure out why operators didn't share their learning. One operator explained that the managers would "get mad" if employees weren't working in the prescribed way. "We have all of these ideas," another said, "but how do we feel safe to try them?"

"It's easy for workers to find something that works better . . . ," explained another employee, who over nine years had risen from the factory floor to a position as a trainer. "But when you tell others, they'll say, 'How do we know how much value this has?' We don't have the kind of data they want, and we can't make a case for our findings."

Another worker talked about the value of implementing changes in real time. "Even if we had the time to explain, and they had the time to listen, it wouldn't be as efficient as just solving the problem now and then discussing it later. Because there is so much variation, we need to fix first, explain later."

"Wouldn't it be nice if they hung up curtains all around the line, so we can be completely closed off?" joked one operator to an embed. "We could be so much more productive if they did that." The operator's dream was to be hidden from management so the team could be *more* productive.

Precision was facing a problem that confronts many organizations that are building highly adaptive cultures. Cultures are ecosystems. Their parts all affect one another. By not adequately implementing high-ToMo job design, leadership, performance management, and resource planning, Precision wasn't able to create as much adaptive performance as it should have, given all their other investments.

After gathering all of these observations, Bernstein demonstrated how much adaptive performance was still unexploited. He conducted a controlled experiment at Precision. He designated some assembly lines "experimental" and separated them from the control lines with curtains, making the operator's dream a reality.

Now four of the company's thirty-two shifts could work in privacy. The operators experimented with sixteen innovations in the first week alone. When problems occurred, they gathered together to discuss solutions. When bottlenecks formed on the line, they moved around the floor to fix them. They could never have made those adaptations before.

Production increased by 10 to 15 percent after only a few weeks, and remained higher than the control lines for the full five months the experiment lasted. That's a huge improvement for a process that was supposed to be optimized already. It was also a major victory for the operators, workers who weren't trained as engineers or managers. And it translated into significant benefits for a company that operated on slim margins.

In a different experiment at a different kind of company, Wharton professor Adam Grant separated call center operators into three groups. One was given a leader taught to increase total motivation. The second group experienced a high–total motivation role design change in which they were given direct contact with the beneficiaries of their work. The third group got both. Grant found that neither leadership nor beneficiary contact alone resulted in better performance. Yet both together resulted in a 28 percent increase in sales per shift.[3]

A similar experiment was conducted with nurses in Italy who were in a training program that required them to assemble surgical kits from donated medicines and tools.[4] As in the call center, some of the nurses were exposed to a high-ToMo leader. Others were able to interact with a patient who had benefited from a similar effort in the past. Another group was asked to think deeply about the purpose of their work by writing an essay on the good their work did and why other hospitals should join the program. While each of the interventions alone had only a slight positive impact on performance, performance almost doubled when they were combined.

Experiments like these and our own research have shown us that the keys of culture are not additive but synergistic. You need to turn them all to unlock the door of high performance. One plus one equals five. Leadership helps, but it isn't enough. An inspirational mission statement won't do it. A great behavioral code alone won't move the needle. Great cultures are ecosystems whose components all need to work together to inspire the highest levels of performance.

According to our measurements, believing in either your job or your organization creates a maximum ToMo of between 5 and 10. Believing in both together creates a maximum ToMo of about 40. Having a confidant at work without having the ability to play results in a ToMo of about 3. Having the ability to experiment without having a confidant at work results in a maximum ToMo of about 16. Having both results in a ToMo of about 46.

In the previous chapter, we described companies that operate on indirect motivators as "marketplaces" and those that operate on total motivation as "societies." What the scientific community and we have found is that the marketplace is the default. So long as any of the powerful keys of culture are still based on indirect motivators, the whole culture tends to stay locked in a marketplace mentality. To unlock the door to high performance, the keys of culture must work together. This requires consistency and coordination.

DIVIDE AND CRUMBLE

Unfortunately, we're all bad at consistency and coordination.

For example, companies will invest years of effort to create new and innovative products. But when it comes time to sell them, they don't consider the impact the launch will have on their sales force or their service team or even their other brands. They will create a new sales incentive, run some training, and assume the rest of the ecosystem will remain as it was. This is the "coordination neglect."

As a technology entrepreneur, Neel saw this exact issue play out while developing software. The work was divided among various experts, including a designer, a web developer, a back-end programmer, and a database administrator. As often as not, the work was divided too soon and reintegrated too late, costing expensive rework and lots of wasted time. "Software engineers partition the project crudely and then proceed immediately into implementation," wrote Stanford University's Chip Heath and Nancy Staudenmayer in a study about coordination neglect. "Unfortunately, this inevitably results in greater integration problems later on because they must continuously loop back and make unanticipated changes to the original inadequate design."[5]

This problem is especially acute when building and sustaining high-performing cultures. Building a culture ecosystem that is internally consistent requires many cultural keys to be aligned. Career ladders, performance management systems, compensation, village identity, leadership behaviors, and all the other keys described so far need to be designed to increase total motivation. In most organizations, the keys are either managed by separate people or they are not managed by anyone.

Think about your own organization for a moment. Is your leadership program designed to be consistent with your performance dialogues? Is your job design approach consistent with your identity and your compensation philosophy? Most organizations' cultures suffer from a lack of consistency in their design.

Each of the keys that motivate people is designed independently, without a common goal or methodology. A group's compensation plan may have been designed with a focus on short-term sales growth. An HR manager may be responsible for designing career paths focused on employee satisfaction. Neither was built to maximize adaptive performance.

Herein lies the challenge: how can we build tightly integrated and internally consistent cultures when we have a bias toward disintegration? To keep the fire of a high-ToMo culture burning hot, you need fire watchers.

THE FIRE WATCHERS

Now that we understand that the objective of culture is adaptability, and know how culture works, who is responsible for it? In most organizations, no one is. At best we have HR departments that own some of the keys of culture, like compensation and benefits. But HR departments are almost never perceived to be the custodians of adaptive performance.

This is where fire watchers come in. Their job can be broken down along six dimensions:

1. The Mandate

The mandate of the fire watchers is not to make employees happy or satisfied, nor is it to drive employee retention. These are all outcomes of high-performing cultures, but they shouldn't be the team's objective.

The focus of the fire watchers is to build a culture and a system for continuously improving adaptive performance in every role in the organization.

In order to be responsible for adaptive performance, the fire watchers must study how their organization benefits from adaptive performance. They must learn where VUCA threatens the overall strategy or creates a competitive opportunity.

For example, while a Starbucks store must adhere to consistency in food preparation, each store has to handle machines that break, customers with unique needs, and markets with varied competition. The culture officer must consider how ToMo and the keys of culture can maximize adaptive performance to address each of those specific forms of variability.

A portfolio manager at an asset management fund, on the other hand, knows that the fund's strategy requires him to study energy companies. The strategy also dictates that he and his team produce a certain number of unique investment ideas per week. But the quality of those ideas is adaptive performance. Culture also plays a role in how well he resists the temptation to cheat. Their fire watcher must learn how to use the keys to optimize their unique form of adaptive performance.

2. Adaptive Performance Metrics
We've already seen how companies tend to make the grave error of focusing on easy-to-measure tactical performance at the expense of adaptive performance. Because the ToMo factor measures the motivational state that leads to adaptive performance, it can be used as the primary performance metric for the culture team. The culture team should be constantly seeking to improve the measurement and to see if there are better ways to use it to drive change and experimentation.

3. Budget and Return on Investment
Like the pheromones termites use to attract the resources of their mound, organizations use financial metrics to attract and justify investment. Historically, it has been very difficult to justify the expense required to drive adaptive performance and culture because neither have been easy to measure.

One organization we worked with spent around $1 billion per year on marketing. To carefully manage and optimize the tactical performance of that investment, they have about five hundred full-time people. This same company spends about $5 billion on human capital. When we asked them how many analysts they'd assigned to manage and optimize the adaptive performance of that much larger investment, they told us they didn't have anyone.

If you spend roughly one percent of your total compensation expenses to optimize your organization's return on investment (ROI), you could hire a dedicated fire watcher for each village. If you invested roughly 2 to 5 percent of total compensation expenses on performance, you could create the career paths, leadership training, tools, and more that are needed to support a high-ToMo system.

Usually, not all of this is additional spending. Existing programs for leadership training, process improvement, and more can incorporate the lessons of total motivation.

In any case, the fire watchers will need to justify their expense. Using the ToMo factor, they can begin to estimate how much adaptive performance they are creating. Using other metrics (like the value of a satisfied customer), they can quantify the dollar value of each point of ToMo. Through controlled experiments for each key to culture, impact estimates can be further refined.

4. The Team

The fire watchers should be led by a chief culture officer, who reports directly to the CEO.

The fire watcher team comprises core members and rotational members.

Core members include the traditional HR department, which already manages a number of culture keys. Additional core members may be required depending on who currently manages the keys to culture.

The fire watcher team should also include members from throughout the organization on a rotational basis. As a starting point, natural ToMo leaders from every major job category should be offered the opportunity to join for a two-year tour of duty. The rotational group may be called to implement keys in their part of the organization, conduct culture interviews, apprentice to be core team members, or lead induction programs. Successful rotation through the noncore team of fire watchers should be part of the managerial career ladder. You wouldn't want to create leaders who didn't understand how to build great cultures.

Collectively, the group of fire watchers should have ownership across all the keys to culture in their organization. This collective ownership is the first step to solving the coordination challenge.

5. Apprenticeship and Skill Building

Maximizing adaptive performance isn't easy. For one thing, it is difficult to predict where it will be required. Every job is different and every strategy is different. A frontline salesperson requires adaptability in different ways than a middle manager does. The culture team must become students of adaptive performance and its muse, total motivation.

Culture officers must be given the training and support they need to learn these skills. In the finance function, many workers are certified accountants; some have advanced degrees in finance. In the quality function, individuals are certified at various levels of Six Sigma. Strategists often have MBAs. Culture officers should be similarly trained in the art and science of fire watching, most effectively through apprenticeships. Apprenticeship is the second step to solving the coordination challenge. And while formal certification should be a part of the process, it's important to take care to not make it an indirect motivator.

6. Habits

Cultures, like all ecosystems, are very difficult to design. There are simply too many imponderables.

When sailors brought rabbits to New Zealand, they didn't anticipate the devastating effect the animals would have on farms. In response, locals illegally imported a virus that kills rabbits (quite brutally). Yet the result was an even hardier breed of rabbits that had gained an immunity to the virus.[6]

Organizational cultures are similarly unpredictable, especially when you're fine-tuning the balance between strategic and adaptive performance. Rather than try to get it right in one go, culture itself must be adaptive. As Winston Churchill is thought to have said, "To improve is to change. To be perfect is to change often."

Constant optimization requires a process. Consider the well-thought-through processes that manage your finance function. Culture management also requires an ongoing rhythm, and a set of tools, metrics, and people certified in the science of culture building.

Here is one possible cadence:

a. Monthly: Each culture officer reviews the individual learning goals of each person in their village and analyzes the progress of ongoing experiments and projects.

b. Quarterly culture officer goals development: Culture officers come together to prioritize the magnets for investment.

c. Quarterly culture team problem-solving session: Culture officers meet to review ToMo measurements, experiments, and adaptive performance outcomes.

d. Quarterly problem solving on the state of culture with the executive team: Review of ToMo and quality of culture keys.

e. Annual problem solving on state of culture with the board of directors.

The point of the cadence is not evaluation. The purpose is to drive adaptive performance by elevating and encouraging problem solving at every level of the organization. This rhythm of constant experimentation is the third step for solving for the coordination challenge.

THE MANIFESTO OF THE FIRE WATCHERS

The world today has more VUCA than ever before. New technologies are constantly springing up. Laws and regulatory regimes are in a constant state of flux. Incredibly fast flows of information affect customers' decisions and competitive dynamics. Adaptive performance is critical; fire watchers must be recruited and trained to manage and optimize it at every level.

To help you form your team of fire watchers, we leave you with a manifesto of the fire watchers. You can find this manifesto online at www.primedtoperform.com, along with a community of people forming around the practice of culture building.

THE MANIFESTO OF THE FIRE WATCHERS

WHAT WE DO

- We own the adaptive performance of our organization
- We increase adaptive performance by building cultures that inspire total motivation

HOW WE DO IT

- We own or influence the aspects of our culture that affect total motivation
- We continuously iterate our culture through routine measurement and experimentation
- We work in monthly performance cycles with two weeks of integrated design and two weeks of execution
- We constantly study our colleagues' work to understand where adaptive performance is important
- We constantly study how mindset and motivation drive performance
- We develop new knowledge and contribute to our craft
- We organize ourselves to maximize our own adaptive performance and total motivation

HOW WE CHOOSE

- We prioritize creating integrated and consistent cultures even if the design takes longer to create
- We prioritize creating sustainable cultures versus cultures that require constant oversight
- We prioritize fast execution provided we learn from mistakes
- We prioritize learning over knowing
- We prioritize grass roots change over big branded change programs

GOING FORWARD

Culture can't be managed by chance. Assemble a team of people who are explicitly charged with culture building. Create your own, personal manifesto. Then go light some (metaphorical) fires!

Performance Calibration

| *Don't Change the Player, Change the Game*

So far, we've focused on creating adaptive performance—enhancing total motivation so that an organization can innovate when things don't go according to plan. But an organization also needs tactical performance. It needs to meet daily and weekly production goals to satisfy its customers; it needs to accurately forecast sales so it can manage its money effectively and satisfy its shareholders' expectations; and it needs to meet deadlines to beat the competition. How do you balance adaptive and tactical performance for your whole organization?

The answer lies in your performance management system. In the pursuit of predictability, many performance management systems completely crush total motivation. On the opposite extreme, some organizations have no performance management systems at all; they are as unfocused and chaotic as a cloud of steam. But a well-managed, high-ToMo performance management system balances the yin and the yang of adaptive and tactical performance, balancing creativity and practicality, values and valuations, aspirations and economics.

THE DEADLY SINS OF PERFORMANCE MANAGEMENT
Building Cobra Farms

Many organizations get performance management wrong. They believe that performance reviews will motivate people to the highest levels of performance and produce predictable financial returns. But more often than not, performance management systems create gigantic cobra farms.

Take Microsoft, for example, a company that hires some of the smartest people in the world. Despite its incredible talent pool, from 2003 to 2012, its stock remained stuck below $30. Though it blazed a trail into the personal computing era in the 1980s and '90s, Microsoft came late to a number of the defining tech trends of the last fifteen years, like the Internet, mobile computing, and social networking. Investigative reporter Kurt Eichenwald wanted to find out what had caused the company's "lost decade."[1] The culprit, he concluded, was its performance management system.

"Every current and former Microsoft employee I interviewed—*every one*—cited stack ranking as the most destructive process inside of Microsoft," he reported. Every manager in every department had to rank their reports from the highest to the lowest performers. Those at the top got bonuses and promotions. Those at the bottom didn't last very long.

The process might seem logical at first glance. Why shouldn't ranking inspire people to do their best? And isn't it meritocratic? The people who contribute the most receive the highest levels of rewards. Those who can't contribute leave the organization. Shouldn't this raise overall performance? But stack ranking shifts motives from play and purpose to emotional pressure and economic pressure. Total motivation falls and, with it, adaptive performance.

First the distraction effect: "People planned their days and their years around the review rather than around products," one software designer told Eichenwald.

Then the cancellation effect: "You really had to focus on the six-month performance, rather than on doing what was right for the company."

And last, the cobra effect. In some cases, Microsoft employees prevented high performers from joining their teams, so they wouldn't lower their own rankings. The ability to play politics became a survival skill. "One of the most valuable things I learned was to give the appearance of being courteous while withholding just enough information from colleagues to ensure they didn't get ahead of me on the rankings," said one engineer. In a different company with a similar performance management system, managers told us that they would purposely keep low performers on their teams until the reviews so that they would protect high performers from low ratings.

Even a high performer we interviewed told us he had mixed feelings about the ranking system. While he was in the top decile of performance, he didn't feel like his colleagues were compensated fairly. His whole team worked harder than most of the company, yet its lowest performers faced negative consequences. Imagine if "Steve Jobs of Apple, Mark Zuckerberg of Facebook, Larry Page of Google, Larry Ellison of Oracle, and Jeff Bezos of Amazon" were all on the same team, Eichenwald wrote. "Regardless of performance . . . two of them would have to be rated as below average, with one deemed disastrous."

Microsoft's former review system was supposed to keep everyone on track toward the organization's business objectives. But by creating extremely high levels of emotional and economic pressure, it undermined total motivation—and with it, adaptive performance.

Luck Takes the Lead

Performance management systems can create indirect motives in a few different ways. One is the emotional pressure that comes from feeling judged for outcomes out of your control. These systems allow luck to play a starring role.

Experiments have proven this in multiple situations. Imagine that you supervise a group of nurses in a hospital wing. One afternoon you learn that Jackie, a competent nurse whom you've worked with for many years, accidentally left the railing down on a patient's bed. A patient could have fallen to the ground, but didn't. What would you tell Jackie in her performance review?

You'd probably give her a light warning. "Jackie, remember how you left that railing down? I know it was a small, onetime mistake, and that you are a competent and caring nurse. The odds of someone falling are really low, and I don't think it's a big enough deal to affect your performance evaluation, but watch out for it next time."

Now suppose that Jackie has a twin brother, Jackson. Jackson is as experienced and as competent as Jackie and he made the exact same mistake. Yet unfortunately for Jackson (and his patient), someone did fall out of bed. What would you say to Jackson? Should he receive a light warning as his sister had, or a serious punishment?

An experiment with fifty-five nurses found that the blame bias is alive and well.[2] When presented with these two scenarios, test subjects could not help but be swayed by the outcome even though the behaviors were the same. They believed that Jackson's mistake was major and that the odds of a patient falling were high, not low as in Jackie's case. They blamed Jackson for being a careless nurse, ascribing his mistake to his intrinsic character. This was true even though the two made the exact same mistake. We're biased to evaluate behavior based on its outcome, not the input, even if the outcome was driven by luck.

People demonstrate this "outcome bias" in experiment after experiment. It applies to doctors and surgeons, salespeople and homebuyers.[3] We exaggerate what someone "should have known."

Ninety percent of HR executives believe that their performance management systems yield inaccurate results.[4] Imagine that. The very people who run the systems believe that they are flawed. In our own research, we've found that unfair review processes reduce ToMo by a whopping 33 points.

Not only do people become disgruntled, the organization loses a valuable source of information. Because the system is prosecutorial, organizations lose the ability to find out what's blocking performance.

Consider two salespeople, one with outstanding sales and one with poor sales, both due to factors outside their control. We celebrate and promote the person who had good luck, believing she's talented, and punish the person whose performance was low. As a result, we might not see that the lucky salesperson made some incredibly risky decisions that could endanger our reputation in the future. Or we may miss the ingenuity of the lower-performing salesperson, and end up firing someone who could have been extremely valuable to the team.

Ironically, the outcome bias ensures that many performance reviews don't do anything to improve performance. They don't acknowledge the person who had an innovative idea and figure out how to scale it. They don't analyze patterns across people, realize that many people are struggling with one particular skill, and design tools or training to strengthen it. Most review processes result in a grade, but not a plan to lift any, never mind all, boats.

All Yang, No Yin

Most performance review systems prioritize tactical performance. They look at calls per hour, without considering the creativity someone used to win the loyalty of a tricky but important customer, which took twice as long as a normal call. They consider the productivity of an individual, not the time spent helping a colleague get up to speed. They consider the profitability of a business unit without considering the costs that might have been slashed to meet those targets. When reviews holistically incorporate everything it takes to be excellent in a job, organizations can have up to 28 points higher ToMo.

YOU ARE NOT ALONE

We are not the first to have recognized the internal inconsistencies of so many of today's performance management systems. The stacking dogma in particular has come under sharp scrutiny. *Forbes* magazine reported that "By 2012, 60% of Fortune 500 firms used Rank and Yank—giving it more politically correct labels." But they went on to report that the number was decreasing.[5] A number of notable organizations have gotten rid of performance rankings and ratings altogether, like Minneapolis-based Medtronic. A $64 billion company that manufactures medical devices like pacemakers and insulin pumps, Medtronic used to rate each of its 64,000 employees on a scale from one to five.

The entire company became obsessed with ratings rather than true performance. "Ratings detract from the conversation," Caroline Stockdale, formerly Medtronic's chief talent officer, told the *Washington Post.*[6] "If an employee is sitting there waiting for the number to drop, they're not engaged in the conversation, at best. At worst, it can make them angry and disaffected for a period of up to a year."

In 2011, Medtronic replaced its forced bell curve with what they call "performance acceleration." The process focuses not on evaluating past performance, but on helping each employee figure out how he or she can meet future goals. While some were concerned that managers wouldn't terminate low performers under the new system, "involuntary turnover," the number of people the company dismisses, remained steady.[7]

Other companies have made similar moves, including Expedia, Adobe, and Motorola.[8] Microsoft itself scrapped its stack ranking system in 2013. Their traditional performance review processes were doing the opposite of what they were intended to.

Yet the question remains—what do we do instead?

BALANCING YIN AND YANG

You might think that the best way to improve performance management systems is to eliminate them altogether. But we've found that employees without performance management systems also have lower total motivation. Absent a formal process, assignments and promotions appear to be based on favoritism, or whoever makes the most noise. Lack of transparency creates new forms of emotional and economic pressure. What's needed is a new kind of system, one that's designed to avoid the most common pitfalls while improving performance for all.

A highly effective performance management system can only exist, however, if the other elements of a ToMo culture are in place. Each individual must be working toward adaptive goals. Leaders must understand total motivation. Roles must enable experimentation and allow people to see the impact of their work. Career ladders must demonstrate that skills and learning are the primary drivers of differentiated compensation. A strong sense of citizenship must shift the organization from one that feels like a marketplace to one that feels like a community.

But after yin is optimized, the reality is that our organizations live in a yang world of tactical performance. Economic stakeholders prize tactical performance and predictability. Long-term capital investment projects and simple financial prudence require them. Competitive forces require us to consider outcomes such as market share. In a high-performing culture, where and how do we ensure that yin and yang are constantly kept in balance? Where are culture and strategy calibrated?

PERFORMANCE CALIBRATION

We saved this chapter for the end for a reason. The performance management system is the calibrator of yin and yang. It is what keeps the whole ecosystem operating in harmony with the tactical performance obligations of the organization.

To explain, let's start with a hypothetical. If each individual is on a continual journey of self-improvement, how do we make sure that self-improvement aligns with the tactical performance the company requires? If the employees of a department store have all set personal goals to become better at selling clothing when the best strategy for the business overall is to sell more refrigerators, there will be a problem.

As you look at the competing forces of yin (adaptive performance through culture) and yang (predictable tactical performance), you will find many places where they will be in tension. Perhaps even more concerning is that, unlike natural ecosystems that eventually achieve equilibrium, business cultures never do. There are too many changes in the environment and too many shocks to the system. A new executive is a shock. Changing regulations or technology are shocks. A new customer need is a shock. All of these shocks constantly threaten the balance between yin and yang. As such, we need a process that keeps the two in balance. This process is called performance calibration.

First and foremost, performance calibration must manage the career ladders. Every six months the calibration team, which comprises executives, fire watchers, and finance professionals, convenes. During this session they see who should move to the next rung, and independently test that each rung is creating additional economic value. If the rungs do not create more value than they cost, the system will be out of equilibrium and eventually lead to major problems. The fire watchers and finance professionals complete this analysis before the meeting even begins.

In the cases where there is doubt that the rungs are driving additional value, this group must understand why, and launch experiments to fix it. Perhaps a person advancing on the expertise career ladder isn't able to leverage his or her knowledge across the whole organization. Perhaps the culture is in some way blocking them. The calibrators must ensure that the tactical and adaptive requirements of the career ladders are in harmony.

Second, performance calibration must manage the connections between the bottom-up adaptive goals set as part of the daily rhythm and the tactical goals being communicated to parties outside of their society. Again, the fire watchers and finance team come to the table prepared to answer this question. They need to understand where performance is improving at pace and where it is not. They need to compare the improvement in performance they expect from local adaptability with the expectations of their stakeholders.

Rather than a blame bias approach of prodding individuals, the calibrators must be scrupulous to consider the whole context, wherever they see gaps in performance. When they see ideas worth scaling from one person or team to another, they must make it happen. When they see a systemic problem with performance, they must either launch their own experiments or provide guidance to their people on where they should themselves be experimenting to improve performance.

Of course, there will be times when someone is simply a poor fit and would be better off working elsewhere. But identifying these situations isn't the purpose of performance calibration, it is simply one of its by-products. When such a candidate is identified, a separate process should be launched to address the situation. Performance calibration is positive in its intent, not punitive.

As a fire watcher, you need to understand where yin and yang threaten each other, potentially resulting in a frozen or chaotic organization. These areas should be incorporated into your performance calibration system.

PERFORMANCE TURNAROUND

As passionate engineers of culture, we are constantly looking for live experiments—places where cultures are actively being built. We found one in an industry where millions of dollars ride on everyday decisions—the hedge fund industry.

Hedge funds pool money from investors and develop strategies to invest it. Each hedge fund typically has its own strategy and approach, supported by terabytes of information, sophisticated mathematical models and brilliant analysts. Portfolio managers (PMs) at some firms can fly to Japan at the drop of a hat to interview experts in solar power, or access massive databases of consumer credit card information. Speaking about a hedge fund that invests based on macroeconomic trends, Paul A. Volcker, the former chair of the Federal Reserve, said it had "a bigger staff, and produces more relevant statistics and analyses, than the Federal Reserve."[9]

SAC Capital was founded in 1992 by Steven A. Cohen to invest primarily in the US stock market. It became famous for its returns during the tech-stock boom of the late 1990s. In 2000, it bet against the tech industry, believing the stocks were massively overvalued. Sure enough, the dotcom bubble burst. Cohen was on his way to being "regarded by many as one of the premier stock traders of his generation," according to the *New York Times*.[10]

We spoke with Cohen on a Sunday morning to understand the motives of one of the wealthiest men in the world, and the story of SAC Capital. It's easy to assume that Cohen is a real-life Gordon Gekko, one of those who believes that "greed is good." Instead, we found something very different. Even in the high pressure, highly lucrative world of investing, ToMo is still king.

Cohen was born and raised in Long Island, New York. At the age of thirteen, he bought his first stock. "My first pick was a loser," Cohen said. Yet he wasn't deterred. Instead, he was curious. He began to follow stocks in the *New York Post* his father brought home every evening. By fourteen, he was hanging out at the local brokerage firm. "I used to go to a brokerage firm and sit there all day when I wasn't at school, and during the summer. If I was sick for a day, I would sit and watch the tape going across and just loved it," he remembered, referring to the "tape" that showed how stock prices were moving.

Trying to find the hidden pattern was play for Cohen. The better he got at seeing the patterns, the more he wanted to challenge himself. While still in high school, he graduated from just watching the patterns to testing himself under the pressure of real risk—through his neighborhood poker game. With the cards in his hands and his opponents across the table, again Cohen saw patterns where others did not. He began to earn so much from the game that he quit his part-time job as a grocery store clerk, where he made $1.85 an hour. Even before graduating from high school, Cohen had found his source of play: detecting patterns, and managing risk.

After college, Cohen became a successful trader on Wall Street, and then eventually branched out on his own, founding SAC Capital.

He wanted to build a firm that could adapt. While many other hedge funds had one portfolio manager, fed by many analysts, Cohen built a firm where many traders could make their own decisions. They all benefited from a common platform, sharing the best tools and processes in the industry. "I have a lot of trust that if you give someone the ball, they'll figure it out," Cohen said.

His hedge fund model worked. For almost a decade, SAC Capital delivered high returns. But over time, the world began to change. The number of hedge funds started growing, from about 1,600 in 1994 to over 6,500 in 2005. More and more sophisticated investors entered the market. Tape watching was no longer enough.

Many people facing the fact that their once lucrative skill has become obsolete simply dig in. As performance suffers, their blame bias causes them to want to apply more pressure to squeeze out more performance. Instead, Cohen realized that the world was too different. It was adapt or die.

Cohen navigated his Firm towards a strategy that focused on fundamental analysis. While previously PMs detected patterns in trading, they began to focus on building deep expertise in a set of companies. Today, fundamental analysis has become standard in the industry, and the cutting edge includes even more quantitative, computer-enabled strategies. "I think that it's important that the Firm is always dynamic, always changing, always adaptable," Cohen explained. "Because the world is changing, what worked ten years ago may not work ten years from now."

Yet despite its success, SAC Capital was not immune from cobra effects. Economic pressure is a real risk. The best portfolio managers are often wrong 45 percent of the time. "It's like getting punched in the face every day," said one PM.

In 2013, the government filed suit against SAC. Several current and former employees were convicted or pled guilty to insider trading. SAC Capital paid $1.8 billion in penalties, and gave up the right to trade other people's money.

In 2014, SAC became Point72 Asset Management, and recruited Doug Haynes, a former senior partner at McKinsey & Company, to lead the organization into a new era. "I know we have the greatest people in the industry," said Cohen, "but we don't have the greatest management process to take Point72 to the next level. Doug is here to change that."

Born and raised in West Virginia, Haynes is a leader with a natural gift for understanding motivation. He's been known to provide his own musical score to his speeches with a banjo, decreasing everyone's emotional pressure and priming play.

In his first year, Haynes wanted to understand what drove the best portfolio managers. He measured the total motivation of the group, and found that the highest performing PMs had 10 points more ToMo than the rest, driven largely by a sense of play.

The sense of play is obvious when watching some portfolio managers at work. One portfolio manager who invests in media and technology companies, whom we'll call Nick, leads meetings with his analysts like a kid in a candy store. He suggests new ways to interpret data, and debates investment ideas like there's nothing else he'd rather be doing. A high school chess champion, he has loved the stock market ever since he went on a school field trip to the New York Stock Exchange. "I don't really think about success and failure in terms of dollars and cents because that's not what motivates me. It's really more about 'did I figure out the puzzle?'" he said. "My work isn't just a job, it's a passion. I love what I do and I want to do it all the time—even on Sundays, even on vacation."

But Nick knows that emotional pressure can get to his team. "A big loss can shut them down," he said. "They can't work on the next idea. They sit silently at their desk staring at the chart of the investment gone wrong." Nick tries to build their "loss muscle" over time. He points to his own shared responsibility for the mistake. He tries to relieve the pressure through humor and stories, including his team's favorite, about how he didn't know the meaning of some basic financial terms on his first day on the job. He assures them that it's okay to make mistakes.

One day, Nick realized he was making a series of bad decisions while investing in a particular subsector of Internet stocks. This particular slice of the market behaved unpredictably, and he wasn't generating good returns. His analysts and trader thought they should not invest in these stocks, but were reluctant to say so to their boss. Nick realized that adaptive performance requires a team to contribute all of their ideas. So he wrote a letter to himself from the team. He called the team into his office, gave the letter to his trader, and asked him to read it aloud. It said:

> *Nick. What the @#$%, you stupid @#$%. You promised you were going to get out of these ridiculous . . . stocks. If I have to hear about [these stocks] one more time, I'm going to punch you in the face.*

"The team was cracking up," Nick said. It was a good reminder that everyone makes bad decisions, and that the team needed to speak up and help their boss deal with a mistake, just as he would help them. To this day, the trader keeps the letter within arm's reach for the moment he'll need to read it back to his portfolio manager.

One of the first questions Haynes set out to answer as he began to transform Point72 for the new era of investing was how to create a performance management system that didn't ratchet up the emotional and economic pressure even further.

Previously, performance reviews occurred like they do at most companies. A PM sat down with management, management gave the PM lots of feedback, and that was that.

Except at Point72 a few things are different. Management has a trove of data on each PM's performance. They can analyze every trade. Their risk tools can dissect the performance of a portfolio in hundreds of ways. In the old model, a PM came into the meeting having no idea where the conversation would turn.

Second, the stakes in the asset management industry are higher than in some other jobs. At a performance review, a PM is told his "buying power" for the next year, essentially how much money he would have to invest. Buying power can increase or decrease by tens of millions of dollars.

"The old process had several weaknesses. Once they heard the number, PMs often struggled to pay attention to anything else," Head of Equities Perry Boyle said.

The process also failed to reveal the whole picture. While Point72 could see the outputs—the trades a PM made and how much money those trades lost or made—it couldn't see the inputs that led to a trade. "We would look backwards and say to a PM 'tell me what happened,'" Haynes explained. "If things had gone well, it was due to their skill. If things went badly, it was a story of bad luck." The process wasn't set up to detect if the next year would be different. "We used to assume good outputs meant good inputs," Haynes said. "Now we look at the inputs to make sure it wasn't luck but a repeatable process that is driving the outputs."

Take the story of a great trade, for example. In December 2012, an early-tenure PM, whom we'll call Callan, walked the halls at Point72 telling senior executives that the market for potash would crash. Potash is a type of salt used in fertilizer. Big swings in the market were unusual, since a few big producers in Belarus, Canada, and Russia managed two-thirds of the world's supply as an "informal global pricing cartel."[11] But Callan was convinced the market would drop, and invested accordingly. Why?

When Callan learned that Belarus's economy was struggling, he formed a hypothesis that the country would start producing more potash to bring in more revenue. If there's a big increase in the supply of a product without an increase in demand, prices drop.

Callan looked for clues. He read comments from Belarus's prime minister suggesting changes in the country's export strategy. He found a description of an unusual deal between Belarus and Bangladesh in the back of a fertilizer industry trade magazine he subscribed to. He started to read Belarus's local newspapers. As a result, he was one of the first in the investment community to learn of a declaration by the government in Belarus to export potash outside their existing agreements. Meanwhile, he found data on Russian exports to China—it looked like Russia was producing more potash than expected as well. Sure enough, Callan's hypothesis was right. Potash prices plunged.

Was Callan's insight into the potash market skill or luck? Everyone knows about the executive who gets a massive promotion because he was in the right place at the right time and never reproduces that success again. But as one Point72 executive told us, some

PMs do have systems that consistently generate "crazy, overlooked ideas." Perhaps this was not a one-hit wonder. A performance management system needs to understand whether performance is based on a repeatable process. "You have to think about how someone will perform going forward, not just depend on past results," Cohen explained.

The first thing Point72 did to improve its system was to make an organizational change. It created seven new "sector executives," people who would support and oversee PMs in each sector the Firm invested in, like energy or healthcare. With this increase in management capacity, Point72 launched a new business plan process. Each PM worked together with managers and risk experts to analyze performance data in advance of the review process. The PM used those insights to construct a plan for the next year, a plan that in some cases went through multiple iterations. What was working well? What needed to change? What strategy would deliver the highest returns in the coming year? After the PM submitted the plan to management, a meeting was held in which the PM and management could discuss the plan. After the management team had considered all the plans, it made buying power decisions, and shared the results.

"It isn't evolutionary, it's revolutionary," the Firm's chief risk officer said. For the first time, there was a formal process for the Firm to understand not just the outputs, but also the inputs.

"There was some groaning at the beginning," one sector executive told us. "But as we started to do it, people said, 'You know what? This is kind of helpful.'"

About 15 percent of the business plans were "eye-popping, completely innovative," one executive noted. "The process fundamentally changed our view of a few guys." Two PMs, for example, had had a bad year. In the past, they would have been treated exactly the same. But one "was so introspective and thoughtful" on how he proposed to adapt that the Firm decided to increase its investment in him.

The process reduced the impact of personality, the chief risk officer explained, and focused on whether a PM had created a "repeatable machine." The reviews helped identify which teams had strong, consistent processes for examining the fundamental values of the companies they invest in. "Strong fundamental processes go hand in hand with compliant behavior and high returns," Haynes explained.

The new review process shifted the focus from the outputs to the inputs—the work that portfolio managers can control and refine over time. It also uncovered areas where PMs often struggle. The management team was able to make suggestions for common problems, like overtrading. The process generated ideas for how the Firm could build new tools to help all PMs improve their processes, for example, by building new risk capabilities. Even though Point72 had higher returns than most hedge funds in 2014, according to the *New York Times*, the Firm identified many opportunities to improve performance even further.

Haynes calls it "predictive performance management." Point72 doesn't just judge past performance, it assesses which PMs will be high performers in the future. And by providing data, counseling, and advice, it increases everyone's performance going forward.

The process is in its first iteration, and more time is needed to see its full potential. Some PMs said that the new process was highly valuable. Others complained that their track records should speak for themselves. Point72's management answers them with a sports analogy. "I would challenge them to go talk to a top golfer, top tennis player," said the sector executive, "and ask them, 'When you got to number five, did you stop getting coaching? Did you stop learning?'"

GOING FORWARD

Getting performance management right is one of the hardest things to do when building a great culture. Yet once you build a performance calibration system, you can use it to chart your course forward. You can balance tactical and adaptive performance. As you walk away from this chapter, ask yourself a simple question. "How does my organization balance the yin and the yang of performance?"

Igniting a Movement

Creating ToMo through ToMo

Many of the readers of this book work in large organizations that are stuck with cultures that are low performing. It may be tempting to try to force your company to adopt all of the principles you've learned about right away, but using indirect motivators to build a high-ToMo culture doesn't work. As Martin Luther King Jr. said, "Darkness cannot drive out darkness; only light can do that."

The process by which you build or rebuild your culture must itself be high ToMo. You have to lead change in ways that create play, purpose, and potential, not pressure. As the motivation guru Edward Deci wrote, "The proper question is not, 'How can people motivate others?,' but rather, 'How can people create the conditions within which others will motivate themselves?'"[1]

So where do we begin? Nature yet again provides a clue.

ORGANIC CHANGE

Off the coast of Japan is the island of Kōjima, a utopia for the macaque, a monkey-like primate. Kōjima has been the home of a primate research center for over half a century. Since 1952, all the primates on the island have been individually marked and have names, histories, and recognizable personalities. In 1953, one particularly industrious macaque named Imo became an inventor, the Thomas Edison of the macaque community.[2] At the time, the other macaques in Imo's tribe would rub the dirt off their sweet potatoes by hand before eating them. One day, at just eighteen months of age, Imo tried something different. She walked up to a stream and used water to wash the dirt off her sweet potato. This was her lightbulb moment.

Macaques haven't developed culture like humans have. They don't have language or schools or the Internet to facilitate the spread of ideas. Nevertheless, ideas do spread. About a month after Imo introduced her innovation, Imo's playmate Semushi began to wash her sweet potatoes with water. Three months after Semushi, Eba, Imo's mother, and Uni, another playmate, were also observed washing their sweet potatoes. While Imo was the inventor, her group of confidants became the first to adopt. Within the next two years, seven more young macaques started washing their sweet potatoes. Within the fifth year, fourteen of the fifteen juveniles and two of the eleven adults were washing potatoes. Her band had been converted. Within five more years, potato washing became the norm. By 1983, thirty years after the invention, the idea had completely diffused throughout the village.

Imo wasn't a one-hit wonder. In 1956, she did it again.[3] Rather than eating dirty grain, Imo discovered that when she threw a handful of grain in water, the sand would sink, and she could simply skim her food off the top. Again, play led to adaptive performance. Eventually grain skimming became the norm in her village.

Humans have far more sophisticated ways to transfer adaptability than "monkey see, monkey do." Language, the way we teach our children, and communications media facilitate our ability to scale adaptive innovations across whole societies. The Internet allows us to scale innovation from one part of the world to another almost instantaneously.

However, all of these scaling mechanisms are just scratching the surface compared to the ultimate form of human adaptability: the social movement. Social movements that enable collective invention have given us tectonic shifts like the American Revolution and the civil rights movement.

The brilliant sociologist Neil Smelser, who studied at Harvard, Oxford, and Berkeley, developed a theory that explains the necessary conditions for collective action to form. There are six prerequisites:[4]

- *Relaxed control.* The dominant authority must not be willing or able to prevent collective action. In the case of culture building, you simply need to make sure that you have enough air support to begin introducing total motivation to your organization.
- *Common belief.* People must share a common view of the problem and a common perspective on the solution. When creating a high-performing culture, common belief requires the most influential people to understand the importance of adaptive performance and the role ToMo plays. Moreover, a common belief inspires change through ToMo itself.
- *Strain.* People must emotionally feel the difference between their current state and their desired future state. This tends to be the easiest of the prerequisites, as most people feel the pain of a low ToMo environment. It also helps to run a total motivation survey and share the data within the organization.
- *Conduciveness.* People must have the ability to interact with one another to enable collective action. Even an informal group of fire watchers can help to ensure that the right set of people are working together to shift the keys of culture. Further, by giving this early group of fire watchers a common language to describe the motives and adaptive performance, their ability to coordinate increases tremendously.

- *The spark.* Some kind of catalyst triggers action. The spark can be very situational. It could be a new mission. It could be a large merger. It could be a ToMo goal. It could even be sharing a copy of *Primed to Perform* (we wrote *Primed to Perform* with the hope that it could serve as a spark for some organizations). The right answer depends on the organization.
- *Mobilization.* Processes mobilize people within the system to act collectively, while still enabling individuality and adaptability. The fire watchers will eventually need to launch their own rhythm for managing the keys of culture. This rhythm serves as the drumbeat of broad mobilization.

Borrowing from the pattern of social movement formation, we can create a process to build a high-ToMo culture, even when the organization's starting point is low ToMo.

MIDDLE-FIRST

We had just wrapped up a four-hour workshop on total motivation and its implications on leadership behaviors. Over the previous four months, we had been doing two of these workshops per week to help a retail institution—let's call it Omicron—build its own high-performing culture.

This workshop was with sixty of its highest performing store managers. From our vantage point on stage, the workshop appeared to be going well. That is, except for one member of the audience. This gentleman was perhaps their most tenured and experienced store manager. Throughout the entire workshop, he sat in his seat with his arms folded and a scowl on his face.

When we opened the discussion for questions, we weren't thrilled to see his hand go up. He stood up and said, "I've been doing this for a long time, and I have to say, this talk really opened my eyes!" We learned something that day. Even accomplished leaders can enjoy for learning how to up their game. This very instinct is at the core of how Omicron has been developing a social movement to change its culture across its twenty thousand employees.

The torch metaphor could not have been more apt when we first started sharing our research with the head of culture for Omicron. She was naturally a high-ToMo leader, but by giving her a framework, metrics, and language for adaptive performance, she was able to see the whole problem at once.

At the time, the entire economy was in a slump, as was Omicron. They were going through tough cost-cutting measures, and morale had taken a hit. It took real courage for her to choose that moment to build a legendary culture at Omicron, but, in fact, there was no better time.

Omicron set out to build a social movement to take its culture to the next level. First, they worked to build common belief. The most influential leaders throughout the organization—about one thousand people—all went through a half-day workshop to learn the science of total motivation. They were given tools, a common language, and encouragement to play in their own playgrounds. Simultaneously they ensured relaxed control. All the key executives went through individual one-hour workshops so they too would learn the science of total motivation and understand the facts and data for themselves.

Lastly, the organization created its own spark by crafting a new mission for itself, one that is genuinely meant to be positive for its customers and society as a whole. This was Phase 1.

Phase 2 began to add structure to the movement. The fire watchers were formed from a combination of the HR team, an informal culture council, and a group of others who naturally managed some of the keys of culture.

Their culture team then began the hard process of ensuring that someone was managing each of the keys to culture. To help speed up the process, they launched a set of pilots meant to demonstrate the impact of an adaptive culture.

The other major effort of Phase 2 was focused on cohesiveness. Taking an inventory of the cultural messages that were being delivered throughout the organization, they found that about half the messaging was contrary to the objective of maximizing total motivation. With the best of intentions, a number of people within the organization were sharing contrary advice and values. To maximize the cohesiveness of a new culture mandate, they aligned on a new set of messages, and ultimately a new cultural identity.

Omicron's approach to launching a social movement is incredibly powerful. No one feels forced to change. Instead, they are naturally moving from a spot of low ToMo to a spot of high ToMo. The fire watchers are doing their best to ensure that the transition occurs without any interim loss of performance.

However, this is only one of an infinite variety of ways to launch a social movement.

ENGINEERING ICONIC CULTURES

Most of us do not have the luxury of building a culture from scratch. Most of us work in cultures whose total motivation may already have been weighed down by decades of baggage. The science addresses this as well. It's never too late to change.

But as with so many things, you have to recognize that you have a problem first. Three decades ago, when Toyota and General Motors combined forces in the New United Motor Manufacturing Inc. (NUMMI), GM was given a golden opportunity to improve its culture. The story reads almost like the plotline of one of those classic movies in the mold of *The Dirty Dozen* or *The Revenge of the Nerds*, in which the underdogs come out on top and teach the overdogs a lesson. Only it didn't turn out that way.

GM had recently closed its factory in Fremont, California, which had been plagued with "poor productivity, poor quality, and a history of extensive labor troubles, including strikes, high levels of absenteeism and turnover, and problems with alcoholism and drug abuse," as Jeffrey Pfeffer, a Stanford University professor and expert on human relations at work, tells the story.[5] "When I was mounting tires, we'd drink," said plant employee Rick Madrid in an interview with *This American Life*, on National Public Radio. "You know, I'd bring a thermos of screwdrivers with me."[6]

The factory was a textbook model of a low–total motivation organization; economic pressure and inertia were the only reasons people came to work. "The analogy to prison is a good [one]," said Toyota production expert Jeffrey Liker, "because the workers were stuck there, because they could not find anything close to that level of job, and pay, and benefits, at their level of education and skill."

The predictable consequence of low–total motivation cultures is poor adaptive performance, and in the worse cases, maladaptive performance. At this factory, workers would go so far as to sabotage cars on the line. "They'd intentionally screw up the vehicles," reported *This American Life*. "Put Coke bottles or loose bolts inside the door panels so they'd rattle and annoy the customer."

To kick off their joint venture, Toyota reopened the plant in 1984, two years after it had closed, and hired back 85 percent of those who had originally worked there. Not only were the people the same, but the United Auto Workers still organized the employees, and the majority of the equipment was the same.

Toyota's takeover was an incredible success. The plant was 49 percent more productive than it had been under GM's leadership. By 1986, it would achieve levels of performance that came within striking distance of the famous Toyota plant in Takaoka, Japan.

Toyota's approach to NUMMI was consistent with the lessons of *Primed to Perform*. First and foremost, it understood that adaptability is an everyday necessity in an automobile plant. New car models are introduced every year; changes in the supply chain lead to variations in components. Tools wear out and break. A newly hired employee may perform his job slightly differently from his predecessor. This degree of VUCA cannot be anticipated by an engineer who's designing a production process. It is simply too complicated.

Second, Toyota realized that creating a highly adaptive culture can be done only through ToMo. Fear and pressure do not make for adaptive people. They began their process by investing heavily in creating *common belief* and helping their people self-diagnose their *strain.*

Toyota had the American factory workers spend two weeks in Japan, where they learned, in teams of about five people (the size of a confidant clique) how Toyota implemented the performance cycle through the Toyota production system. They learned the language of the system. Terms like *hansei* (relentless reflection), *kaizen* (continuous improvement), *genchi genbutsu* (see for yourself), *heijunka* (work like the tortoise, not the hare), became part of their daily vocabulary.

They saw for themselves what it meant to be adaptive on the assembly line and understood why their previous work environment felt so bad. For the first time in their careers, these veteran autoworkers felt play and purpose at work. "You had union workers— grizzled old folks that had worked on the plant floor for thirty years, and they were hugging their Japanese counterparts, just absolutely in tears," one of the trainers related.[7]

Toyota also understood that no one silver bullet creates a high-ToMo culture. While they didn't change the workers or the equipment at the NUMMI plant, the culture and the processes were both turned upside down.

Everyone worked in small teams, increasing the sense of community. Managers and workers formed a village. The two groups symbolically parked in the same lots and ate in the same cafeterias. The dividing lines disappeared. Automobile components were improved, giving people better raw ingredients to work with, increasing the sense of purpose. The language of the Toyota Way was introduced to eliminate the blame bias and remind the workers that quality comes from the system.[8]

Toyota also introduced the factory to the famed andon cord, "a thin nylon rope that hangs on hooks along the assembly line, which became a symbol of everything that was different about the Japanese way of making cars," reported *This American Life*. Workers were encouraged to pull the cord if they saw a quality problem or had an idea for an improvement. This cord is an incredible example of framing the playground. "I can't remember any time in my working life where anybody asked for my ideas to solve a problem," said Liker. "And they literally want to know, and when I tell them, they listen, and then suddenly, they disappear and somebody comes back with the tool that I just described—it's built—and they say, 'Try this.'"

The andon cord itself was designed to reduce emotional pressure and increase the sense of play and purpose. Whenever it was pulled, a song of the worker's choice came on the loudspeakers. If a worker and manager could not solve a quality problem alone, the whole line stopped. "You just don't see the line stop," Madrid said about the old ways. "I saw a guy fall in the pit and they didn't stop the line."[9]

It's worth asking: why would Toyota give a major competitor the keys to its kingdom? Without an understanding of the yin and yang of performance or total motivation, the keys themselves were useless.

Even with the keys, GM's managers didn't know how to unlock the door. They thought the secret of Toyota's productivity was its technology.

"There was no vocabulary, even, to explain it," Liker recalled. "I remember, one of the GM managers was ordered, from a very senior level . . . to make a GM plant look like NUMMI. And he said, 'I want you to go there with cameras and take a picture of every square inch. And whatever you take a picture of, I want it to look like that in our plant. There should be no excuse for why we're different than NUMMI, why our quality is lower, why our productivity isn't as high, because you're going to copy everything you see.' Immediately, this guy knew that was crazy. We can't copy employee motivation, we can't copy good relationships between the union and management. That's not something you can copy, and you can't even take a photograph of it."[10] You have to build a great culture for yourself.

GOING FORWARD

Through *Primed to Perform*, you have learned a powerful theory of impact for culture itself.

You've seen that performance is more than meets the eye. To create the highest levels of performance, you must balance two opposing forces—tactical and adaptive performance—in every single person and process.

You've seen how and why total motivation increases adaptive performance. You've also seen how and why reducing total motivation destroys adaptive performance.

Figure 20: The *Primed to Perform* theory of impact revisited.

Total motivation maximizes adaptive performance. ToMo requires your people to feel the direct motives and not the indirect motives.

The highest levels of organizational or team performance require a balance between the opposing forces of tactical and adaptive performance.

Culture is the ecosystem that maximizes adaptive performance through total motivation. The many keys to culture must be used together to unlock performance.

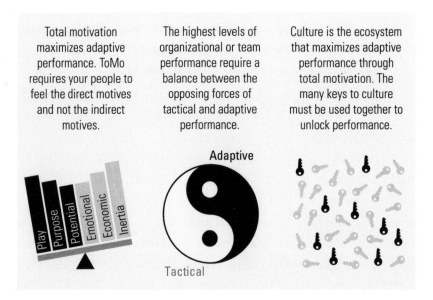

Finally, you've seen how a whole set of keys to culture can maximize total motivation in your organization.

Now it is your turn. If you're still looking for a place to start, here are a few simple ideas:

1. Join the broader community of practitioners at www.primedtoperform.com and follow us on Twitter at @NeelVF or @McGregorLE.
2. Measure your own ToMo, or the ToMo of your team or organization. The survey at www.primedtoperform.com is an easy and free-of-cost starting point. You can use the survey to measure your own or your team's ToMo.
3. Begin teaching all your leaders the concepts in this book, as deeply as you now understand them. You're creating a common language, which will ultimately help to accelerate the process of change.
4. Understand exactly how much you're spending on all the keys to culture today, in time and in money. You'll find that when you look at this investment through the lens of ToMo and adaptive performance, you'll want to repurpose much of it. In many cases, you can launch the process of building a high-ToMo culture without spending any additional money.

Good luck, fire watchers. We are excited to see all the amazing things your cultures will create.

Appendix: The Scientist's Toothbrush

| Primed to Perform *Builds on the Insights, Courage, and Hard Work of Brilliant Thinkers*

Primed to Perform is about engineering the highest-performing cultures. Its premises rest on a science that was pioneered by a hardy band of researchers, many of them mentioned in the pages of this book, who were brilliant and courageous enough to dedicate their careers to the study of something that was far from mainstream thinking.

"A scientist would rather use someone else's toothbrush than another scientist's terminology," writes Murray Gell-Mann, a Nobel laureate physicist and a leader in the field that studies emergence.[1] Ironically, even in that statement, Gell-Mann mentions he's paraphrasing another "distinguished professor." In its presentation of the science of performance, *Primed to Perform* is guilty of the same accusation (without borrowing anyone's toothbrush).

This appendix pays homage and respect to the scientists who came before us. It also explains our rationale for changing the terminology that many of these pioneering researchers used.

SELF-DETERMINATION THEORY
The motive spectrum described in the introduction is a rephrasing of the Self-Determination Continuum,[2] developed by Richard Ryan and Edward Deci while at the University of Rochester.

As we studied the vast body of research on the Self-Determination Continuum, we saw its potential as the root of great cultures and as the basis of the total motivation factor. In our early conversations with business leaders, we attempted to describe the Self-Determination Continuum exactly as Deci and Ryan did:

Motivation was divided into three types—Intrinsic, Extrinsic, and Amotivation. Those types were in turn divided into other "regulatory styles":

- Play was "Intrinsic Motivation—Intrinsic Regulation"
- Purpose was "Extrinsic Motivation—Integrated Regulation"
- Potential was "Extrinsic Motivation—Identified Regulation"
- Emotional pressure was "Extrinsic Motivation—Introjected Regulation"
- Economic pressure was "Extrinsic Motivation—External Regulation"
- Inertia was "Amotivation—Non-regulation"

Executives found the language too complex. We realized we needed to find a simpler way to communicate.

Many business leaders have already been exposed to portions of this theory either through their reading or their studies. However, when asked what they recall, most would say "intrinsic motivation is good and extrinsic motivation is bad." According to the terminology of the theory's developers, however, this extremely widespread belief is not correct. The purpose and potential motives typically increase adaptive performance despite being called "extrinsic motivation."

At first we tried to correct the people we interacted with, but we found that was a losing strategy. Instead, we simply changed the language that was the source of the misunderstanding.

We renamed the six motives using terminology that was easier for the layperson to understand because they already use those words. Hence play, purpose, potential, etc.

We wanted to provide a shorthand way to explain that play, purpose, and potential typically increase adaptive performance while emotional pressure, economic pressure, and inertia typically decrease adaptive performance. Since play, purpose, and potential are still in some way directly connected to the work, we call them the direct motives. The other three similarly became the indirect motives.

If you would like to read more about Self-Determination Theory, there are many resources to check. We are posting articles, links, and new ideas on www.primedtoperform.com. You can find a survey there that you can administer to your teams to understand their motives. If you are really curious, www.selfdeterminationtheory.org is a hub of much of the most serious academic research on the topic.

JOB ENRICHMENT

In the 1970s, two researchers realized that the way most jobs were designed inherently led to poor performance.[3] Richard Hackman and Greg Oldham called their field "job enrichment." The keypuncher experiment that you read about is an example of their groundbreaking insight.

We departed from their terminology for strictly practical reasons.

When we studied their work and their findings, we found that it was very consistent with the predictions of the motive spectrum. For example, Hackman and Oldham speak of the importance of a job's meaningfulness, which they divide into three types:

- Skill variety, which we believe aligns well to the play and potential motives.
- Task identity, or the degree to which a job is responsible for a whole, identifiable piece of work. True task identity requires

a job to be structured in such a way that people feel that they own the right scope of work, that they have the degrees of freedom to allow for adaptability where required, and that the work itself provides feedback on performance. From our own data and analysis, we can clearly see that task identity is a critical driver of play. It increases curiosity to find new ideas, and the ability to fulfill that curiosity.

- Task significance, or the degree to which a job has impact on other people. This is squarely a driver of the purpose motive. True task significance requires people to see for themselves the value that is created for their customer.

Upon review, we found their research to be consistent with the view that cultures drive adaptive performance through total motivation.

At this point, we had a choice. We could introduce Hackman and Oldham's terminology, presenting business leaders with another framework to learn. Alternatively, we could continue to reinforce the common messages of adaptive performance through ToMo. For the sake of simplicity we chose the latter.

TRANSFORMATIONAL LEADERSHIP

The field of transformational leadership began in the 1970s when Pulitzer Prize–winning presidential biographer James MacGregor Burns introduced his theory of leadership. Burns described two types of leaders—transactional and transforming. The transactional leader focuses on an exchange of some kind with his or her followers. The transformational leader, on the other hand, focuses on a common vision.

Bernard Bass, from the State University of New York, advanced Burns's thinking considerably, adding a quantitative and psychological underpinning to his historical analysis.[4]

Bass surveyed thousands of workers to understand common leadership behaviors in their bosses. He was able to group those behaviors into a handful of categories. According to his work, a transformational leader exhibits the following traits:

- *"Charisma: Provides vision and sense of mission, instills pride, gains respect and trust."* These are the characteristics of leaders who create the purpose motive.
- *"Inspiration: Communicates high expectations, uses symbols to focus efforts, expresses important purposes in simple ways."* These too are behaviors of leaders that create the purpose motive.
- *"Intellectual stimulation: Promotes intelligence, rationality, and careful problem solving."* These are some of the aspects of a leader that creates the play motive.
- *"Individualized consideration: Gives personal attention, treats each employee individually, coaches, advises."* These traits are all consistent with creating a sense of play and potential while also reducing emotional pressure.

Meanwhile, Bass goes on to describe the traits of transactional leaders:

- *"Contingent reward: Contracts exchange of rewards for effort, promises rewards for good performance, recognizes accomplishments."* These are leadership traits that lead to economic and emotional pressure.
- *"Management by exception—active: Watches and searches for deviations from rules and standards. Takes corrective action."* These behaviors extinguish play and add to emotional pressure.
- *"Management by exception—passive: Intervenes only if standards are not met."* This is a leader who is neutral, driving

neither direct nor indirect motives. In the worst case, this trait creates a sense of inertia.

- *"Laissez-faire: Abdicates responsibility, and avoids making decisions."* This leader reduces play and increases inertia.

There is much compelling research on Transformational Leadership. Like job enrichment, it too has been linked to better adaptive performance and higher levels of satisfaction. The theory of total motivation predicts this should be the case. If a transformational leader increases the ToMo of his or her followers, we should see an increase in adaptive performance. The research that compares these two disciplines confirms this.[5]

Similar to job enrichment, we found the theory of transformational leadership to be completely consistent with the motive spectrum. Again, we were confronted with the decision to add another new framework, or keep the message simple. Given our goal to help business leaders at every level build high-performing cultures, we opted to keep the message as simple as possible.

FUNDAMENTAL ATTRIBUTION ERROR

The blame bias presented earlier in this book is a renaming of the sociological phenomenon known as the Fundamental Attribution Error. The theory suggests that people have a natural bias to place blame on people for outcomes that may be better explained by the context. The further a person is from the situation, the more likely they are to have this attribution error.

The importance of this theory cannot be emphasized enough. It is at the core of why laypeople are quick to blame factors like race or ethnicity or gender for outcomes when, in fact, the context is actually to blame.

Again, we chose to rename it to make the message simpler and more obvious to a business leader. It is one thing to say to a person,

"Don't commit the fundamental attribution error." We found it easier to say, "Don't blame people for outcomes that are out of their control."

COMPLEX ADAPTIVE SYSTEMS

The core premise of the high-performing culture is that adaptive performance is critical to ongoing success in an environment that is itself highly variable. It is simple Darwinian logic.

However, the other core premise is that when you couple highly adaptive individuals (who play with purpose) with a system that is able to scale their adaptability, you create the highest levels of performance. This premise comes directly from the study of complex adaptive systems.

The fields of chaos and complexity theory study a very curious phenomenon. How can seemingly simple rules result in extremely complex outcomes? For example, how can termites with brains the size of a grain of sand create such complex behaviors as a group? How do individual neurons create something as adaptive and complex as human consciousness when combined?

The field itself is in its relative infancy, but it has already discovered many of the patterns of these "complex adaptive systems."

Again, we were confronted with the decision to introduce a new framework, new vocabulary, and technical terminology or to simplify the message to focus on what is required to engineer great cultures. Again, we opted for the latter, focusing on the distinction between tactical and adaptive performance.

GREAT THANKS

We've drawn on hundreds of great thinkers in writing *Primed to Perform*, and we want to thank them for pioneering the research we draw on. Their creativity, thoughtfulness, and citizenship shine through. We owe them a vast debt of gratitude.

Also, Teresa M. Amabile, Dan Ariely, Bruce J. Avolio, Bernard M. Bass, Marc R. Blais, Céline M. Blanchard, Robert Boyd, James Mac-Gregor Burns, James Connell, W. Edwards Deming, Dov Eden, M.S. Fortier, Marylène Gagné, Murray Gell-Mann, Adam M. Grant, Wendy S. Grolnick, Frederic Guay, J. Richard Hackman, Chip Heath, James Heskett, John Kotter, Chris Lonsdale, Greg Oldham, Luc G. Pelletier, Ronald F. Piccolo, Rémi Radel, Peter J. Richerson, Lee Ross, Rajendra Sisodia, Maxime A. Tremblay, and Robert J. Vallerand. Thank you also to thought leaders John Mackey, Thomas J. Peters, Dan Pink, Simon Sinek, Robert H. Waterman Jr., Ira Glass, Frank Lagfitt, and *This American Life*.

Fourth, the large group of researchers who have contributed to the knowledge. While there are more than we can list, this includes: Sumit Agarwal, Leslie C. Aiello, W. C. Aird, Susan J Ashford, Ann Kristin Aspeli, Anat Bardi, Julian Barling, J. Barling, Kathryn M. Bartol, Roy F Baumeister, Max H. Bazerman, Linda Beckman, Nicola Bellé, Jenny Bellerose, Ethan S. Bernstein, James W. Berry, Robert L. Bettinger, Colette Boucher, Robert D. Bretz, James H. Bryan, Joseph Bulbulia, Rohan Callander, Priyanka B. Carr, D. Charbonneau, Todd H. Chiles, Thomas Y. Choi, Jason A. Colquitt, Laurence Crevier-Braud, Kathryn Dekas, Ülkü D. Demirdögˇen, David DeSteno, Tom DiDonato, Stéphane G. Dion, Kevin J. Dooley, Robin Dunbar, Taly Dvir, Florian Ederer, Elizabeth Haas Edersheim, A. J. Elliot, Lisa Endlich, Glenda Holladay Eoyang, Claude Fernet, Ronald Fischer, Richard Flaste, Jacques Forest, Roland G. Fryer, Kentaro Fujita, Bennett G. Galef, Adam D. Galinsky, David A. Garvin, Francesco Ginio, Uri Gneezy, Jeffrey Goldstein, John R. Graham, Frédéric Guay, Lale Gumusluoglu, Seth Ayim Gyekye, Mason Haire, Bronwyn H. Hall, Joseph Harder, Campbell R. Harvey, Donald Hedeker, Thomas J. Hench, Guido Hertel, Ken Hodge, John H. Holland, Arzu Ilsev, Alice M. Isen, Robert Janson, Marie Jehu, Timothy A. Judge, Laura S. Kalb, Robert

Kanigel, Steven Karau, Scott Keller, E. Kevin Kelloway, Kyung Hee Kim, R. Koestner, David A. Kravitz, J. S. Lansing, Simon Larose, Gary P. Latham, Brandon W. Latham, Edward P. Lazear, Paula F. Levin, Ning Li, Benyamin B. Lichtenstein, Jeffrey Liker, Daniel Y. Lin, Lorraine E. Lisiecki, George Loewenstein, P. D. Magnus, Gustavo Manso, Max Marmer, Barbara Martin, Nina Mazar, H. Gene McFadden, Leon C. Megginson, David Meier, Alan D. Meyer, Terence R. Mitchell, Arlen C. Moller, Don A. Moore, Mark Muraven, Kou Murayama, William H. Murphy, Nikos Ntoumanis, Samir Nurmohamed, Lisa D. Ordóñez, Jennifer Ouyang, S. J. Peterson, Jeffrey Pfeffer, Paul Piff, Donde Ashmos Plowman, Colin Price, Emily Pronin, Kenneth Purdy, Shiva Rajgopal, Jay Rao, Catherine F. Ratelle, L. J. Rawthorne, Maureen E. Raymo, Paul Reddish, Robert Reid, Max Ringelmann, Elaine Rose, Sherwin Rosen, Manus Rungtusanathan, Stéphane Sabourin, Simo Salminen, Philippe Sarrazin, Joachim Schroer, Shalom H. Schwartz, Maurice E. Schweitzer, Gerard H. Seijts, Caroline Senécal, Boas Shamir, Abraham B. Shani, Monika Slovinec-D'Angelo, Bonnie Spring, Susan E. Squires, Nancy Staudenmayer, Jim Storr, Hikaru Takeuchi, Kevin Tasa, Sara Taylor, Cecilie Thøgersen-Ntoumani, Dianne M. Tice, Michael Tomasello, D. Reid Townsend, Scott J. Turner, Piercarlo Valdesolo, Anja Van Den Broeck, Maarten Vansteenkiste, Martin Villeneuve, Nancy Hodges Walbek, Gregory M. Walton, Faye H. Wang, Felix Warneken, Tom Weber, Peter Wheeler, Kipling D. Williams, Philip M. Wilson, Xiaomeng Zhang, and P. R. Zimmerman. Thank you also to Kurt Eichenwald, Kevin Freiberg, Jackie Freiberg, Ben Horowitz, Bruce Temkin, and the creators of the Agile Manifesto.

Fifth, the supporters who have helped us bring the book to you, including Shawn Achor, Sumit Agarwal, Joanna Barsh, Alexandra Cavoulacos, Jeff DeGraff, Tom Doctoroff, Jeremy Eden, Adam M. Grant, Brian Halloran, Fred Kiel, Joel Klein, Patrick Lencioni, Terri Long, Kathryn Minshew, Max Neukirchen, Jen Porter, John Reed,

Shruti Sehra, Barry Sternlicht, Angela Sun, Jamie Warder, and Liz Wiseman. Thank you also to the authors who gave us invaluable advice, including Nicole Avena, Lindsey Pollak, Ken Roman, Rachel Romano, Geoff Smart, and Shane Snow.

Sixth, thank you to the thousands of people who have taken our total motivation survey and shared their thoughts on their workplace cultures, as well as the people who've taken time to share their stories and experiences, including: Andreea Akerele; Alex Anton; Nadav Benbarak; Jordan Bird; E. Kyle Bisutti; David Bolotsky and Melissa Bishop at Uncommon Goods; Anat Bracha and the Federal Reserve Bank of Boston; Donna Carrea; Steve Cohen and the team at Point72; James Coker; Curt Daniels; Amy Diaz; Sarah Ekeberg, Fabrice Enderlin and UCB; Doug Fearing; Daniel Thabo Fisher; Steve Ford; Sam Franklin; Steve Greene; Mark Haggarty; Jennifer Hines and the team at YES Prep Public Schools; Rotem Iram; Angela Jillson; Leslie Bernard Joseph; Aaron Kletzing; Tricia Lee; Christine Loggins, Michael McGurk; Dave Meller and Belron; Martín Migoya; Guibert Englebienne and the team at Globant; Catherine Newcombe; Marni Pastor; Amy Pressman, Borge Hald, David Reese, Josh Budway and the team at Medallia; Tim Prugar; Vidal Sadaka; David Saltzman, Michael M. Weinstein, Eric Weingartner, Emary Aronson, Steven Lee, Jamie Elfenbein, and Veyom Bahl at the Robin Hood Foundation; the team at Shape Security; Jenny So; Jon Stein, Dustin Lucien, Lucy Babbage, Joe Ziemer and the team at Betterment; and Nitin Walia.

Seventh, the mentors and teammates who have given us much guidance and inspiration over the past twenty years: Doug Haynes and Ramesh Srinivasan, for supporting the early versions of this work, as well as Dana Ashfield, Mogolodi Bond, Josh Budway, Michael Buman, Michael Butler, Frank V. Cespedes, Clay Christensen, Ron Daniel, Ajay Gupta, Rebecca M. Henderson, Somesh Khanna, Rik Kirkland, Janet Kraus, Ida Kristensen, Nick Malik,

Asheet Mehta, Felicia Mitchell, Fritz Nauck, Amit Paley, Michael Rennie, Liz Hilton Segel, Chris Sergeant, Dan Singer, Dan Stevens, Kurt Strovink, Zubin Taraporevala, Vivek Wadhwa, Allen Webb, and Joy Zaben. Thank you to the readers who advised us on our earliest drafts, Melisa Gao, and Jake Loggins. Thank you to our summer fellows, Zara Malik, Jenner Deal, Mina Asayesh-Brown, and Charlotte Lepic.

Second to last, but certainly not least, thank you to our core team at Vega Factor for pushing forward the thinking each and every day: Mary Winn Miller, Ekene Agu, Erin Wayne, Courtney Kaplan, Deborah Moe, and Anneli Tostar.

And finally, to our friends and family members, who have supported us through this journey and encouraged us to spread the word.

Notes

INTRODUCTION: PRIMED TO PERFORM

1. Deloitte, "Core Beliefs and Culture. Chairman's Survey Findings," 2012, http://ow.ly/Gf8rQ.
2. H. L. Roediger, M. S. Weldon, M. L. Stadler, and G. L. Riegler, "Direct Comparison of Two Implicit Memory Tests: Word Fragment and Word Stem Completion." *Journal of Experimental Psychology. Learning, Memory, and Cognition* 18 (1992): 1251–69.
3. Rémi Radel, Philippe Sarrazin, Marie Jehu, and Luc Pelletier, "Priming Motivation Through Unattended Speech." *British Journal of Social Psychology* 52 (2013): 763–72, http://ow.ly/L5Nap.
4. For those of you who have studied the science already, you'll notice that in many cases we have opted to use less technical nomenclature. Please feel free to read through the Appendix for a decoder key to the nomenclature, and our rationale for changing it.
5. Thomas J. Peters and Robert H. Waterman Jr., *In Search of Excellence: Lessons from America's Best-Run Companies* (New York: HarperCollins, 1982), http://ow.ly/Gg54N.
6. John P. Kotter and James L. Heskett, *Corporate Culture and Performance* (New York: Free Press, 1992), http://ow.ly/Gg4l0.
7. "Whole Foods Fast Facts." Whole Foods Market, March 14, 2015, http://ow.ly/KkMej.
8. "Whole Foods Market History." Whole Foods Market, March 14, 2015, http://ow.ly/KkMvc.
9. John Mackey and Rajendra Sisodia, *Conscious Capitalism: Liberating the Heroic Spirit of Business* (Cambridge: Harvard Business Review Press, 2014), http://ow.ly/Gg4Eq.
10. "Most Admired Companies 2015." *Fortune*, 2015. http://ow.ly/L9gUQ; "John Mackey: Co-Chief Executive Officer and Co-Founder." *Whole Foods Market*, March 14, 2015, http://ow.ly/KkN7A.

11. John Mackey, "'I No Longer Want to Work for Money.'" *Fast Company*, 2007, http://ow.ly/KkO8C.

12. The ToMo research into Whole Foods and other named companies comes from our 2015 database. Unless otherwise stated, it was conducted "outside in." A professional market research firm sought out employees of these firms and gathered their responses to the total motivation questions.

13. Charles Fishman, "Whole Foods Is All Teams," *Fast Company*, April 30, 1996, http://ow.ly/Gg44D.

14. Ibid.

15. Mackey and Sisodia, *Conscious Capitalism*.

16. "The American Customer Satisfaction Index," accessed February 4, 2015, http://ow.ly/L9ahN.

17. "Dewey Ballantine and LeBoeuf, Lamb, Greene & MacRae Announce Completion of Merger." *PR Newswire*, September 26, 2007, http://ow.ly/KkOvz.

18. Jennifer Peltz, (Associated Press), "Dewey & LeBoeuf Executives Lied as Their Law Firm Failed, Say Prosecutors." *The Christian Science Monitor*, March 6, 2014, http://ow.ly/KkOKU.

19. "Dewey Defeats Truman: The World's Most Famous Newspaper Error," n.d. http://ow.ly/KkOXb.

20. Peter Lattman, "Dewey & LeBoeuf Files for Bankruptcy." *New York Times*, May 28, 2012, http://ow.ly/Gg4nQ.

21. Ibid.

22. Marc R. Blais, Stéphane Sabourin, Colette Boucher, and Robert J. Vallerand, "Toward a Motivational Model of Couple Happiness." *Journal of Personality and Social Psychology* 59 (1990): 1021–31, http://ow.ly/KkPpW.

23. Luc G. Pelletier, Stéphanie C. Dion, Monika Slovinec-D'Angelo, and Robert Reid, "Why Do You Regulate What You Eat? Relationships Between Forms of Regulation, Eating Behaviors, Sustained Dietary Behavior Change, and Psychological Adjustment." *Motivation and Emotion* 28 (2004): 245–77, http://ow.ly/Gjrkw.

24. Chris Lonsdale, Ken Hodge, and Elaine Rose, "Athlete Burnout in Elite Sport: A Self-Determination Perspective." *Journal of Sports Sciences* 27 (2009): 785–95, http://ow.ly/GjBjC.

25. R. J. Vallerand, M. S. Fortier, and F. Guay, "Self-Determination and Persistence in a Real-Life Setting: Toward a Motivational Model of High School Dropout." *Journal of Personality and Social Psychology* 72 (1997): 1161–76, http://ow.ly/KkPG9.

CHAPTER 1: THE MOTIVE SPECTRUM

1. Marie Ng et al., "Global, Regional, and National Prevalence of Overweight and Obesity in Children and Adults During 1980–2013: A Systematic Analysis for the Global Burden of Disease Study 2013," *Lancet* 6736 (2014): 1–16, http://ow.ly/GFMaz.

2. Praveen Menon, Belinda Goldsmith, and Tom Pfeiffer, "Dubai Offers Gold to Fight Obesity Epidemic," Reuters, July 19, 2013, http://ow.ly/Gj1Rm.

3. Asa Fitch, "Lose Weight, Get Gold in Dubai," *Wall Street Journal*, November 17, 2013, http://ow.ly/Gj20v.

4. Agence France-Presse, "Dubai's 'Your Weight in Gold' Campaign Rewards Weight Losers with Gold," News.com.au, November 8, 2013, http://ow.ly/Gj2ke.

5. Arlen C. Moller, H. Gene McFadden, Donald Hedeker, and Bonnie Spring. "Financial Motivation Undermines Maintenance in an Intensive Diet and Activity Intervention." *Journal of Obesity* 2012 (2012), http://ow.ly/KkTc7.

6. Approximate value of a gram of gold during the time period of the Dubai weight-loss program.

7. B. M. Kedrov, "On the Question of the Psychology of Scientific Creativity (On the Occasion of the Discovery by D. I. Mendeleev of the Periodic Law)," *The Soviet Review: A Journal of Translations* 8, no. 2 (1967): 91–113, http://ow.ly/GFN70.

8. Bernadette Bensaude-Vincent, "Dmitry Ivanovich Mendeleyev." *Encyclopædia Britannica*, 2014. http://ow.ly/KkUnr.

9. Note, this book substitutes some of Deci and Ryan's technical terms with more common phrases, with the hopes of making the knowledge more intuitive for business leaders. Please see the appendix for further explanation.

10. "Citation Averages, 2000–2010, by Fields and Years | General | Times Higher Education," *Times Higher Education*, March 31, 2011, http://ow.ly/Gj3YR.

11. Dan Pink in his inspirational book, *Drive*, introduces us to the "the Purpose Motive." It is worth noting that our definitions differ slightly. The *Primed to Perform* definition of "purpose" is when the outcome of the work aligns with the person's identity. Daniel H. Pink, *Drive: The Surprising Truth About What Motivates Us*. (New York: Penguin, 2011).

12. Adam M Grant, "How Customers Can Rally Your Troops: End Users Can Energize Your Workforce Far Better Than Your Managers Can," *Harvard Business Review* 89, no. 6 (2011): 97–103, http://ow.ly/Gj4EL.

13. Interview with former Walmart executive, 2014.

14. Steve Arneson, "The Top Leadership Factories," *Examiner*, February 1, 2011, http://ow.ly/Gj9gW; Del Jones, "Some Firms' Fertile Soil Grows Crop of Future CEOs," *USA Today*, January 9, 2008, http://ow.ly/Gj8G4.

15. Keith McFarland, "Why Zappos Offers New Hires $2,000 to Quit," *Businessweek*, September 16, 2008, http://ow.ly/Gjby8; Fact confirmed and updated through interviews with Zappos personnel.

16. Luc G. Pelletier et al., "Why Do You Regulate What You Eat? Relationships Between Forms of Regulation, Eating Behaviors, Sustained Dietary Behavior Change, and Psychological Adjustment," *Motivation and Emotion* 28 (2004): 245–77, http://ow.ly/Gjrkw.

17. Correlations between play, purpose, and potential to healthy eating behaviors were 0.4, 0.6, and 0.3, respectively. Correlations between emotional pressure, economic pressure, and inertia to unhealthy eating behaviors were 0.7, 0.4, and 0.3, respectively. Each correlation had a 95 percent confidence level. To give you an intuitive sense of how to read the correlations, consider a statement from happiness author

and researcher Shawn Achor. He has pointed out that the correlation between smoking and cancer is 0.3, suggesting that a correlation of 0.3 is important enough to change behavior and act on the research.

18. Daniel H. Pink, *Drive: The Surprising Truth About What Motivates Us.* (New York: Penguin, 2011).

19. Some details have been disguised to protect the confidentiality of the client.

20. Adam M. Grant et al., "The Performance Implications of Ambivalent Initiative: The Interplay of Autonomous and Controlled Motivations," *Organizational Behavior and Human Decision Processes* 116 (2011): 241–51, http://ow.ly/Gjs3p.

CHAPTER 2: THE TOTAL MOTIVATION FACTOR

1. David Lindley, *Where Does the Weirdness Go? Why Quantum Mechanics Is Strange, but Not as Strange as You Think* (New York: Basic Books, 1996), http://ow.ly/GjB6V.

2. Marylène Gagné, Jacques Forest, Maarten Vansteenkiste, Laurence Crevier-Braud, Anja Van Den Broeck, Ann Kristin Aspeli, Jenny Bellerose, et al, "The Multidimensional Work Motivation Scale: Validation Evidence in Seven Languages and Nine Countries." *European Journal of Work and Organizational Psychology* 24, no. 2 (2015): 178–96, http://ow.ly/HhaTQ.

3. Marc R. Blais et al., "Toward a Motivational Model of Couple Happiness," *Journal of Personality and Social Psychology* 59 (1990): 1021–31, http://ow.ly/GjtFh.

4. Sixty-three couples. Correlations: play (0.4), purpose (0.18), potential (0.17), emotional (-0.25), economic (-0.25), inertia (-0.49).

5. Catherine F. Ratelle, Frédéric Guay, Robert J. Vallerand, Simon Larose, and Caroline Senécal, "Autonomous, Controlled, and Amotivated Types of Academic Motivation: A Person-Oriented Analysis." *Journal of Educational Psychology*, 2007, http://ow.ly/L65Oh.

6. Correlation to academic achievement: play (0.17), purpose/potential (0.15), emotional (-0.2), economic (-0.19), inertia (-0.36). Correlation to classroom distraction: play (-0.49), purpose/potential (-0.26), emotional (-0.35), economic (0), inertia (0.39).

7. Chris Lonsdale, Ken Hodge, and Elaine Rose, "Athlete Burnout in Elite Sport: A Self-Determination Perspective," *Journal of Sports Sciences* 27 (2009): 785–95, http://ow.ly/GjBjC.

8. Two hundred one athletes in the sample. Correlations to athlete burnout: play (-0.59), purpose (-0.3), potential (-0.43), emotional (0.51), economic (0.47), inertia (0.72).

9. Philip M. Wilson et al., " 'It's Who I Am . . . Really!' The Importance of Integrated Regulation in Exercise Contexts," *Journal of Applied Biobehavioral Research* 11 (2006): 79–104, http://ow.ly/GjCdp; Cecilie Thøgersen-Ntoumani and Nikos Ntoumanis, "The Role of Self-Determined Motivation in the Understanding of Exercise-Related Behaviours, Cognitions and Physical Self-Evaluations," *Journal of Sports Sciences* 24 (2006): 393–404, http://ow.ly/GjBQJ.

10. Susan Burkhauser, Susan M. Gates, Laura S. Hamilton, and Gina Schuyler Ikemoto, "First-Year Principals in Urban School Districts." Santa Monica: RAND Corporation, 2012, http://ow.ly/GjAHv.

11. C. Fernet, "Development and Validation of the Work Role Motivation Scale for School Principals (WRMS-SP)," *Educational Administration Quarterly* 47 (2011): 307–31, http://ow.ly/GjAXF.

12. R. J. Vallerand, M. S. Fortier, and F. Guay, "Self-Determination and Persistence in a Real-Life Setting: Toward a Motivational Model of High School Dropout," *Journal of Personality and Social Psychology* 72 (1997): 1161–76, http://ow.ly/Gg5P1.

13. Note: Early research in the field combined the purpose and potential motives with the belief that for children, it would be too difficult to separate the two in a survey. For the sake of our calculation, we treated the researchers' score for potential to be the same score for purpose.

    We recalculated the total motivation factor from the study using the coefficients from later in the chapter to avoid confusion. The original paper includes the original calculations.

14. Luc G. Pelletier et al., "Associations Among Perceived Autonomy Support, Forms of Self-Regulation, and Persistence: A Prospective Study," *Motivation and Emotion* 25 (2001): 279–306, http://ow.ly/GjBuy.

15. Southwest Airlines Communications Department interview, April 2015.

16. Jody Hoffer Gittell, *The Southwest Airlines Way: Using the Power of Relationships to Achieve High Performance* (New York: McGraw-Hill, 2003), http://ow.ly/GjzJ8.

17. Julie Weber, "A Career with a Cause!," *Nuts About Southwest*, May 22, 2014, http://ow.ly/Gjw3o.

18. Marty Cobb, "Hilarious SWA Flight Attendant," *YouTube*, April 12, 2014, http://ow.ly/Gjwl0.

19. Kevin Freiberg and Jackie Freiberg. *Nuts!: Southwest Airlines' Crazy Recipe for Business and Personal Success.* New York: Broadway Books, 1996, http://ow.ly/GjAaF.

20. Ibid.

21. Ibid.

22. "About Southwest." *Southwest.com*, March 14, 2015, http://ow.ly/Gjxiv.

23. Carmine Gallo, "Southwest Airlines Motivates Its Employees with a Purpose Bigger Than a Paycheck," *Forbes*, January 21, 2014, http://ow.ly/Gjy7Z.

24. "'Off the Clock' Service," *Nuts About Southwest,* March 13, 2014, http://ow.ly/GjxsS.

25. Temkin Group, *Temkin Experience Ratings 2015*, http://ow.ly/L66xi.

26. "Most Admired Companies 2015." *Fortune*, 2015, http://ow.ly/L9gUQ.

CHAPTER 3: RETHINKING PERFORMANCE

1. Kyung Hee Kim, "Can We Trust Creativity Tests? A Review of the Torrance Tests of Creative Thinking (TTCT)," *Creativity Research Journal* 18 (2006): 3–14, http://ow.ly/GjIks.

2. Ashley Merryman and Po Bronson, "The Creativity Crisis." *Newsweek*, July 10, 2010, http://ow.ly/GjISH.

3. Kyung Hee Kim, "Can Only Intelligent People Be Creative?," *Journal of Secondary Gifted Education* 16 (2005): 57–66, http://ow.ly/GjIAl; Kyung Hee Kim,

"Meta-Analyses of the Relationship of Creative Achievement to Both IQ and Divergent Thinking Test Scores," *Journal of Creative Behavior* 42 (2008): 106–30, http://ow.ly/GjIqj.

4. Kyung Hee Kim, "The Creativity Crisis: The Decrease in Creative Thinking Scores on the Torrance Tests of Creative Thinking," *Creativity Research Journal* 23 (2011): 285–95, http://ow.ly/GjIui.

5. Teresa M. Amabile, "Motivation and Creativity: Effects of Motivational Orientation on Creative Writers." *Journal of Personality and Social Psychology*, 1985, http://ow.ly/L68vS.

6. Teresa M. Amabile, "Motivation and Creativity: Effects of Motivational Orientation on Creative Writers." *Journal of Personality and Social Psychology*, 1985. http://ow.ly/L68vS; Teresa M. Amabile, B. A. Hennessey, and B. S. Grossman, "Social Influences on Creativity: The Effects of Contracted—for Reward." *Journal of Personality and Social Psychology* 50 (1986): 14–23, http://ow.ly/L68Up.

7. Teresa M. Amabile, "How to Kill Creativity." *Harvard Business Review.* Cambridge: Harvard Business School Publishing, 1998, http://ow.ly/GjHCl.

8. Dan Ariely, Uri Gneezy, George Loewenstein, and Nina Mazar, "Large Stakes and Big Mistakes." *Review of Economic Studies* 76 (2009): 451–69, http://ow.ly/L69tC.

9. Students with the lower incentive on average earned only 40 percent of the maximum payout possible. Students with the higher incentive on average earned 78 percent of the maximum possible payout.

10. "Common Data Set 2013–2014," *MIT Institutional Research*, 2014, http://ow.ly/GjJa8.

11. Ariely et al., "Large Stakes and Big Mistakes." The answer is 3.58 and 6.42.

12. Students with the lower incentive on average earned 63 percent of the maximum payout possible. Students with the higher incentive on average earned only 43 percent of the maximum possible payout.

13. Interestingly, Ariely also found that the students who improved the most with high incentives in the key press experiment also struggled the most with high incentives during the math experiment. In effect, they were most sensitive to the benefits and the harms of indirect motives.

14. Ibid. When solving anagrams publically, students solved 22.2 percent of their total. When solving anagrams privately, students solved 38.5 percent of their total.

15. Ibid.

16. Felix Warneken and Michael Tomasello, "Extrinsic Rewards Undermine Altruistic Tendencies in 20-Month-Olds." *Developmental Psychology* 44 (2008): 1785–88, doi:10.1037/a0013860.

17. Kou Murayama et al., "Neural Basis of the Undermining Effect of Monetary Reward on Intrinsic Motivation," *Proceedings of the National Academy of Sciences of the United States of America* 107 (2010): 20911–16, http://ow.ly/GjJ0O.

18. E. L. Deci, R. Koestner, and R. M. Ryan, "A Meta-Analytic Review of Experiments Examining the Effects of Extrinsic Rewards on Intrinsic Motivation." *Psychological Bulletin* 125 (1999): 627–68; discussion 692–700, http://ow.ly/L6aiQ.

19. Their meta-analysis shows a -0.28 correlation to free-choice behavior, or the amount subjects practiced or continued working when they didn't know they were being watched. We believe free-choice behavior is a nice laboratory analog to "grit" since it measures persistence in an activity. The 95 percent confidence interval for this correlation is -0.38 to -0.18.

20. Their meta-analysis shows a -0.01 correlation to self-reported interest. The 95 percent confidence interval for this correlation is -0.1 to 0.08, suggesting no correlation.

21. Tim Hodges, "Chandrapur: Leopard on the Loose Leaps Through Roof," BBC, April 22, 2014, http://ow.ly/GjI6Z.

22. Stephen J. Dubner, "The Cobra Effect: A New Freakonomics Radio Podcast," *Freakonomics.com*, October 11, 2012, http://ow.ly/GjLIy.

23. Ning Li and William H. Murphy, "A Three-Country Study of Unethical Sales Behaviors," *Journal of Business Ethics* 111 (2012): 219–35, http://ow.ly/L6aEY.

24. Whack-a-mole is a carnival game where mechanical moles randomly pop out of holes in a board. The object of the game is to whack as many moles as possible with a mallet. The more moles you successfully whack, the higher your score.

CHAPTER 4: THE YIN AND YANG OF PERFORMANCE

1. There are many ways things can be defined. You can define a car by what it comprises—like wheels, an engine, seats, and a steering wheel. You can define a car by how it works. "A horseless carriage," for example, adds to the definition a constraint on how the car is meant to operate. Alternatively, you can define a car by its purpose—"a machine to transport an astronaut from the landing vehicle to the crater." Our philosopher friends call this type of definition a "teleological" definition. We believe that to help organizations create the highest performing cultures, we must define "culture" teleologically—that is, by its purpose. Only then does the whole solution space reveal itself to us, while the red herrings can be thrown back into the sea.

2. Mike Berardino, "Mike Tyson Explains One of His Most Famous Quotes," *Sun Sentinel*, November 9, 2012, http://ow.ly/GoXMf.

3. Jason Amareld, "Boxing: The 10 Greatest Heavyweights of All Time," *Bleacher Report*, 2011, http://ow.ly/GoXCt; "Mike Tyson," *Wikipedia*, n.d., http://en.wikipedia.org/wiki/Mike_Tyson.

4. "Strategy: Oxford Dictionaries," accessed January 4, 2015, http://ow.ly/L6Qpw.

5. Craig Johnstone, Garry Pairaudeau, and Jonas A. Pettersson, "Creativity, Innovation and Lean Sigma: A Controversial Combination?" *Drug Discovery Today* 16 (2011): 50–57, http://ow.ly/L6bY4.

6. Adam M. Grant and James W. Berry. "The Necessity of Others Is the Mother of Invention: Intrinsic and Prosocial Motivations, Perspective Taking, and Creativity," *Academy of Management Journal* 54, no. 1 (2011): 73–96, http://ow.ly/GfQ8a.

7. "1993 Milwaukee Cryptosporidiosis Outbreak," *Wikipedia*, January 1, 2015.

8. Grant's research focuses on pro-social purpose. While there are other forms of the "purpose motive," we feel comfortable treating this synonymously. In general, we

have found that pro-social benefit is the most consistent way to build the purpose motive. In this experiment, Grant did not examine inertia.

9. In these experiments, Grant frames "adaptability" as "creativity." However, examination of the questions that were used in his surveys led us to be comfortable with the change in wording.

10. Grant and Berry, "The Necessity of Others Is the Mother of Invention: Intrinsic and Prosocial Motivations, Perspective Taking, and Creativity."

11. Correlations to adaptability (or creativity as Grant calls it): play (.21), purpose (.1), potential (.13), emotional (-0.04), economic (-0.06). Play was the only statistically significant correlation.

12. Note, we excluded cattle as a contender for the biomass throne for this discussion as cattle population is a result of human culture, not cattle culture.

13. "Biomass (ecology)," *Wikipedia*, n.d., http://ow.ly/Gp0bF.

14. For the taxonomists out there, we realize we have committed the cardinal sin of taxonomy by comparing a species to a family to an order. While not apples-to-apples, if we brought humans, ants, and termites to the lowest common denominator of analysis (the order), we suspect the results would largely stay the same. Doing so would create confusion for the reader without much benefit.

15. This study suggests that for every ant, there are almost thirty termites. Assuming that a termite is roughly one-tenth the mass of an ant, we land on a biomass estimate three times larger. P. R. Zimmerman et al., "Termites: A Potentially Large Source of Atmospheric Methane, Carbon Dioxide, and Molecular Hydrogen," *Science* 218 (1982): 563–65, http://ow.ly/GjLAA.

16. Surprisingly, termites are not closely related to ants (or humans for that matter) despite their behavioral similarities.

17. J. Scott Turner, "Ventilation and Thermal Constancy of a Colony of a Southern African Termite (Odontotermes Transvaalensis: Macrotermitinae)," *Journal of Arid Environments* 28, no. 3 (1994): 231–48, http://ow.ly/L6csJ.

18. Termite mounds can be up to 10,000 times a termite's height. If humans built structures 10,000 times our height, they'd be twice the height of Mount Everest.

19. John H. Holland, *Hidden Order: How Adaptation Builds Complexity* (New York: Basic Books, 1995), http://ow.ly/GjLnm.

20. Thomas Y. Choi, Kevin J. Dooley, and Manus Rungtusanatham, "Supply Networks and Complex Adaptive Systems: Control Versus Emergence," *Journal of Operations Management* 19 (2001): 351–66, http://ow.ly/L6cM1.

21. Holland, *Hidden Order: How Adaptation Builds Complexity.*

22. Jeffrey Goldstein, *The Unshackled Organization: Facing the Challenge of Unpredictability Through Spontaneous Reorganization* (Portland: Productivity Press, 1994), http://ow.ly/GjL6k; Todd H. Chiles, Alan D. Meyer, and Thomas J. Hench, "Organizational Emergence: The Origin and Transformation of Branson, Missouri's Musical Theaters," *Organization Science* 15, no. 5 (2004): 499–519, http://ow.ly/L6d7i; J. S. Lansing, "Complex Adaptive Systems," *Annual Review of Anthropology* 32 (2003): 183–204.

23. Benyamin B. Lichtenstein et al., "Complexity Leadership Theory: An Interactive Perspective on Leading in Complex Adaptive Systems," *Emergence: Complexity and Organization* 8, no. 4 (2006): 2–12, http://ow.ly/GoZkG.

24. Benyamin B. Lichtenstein and Donde Ashmos Plowman, "The Leadership of Emergence: A Complex Systems Leadership Theory of Emergence at Successive Organizational Levels," *Leadership Quarterly* 20, no. 4 (2009): 617–30, http://ow.ly/GoYSG.

25. Ibid.

26. Glenda Holladay Eoyang, *Conditions for Self-Organizing in Human Systems* (The Union Institute and University, 2001), http://ow.ly/GoYdC.

27. Murray Gell-Mann, *The Quark and the Jaguar: Adventures in the Simple and the Complex.* (New York: Macmillan, 1995).

28. Leslie C. Aiello and Peter Wheeler, "The Expensive-Tissue Hypothesis: The Brain and the Digestive System in Human and Primate Evolution," *Current Anthropology* 36, no. 2 (1995): 199–221, http://ow.ly/L6dyC.

29. W. C. Aird, "Spatial and Temporal Dynamics of the Endothelium," *Journal of Thrombosis and Haemostasis* 3, no. 7 (2005): 1392–1406, http://ow.ly/GoXus.

30. Aiello and Wheeler, "The Expensive-Tissue Hypothesis: The Brain and the Digestive System in Human and Primate Evolution."

31. Lorraine E. Lisiecki and Maureen E. Raymo, "A Pliocene-Pleistocene Stack of 57 Globally Distributed Benthic $\delta^{18}O$ Records," *Paleoceanography* 20, no. 1 (2005): PA1003, http://ow.ly/L6e3d.

32. Peter J. Richerson and Robert Boyd, "The Pleistocene and the Origins of Human Culture: Built for Speed," *Perspectives in Ethology* 13 (1998): 1–45. http://ow.ly/L6eSZ; Peter J. Richerson, Robert L. Bettinger, and Robert Boyd, "Evolution on a Restless Planet: Were Environmental Variability and Environmental Change Major Drivers of Human Evolution," *Handbook of Evolution* 2 (2005): 223–42, http://ow.ly/L6f8i.

33. Richerson and Boyd, "The Pleistocene and the Origins of Human Culture: Built for Speed."

34. Richerson, Bettinger, and Boyd, "Evolution on a Restless Planet: Were Environmental Variability and Environmental Change Major Drivers of Human Evolution?"

35. Richerson and Boyd, "The Pleistocene and the Origins of Human Culture: Built for Speed."

36. "List of Most Popular Websites," *Wikipedia*, 2014, http://ow.ly/Gp7nC.

37. "New York Times Article Archive," *New York Times*, 2014, http://ow.ly/Gp76r; "Wikipedia:About," *Wikipedia*, accessed January 9, 2014, http://ow.ly/Gp7iS.

38. Ibid.

39. "2013 World Series," *Wikipedia*, n.d., http://ow.ly/Gp71b.

40. P. D. Magnus, "Early Response to False Claims in Wikipedia." *First Monday* 13 (2008): 1–4.

41. "Stigmergy," *Wikipedia*, 2014, http://ow.ly/Gp7b2.

42. "Wikipedia: Getting to Philosophy," *Wikipedia*, 2014, http://ow.ly/Gp7eA.

43. Joachim Schroer and Guido Hertel, "Voluntary Engagement in an Open Web-Based Encyclopedia: Wikipedians and Why They Do It," *Media Psychology* 12, no. 1 (2009): 96–120, http://ow.ly/L6iiK.

44. Leon C. Megginson, "Lessons from Europe for American Business," *Southwestern Social Science Quarterly* 44, no. 1 (1963): 3–13, http://ow.ly/GoZGi.

CHAPTER 5: THE BLAME BIAS

1. Compare that to the 78 percent of toddlers who helped the clumsy researcher from Chapter 3. Is this the cost of adults moving too fast and paying less heed and attention to the world around them?

2. Paula F. Levin and Alice M. Isen, "Effect of Feeling Good on Helping: Cookies and Kindness," *Journal of Personality and Social Psychology* 21 (1972): 384–88, doi:10.1037/h0032317.

3. Paula F. Levin and Alice M. Isen, "Further Studies on the Effect of Feeling Good on Helping," *Sociometry* 38 (1975): 141–47, http://ow.ly/L6iLG.

4. Paul Piff, "Does Money Make You Mean?" *TED*, October 2013, http://ow.ly/L6iQj.

5. Seth Ayim Gyekye and Simo Salminen, "The Self-Defensive Attribution Hypothesis in the Work Environment: Co-Workers' Perspectives," *Safety Science* 44 (2006): 157–68, http://ow.ly/L6jgJ.

6. Lee Ross, "The Intuitive Psychologist and His Shortcomings: Distortions in the Attribution Process," *Advances in Experimental Social Psychology* 10 (1977): 173–220, doi:10.1016/S0065-2601(08)60357-3.

7. Linda Beckman, "Effects of Students' Performance on Teachers' and Observers' Attributions of Causality," *Journal of Educational Psychology* 61 (1970): 76–82, http://ow.ly/L6jtx.

8. We realize there are rare situations where a person is to blame truly because of his intrinsic values and beliefs rather than the context itself. The goal of a high-ToMo recruiting process is to focus on getting this filter exactly right even if it slows down the process or costs more. Thereafter, the purpose of culture should not be to filter, but to increase total motivation.

9. Information sourced from, and Figure 12 re-created from, *Organizational Behavior and Human Decision Processes*, 78, Chip Heath, "On the Social Psychology of Agency Relationships: Lay Theories of Motivation Overemphasize Extrinsic Incentives," 25–62, 1999, with permission from Elsevier.

10. Dov Eden, "Leadership and Expectations: Pygmalion Effects and Other Self-Fulfilling Prophecies in Organizations," *The Leadership Quarterly* 3, no. 4 (1992): 271–305, http://ow.ly/L6jGY; Dov Eden and Abraham B. Shani. "Pygmalion Goes to Boot Camp: Expectancy, Leadership, and Trainee Performance," *Journal of Applied Psychology* 67, no. 2 (1982): 194–99, http://ow.ly/L6jSj.

11. Ibid.

12. George Bernard Shaw, *Pygmalion: A Romance in Five Acts* (London: Penguin Group, 1912).

13. Dov Eden, "Pygmalion Without Interpersonal Contrast Effects: Whole Groups

Gain from Raising Manager Expectations," *Journal of Applied Psychology* 75, no. 4 (1990): 394–98, http://ow.ly/L6lFs.

14. Dov Eden, "Self-Fulfilling Prophecies in Organizations," in *Organizational Behavior: The State of the Science*, ed. Jerald Greenberg (Mahwah, NJ: Lawrence Erlbaum Associates, 2003), 87.

15. Ibid.

16. The paper cited above provides a comprehensive review of the Pygmalion effect: "Two recent meta-analyses of the Pygmalion-at-work research have confirmed the Pygmalion effect and estimated its size. . . . Thus there is solid and consistent evidence for the internal and external validity of the Pygmalion effect among adults in organizations. Moreover, this effect is large."

17. Emily Pronin, Daniel Y. Lin, and Lee Ross, "The Bias Blind Spot: Perceptions of Bias in Self Versus Others," *Personality and Social Psychology Bulletin* 28, no. 3 (2002): 369–81, http://ow.ly/L6lXU.

18. Jeffrey Liker and David Meier. *The Toyota Way Fieldbook*. *McGraw-Hill* (New York: Esensi, 2005), http://ow.ly/L6mxR.

CHAPTER 6: FROZEN OR FLUID

1. Florian Ederer and Gustavo Manso. "Is Pay for Performance Detrimental to Innovation?" *Management Science* 59 (2013): 1496–1513, http://ow.ly/L6mIM.

2. Max Marmer et al., "Startup Genome Report Extra Premature Scaling," *Startup Genome*, 2012, http://ow.ly/GqELl.

3. Zoë Schlanger, "Women Entrepreneurs Fight for Their Piece of the Pie," *Newsweek*, May 7, 2014, http://ow.ly/GqEno.

4. John R. Graham, Campbell R. Harvey, and Shiva Rajgopal, "The Economic Implications of Corporate Financial Reporting," *Journal of Accounting and Economics* 40, no. 1–3 (2005): 3–73, http://ow.ly/L6n5j.

5. Adam Bryant, "Satya Nadella, Chief of Microsoft, on His New Role," *New York Times*, February 20, 2014, http://ow.ly/Gp8P1.

6. Scott Keller and Colin Price, *Beyond Performance: How Great Organizations Build Ultimate Competitive Advantage* (Hoboken, NJ: John Wiley & Sons, 2011), http://ow.ly/Gp8dH.

7. Poornima Gupta, "Dell to Invest More on PCs, Tablets After $25 Billion Buyout Win," Reuters, September 12, 2013, http://ow.ly/Gp8go.

8. Sven Smit, Caroline M. Thompson, and S. Patrick Viguerie, "The Do-or-Die Struggle for Growth," *McKinsey Quarterly* 3 (2005): 34–45, http://ow.ly/Gp7wK.

9. "Email from 3M Corporate Communications," February 16, 2015.

10. Michelle Caruso-Cabrera, "3M CEO: Research Is 'Driving This Company,'" *CNBC*, June 10, 2013, http://ow.ly/Gp8LA.

CHAPTER 7: THE TORCH OF PERFORMANCE

1. Alan Sangster, "The Genesis of Double Entry Bookkeeping," n.d., http://ow.ly/Gpak1.

2. "W. Edwards Deming," *Wikipedia*, accessed April 1, 2015, http://ow.ly/GMaQ9.

3. Thomas J. Peters and Robert H. Waterman, *In Search of Excellence: Lessons from American's Best-Run Companies* (New York: HarperCollins, 1982), http://ow.ly/Gg54N.

4. "The Streetlight Effect," *Wikipedia*, n.d., http://ow.ly/GpaTh.

5. W. S. Grolnick and R. M. Ryan, "Autonomy in Children's Learning: An Experimental and Individual Difference Investigation," *Journal of Personality and Social Psychology* 52 (1987): 890–98, http://ow.ly/Gpadt.

6. Maxime A. Tremblay et al., "Work Extrinsic and Intrinsic Motivation Scale: Its Value for Organizational Psychology Research," *Canadian Journal of Behavioural Science* 41 (2009): 213–26, http://ow.ly/GpaDu.

7. We had a number of choices to make when we developed the size of the scale. We could have kept it from 1 to 7 like the questions, or 0 to 100 like a test grade, or -100 to 100. We chose the latter for a few reasons. First, the negative side of the scale is a very strong reminder of the negative effects of indirect motivators. Second, because the ToMo arithmetic involves subtraction, having a scale with a negative side vastly simplifies the math. Third, many organizations are familiar with the Net Promoter Score, which is also measured on a -100 to 100 scale. Lastly, we did not want the ToMo factor to feel like a grade. Instead, we wanted to maximize its diagnostic potential.

8. Temkin Group, *Temkin Experience Ratings 2015*, http://ow.ly/L66xi.

9. Barbara Thau, "Apple and the Other Most Successful Retailers by Sales Per Square Foot," *Forbes*, May 20, 2014, http://ow.ly/Gp9M1.

10. We've since heard anecdotes from other store employees that sales targets are becoming more pressuring.

CHAPTER 8: THE FIRE STARTERS

1. This analysis was based on research we conducted in the United States. We surveyed people across industries and job types, and asked them whether or not their managers exhibited roughly fifty different leadership behaviors—some of which were indirect motivators and some were direct motivators. We also assessed the total motivation of the survey respondents to see if there is a correlation between manager leadership behaviors and the ToMo of subordinates.

2. The research done on leadership presented here was based on a leadership construct known as Transformational Leadership. In the appendix we detail why we are comfortable explicitly connecting this work to total motivation.

3. Taly Dvir, Dov Eden, Bruce J. Avolio, and Boas Shamir, "Impact of Transformational Leadership on Follower Development and Performance: A Field Experiment," *Academy of Management Journal* 45 (2002): 735–44, http://ow.ly/L6uet.

4. Benyamin B. Lichtenstein and Donde Ashmos Plowman. "The Leadership of Emergence: A Complex Systems Leadership Theory of Emergence at Successive Organizational Levels," *Leadership Quarterly* 20, no. 4 (2009): 617–30, http://ow.ly/GoYSG.

5. S. J. Peterson et al., "CEO Positive Psychological Traits, Transformational

Leadership, and Firm Performance in High-Technology Start-up and Established Firms," *Journal of Management* 35, no. 2 (2008): 348–68, http://ow.ly/GMbP3.

6. Lichtenstein and Plowman, "The Leadership of Emergence: A Complex Systems Leadership Theory of Emergence at Successive Organizational Levels."

7. Starbucks, *Starbucks Global Responsibility Report*, 2013, http://ow.ly/Gpd4O.

8. "Howard Schultz," *The Daily Show* (United States: Comedy Central, June 16, 2014), http://ow.ly/GMcod.

9. Ibid.

10. Howard Schultz and Dori Jones Yang, *Pour Your Heart Into It: How Starbucks Built a Company One Cup at a Time* (New York: Hyperion, 1997), http://ow.ly/GpdHE.

11. Gerard H. Seijts, Gary P. Latham, Kevin Tasa, and Brandon W. Latham, "Goal Setting and Goal Orientation: An Integration of Two Different Yet Related Literatures." *Academy of Management Journal* 47 (2004): 227–39, http://ow.ly/L6yNr.

12. Academic literature uses different terminology to describe these types of goals. However, we found that the individual goal types map cleanly to the motive spectrum. For example "mastery" achievement goals connect more cleanly to play and purpose. On the other hand, a "performance" goal may connect to either direct or indirect motives, thus making the strategy less effective. The study cited below provides a meta-analytic review.

13. L. J. Rawsthorne and A. J. Elliot, "Achievement Goals and Intrinsic Motivation: A Meta-Analytic Review," *Personality and Social Psychology Review* 3 (1999): 326–44, http://ow.ly/GpixA.

14. Verbatim comment from a ToMo survey we conducted.

15. Julian Barling, Tom Weber, and E. Kevin Kelloway, "Effects of Transformational Leadership Training on Attitudinal and Financial Outcomes: A Field Experiment," *Journal of Applied Psychology* 81 (1996): 827–32, http://ow.ly/GpiNV.

16. Alois L. J. Geyery and Johannes M. Steyrer, "Transformational leadership and objective performance in banks," *Applied Psychology* 47.3 (1998): 397–420, http://ow.ly/OzG54.

17. David A. Garvin, "How Google Sold Its Engineers on Management," *Harvard Business Review*, 2013, http://ow.ly/GpiHU.

18. Dominic Field, "Lazlo Bock on Google's Approach to HR," *BCG Perspectives*, July 2010, http://ow.ly/GpgW0.

19. Chris DeRose, "How Google Uses Data to Build a Better Worker," *The Atlantic*, October 7, 2013, http://ow.ly/Gpgim.

20. Adam Bryant, "In Head-Hunting, Big Data May Not Be Such a Big Deal," *New York Times*, June 19, 2013, http://ow.ly/GpfLE.

21. Adam Bryant, "Google's Quest to Build a Better Boss," *New York Times*, March 12, 2011, http://ow.ly/GphLw.

CHAPTER 9: IDENTITY

1. Kentaro Fujita et al., "Construal Levels and Self-Control," *Journal of Personality and Social Psychology* 90 (2006): 351–67, http://ow.ly/Gppir.

2. Mark Muraven, Dianne M. Tice, and Roy F. Baumeister. "Self-Control as a Limited Resource: Regulatory Depletion Patterns." *Journal of Personality and Social Psychology* 74, no. 3 (1998): 774, http://ow.ly/L6zvy.

3. Ülkü D. Demirdöğen, "The Roots of Research in (Political) Persuasion: Ethos, Pathos, Logos and the Yale Studies of Persuasive Communications," *International Journal of Social Inquiry* 3 (2010): 189–201, http://ow.ly/GpldN.

4. Ibid.

5. Ibid. The source provides the quote but, in doing so, references a translation of Aristotle's *Rhetoric*.

6. Anthony Salz and Russell Collins, *Salz Review,* 2013, http://ow.ly/GplXS.

7. Unpublished research report.

8. Simon Sinek, "How Great Leaders Inspire Action," TED, September 2009, http://ow.ly/Gpppl.

9. Major Jim Storr, "A Command Philosophy for the Information Age: The Continuing Relevance of Mission Command," *Defence Studies* 3, no. 3 (2003): 119–29, http://ow.ly/GpmJq.

10. "Order of Battle at the Battle of Trafalgar," *Wikipedia*, n.d., http://ow.ly/Gpn3n.

11. "British Library—Nelson's Trafalgar Memorandum." *British Library*, n.d., http://ow.ly/KWDYK.

12. Ibid.

13. "Trafalgar Signals," *Broadside*, n.d., http://ow.ly/KWFbZ.

14. Andrew Lambert, "The Battle of Trafalgar," *BBC*, February 17, 2011, http://ow.ly/KWGQ8.

15. Rear Admiral Joseph F. Callo, US Naval Reserve (Retired), "Lasting Lessons of Trafalgar," Military.com, September 2005, http://ow.ly/Gpnzy.

16. John T. Kuehn, *16 Cases of Mission Command*, ed. Donald P. Wright (Fort Leavenworth, KS: Combat Studies Institute Press, US Army Combined Arms Center), accessed December 24, 2014, http://ow.ly/Gpof6.

17. Timothy A. Judge and Robert D. Bretz, "Effects of Work Values on Job Choice Decisions," *Journal of Applied Psychology* 77 (1992): 261–71, http://ow.ly/Gpp48.

18. Adam M. Grant, "Leading with Meaning: Beneficiary Contact, Prosocial Impact, and the Performance Effects of Transformational Leadership," *The Academy of Management Journal* 55, no. 2 (2012): 458–76, http://ow.ly/L6A7x; Adam M. Grant and James W. Berry, "The Necessity of Others Is the Mother of Invention: Intrinsic and Prosocial Motivations, Perspective Taking, and Creativity," *Academy of Management Journal* 54, no. 1 (2011): 73–96, http://ow.ly/GfQ8a; Adam M. Grant, "How Customers Can Rally Your Troops: End Users Can Energize Your Workforce Far Better Than Your Managers Can," *Harvard Business Review* 89, no. 6 (2011): 97–103, http://ow.ly/Gj4EL.

19. Shalom H. Schwartz and Anat Bardi, "Value Hierarchies Across Cultures Taking a Similarities Perspective," *Journal of Cross-Cultural Psychology* 32, no. 3 (2001): 268–90, http://ow.ly/L6Aob.

20. McKinsey & Company, "Our Values," accessed December 24, 2014, http://ow.ly/Gpq72.

21. Keller Williams, "Press Release—Keller Williams Realty Reports Record Growth Numbers for 2009," February 22, 2010, http://ow.ly/GpsAi; Keller Williams, "Mission Statement I Keller Williams Realty," accessed December 24, 2014.

22. Keller Williams, "BOLD Law: Are Your Cells Eavesdropping on Your Thoughts?—KW Blog," April 30, 2013, http://ow.ly/GpsOl.

23. Interview with Jordan, Keller Williams specialist, February 2014.

24. Keller Williams, "Drunk Monkey—BOLD Laws," YouTube, September 26, 2012, http://ow.ly/GqUkP.

25. Jessica Guynn, "Steve Jobs' Virtual DNA to be Fostered in Apple University," *Los Angeles Times*, October 6, 2011, http://ow.ly/Gptp6.

26. Brian X. Chen, "Simplifying the Bull: How Picasso Helps to Teach Apple's Style," *New York Times*, August 10, 2014, http://ow.ly/GptiF.

27. Lee Mccoy, "Cailler Chocolaterie," *Chocolatiers*, April 22, 2014, http://ow.ly/KWIGY.

28. James H. Bryan and Nancy Hodges Walbek, "Preaching and Practicing Generosity: Children's Actions and Reactions," *Child Development* 41 (1970): 329–53, http://ow.ly/GptAW.

29. Interview with Dave Meller, Board Director at Belron with Responsibility for People and Leadership, July 2013.

30. Piercarlo Valdesolo, Jennifer Ouyang, and David DeSteno, "The Rhythm of Joint Action: Synchrony Promotes Cooperative Ability," *Journal of Experimental Social Psychology* 46 (2010): 693–95, http://ow.ly/L6AU4.

31. Ronald Fischer, Rohan Callander, Paul Reddish, and Joseph Bulbulia, "How Do Rituals Affect Cooperation?: An Experimental Field Study Comparing Nine Ritual Types," *Human Nature* 24 (2013): 115–25, http://ow.ly/L6B0J.

32. John Warrillow, "The Secret Rituals and Traditions That Bring Teams Together," *CBS News*, December 20, 2010, http://ow.ly/GptLW.

33. Horace Dediu, "Seeing What's Next," *Asymco*, November 18, 2013, http://ow.ly/GqFtO.

34. Interview with Ken Roman, 2014.

35. Kenneth Roman, *The King of Madison Avenue: David Ogilvy and the Making of Modern Advertising* (New York: Palgrave Macmillan, 2009), http://ow.ly/Gpupi.

36. Ken Brown and Ianthe Jeanne Dugan, "Arthur Andersen's Fall from Grace Is a Sad Tale of Greed and Miscues," *Wall Street Journal*, June 7, 2002, http://ow.ly/GqFYD.

37. Ibid.

38. Susan E. Squires et al., *Inside Arthur Andersen: Shifting Values, Unexpected Consequences* (Upper Saddle River, NJ: FT Press, 2003), http://ow.ly/GqGkQ.

39. Elizabeth Haas Edersheim, *McKinsey's Marvin Bower: Vision, Leadership, and the Creation of Management Consulting* (Hoboken, NJ: John Wiley & Sons, 2004), http://ow.ly/Gpu5N.

40. Ibid.

41. Interview with Ron Daniel, June 2014.

42. Robert Lenzner, "Gus Levy: Don't Tell Me What I Can't Do; Tell Me What I Can Do," *Forbes*, March 10, 2011, http://ow.ly/Gppl4.

43. Lisa Endlich, *Goldman Sachs: The Culture of Success* (New York: Simon and Schuster, 2000), http://ow.ly/Gpp7T.

44. "Obituaries: Gustave Levy, Wall Street Wizard," *St. Petersburg Times*, November 5, 1976, http://ow.ly/Gppsi.

45. Endlich, *Goldman Sachs: The Culture of Success.*

CHAPTER 10: THE PLAYGROUND

1. Robert Kanigel, *The One Best Way: Frederick Winslow Taylor and the Enigma of Efficiency* (Cambridge, MA: MIT Press, 2005), http://ow.ly/GqGAa.

2. Ibid.

3. J. Richard Hackman et al., "A New Strategy for Job Enrichment," *California Management Review* 17 (1975): 57–71, http://ow.ly/GqGMH.

4. Hackman and Oldham refer to this work as "Job Characteristics Theory." In the appendix we detail why we are comfortable explicitly connecting this work to total motivation. Hackman, J. Richard, and Greg Oldham. "How Job Characteristics Theory Happened," In *Great Minds in Management: The Process of Theory Development*, edited by K. G. Smith and M. A. Hitt, 151–70 (New York: Oxford University Press, 2005), http://ow.ly/GqUUC.

5. There are a variety of terms describing this concept, including job design, role design, and job enrichment.

6. For a good summary of studies on the link between work and health outcomes, see Gretchen Spreitzer, Kathleen Sutcliffe, Jane Dutton, Scott Sonenshein, and Adam M. Grant, "A Socially Embedded Model of Thriving at Work," *Organization Science* 16, no. 5 (2005): 537–49, http://ow.ly/L6CSs. Spreitzer cites the following study on heart attacks: L. Alfredsson, C. L. Spetz, and T. Theorell, "Type of Occupation and Near-Future Hospitalization for Myocardial Infarction and Some Other Diagnoses," *International Journal of Epidemiology* 14 (1985): 378–88, http://ow.ly/GqUdH.

7. Ben Horowitz, *The Hard Thing About Hard Things* (New York: HarperCollins, 2014).

8. Lionel Vasquez, "Lionel Vasquez, Beer Specialist," *Whole Foods Market*, accessed December 25, 2014, http://ow.ly/GqHhO.

9. Ibid.

10. Robert Reiss, "How Ritz-Carlton Stays at the Top," *Forbes*, October 20, 2009, http://ow.ly/GqH2O.

11. For more, see Adam Grant's excellent article. Adam M. Grant, "How Customers Can Rally Your Troops: End Users Can Energize Your Workforce Far Better Than

Your Managers Can," *Harvard Business Review* 89, no. 6 (2011): 97–103, http://ow.ly/Gj4EL.

12. Interview with Steve Greene, June 2014.

13. Steve Greene and Chris Fry, "Year of Living Dangerously: How Salesforce.com Delivered Extraordinary Results Through a 'Big Bang' Enterprise Agile Revolution," in Scrum Gathering, Stockholm, 2008, http://ow.ly/GqIvq.

14. Kent Beck et al., "History: The Agile Manifesto," *Agile Manifesto*, accessed December 25, 2014, http://ow.ly/GqJ1I.

15. Kent Beck et al., "Principles Behind the Agile Manifesto," accessed December 25, 2014, http://ow.ly/GqJgC.

16. Salesforce.com used a particular type of Agile known as "Scrum."

17. Greene and Fry, "Year of Living Dangerously: How Salesforce.com Delivered Extraordinary Results Through a 'Big Bang' Enterprise Agile Revolution."

18. Salesforce.com, "Transforming Your Organization to Agile," n.d., http://ow.ly/GqK9Q.

19. Ibid.

20. Steve Denning, "Scrum Is a Major Management Discovery," *Forbes*, April 29, 2011, http://ow.ly/GqKkb.

CHAPTER 11: THE LAND OF A THOUSAND LADDERS

1. Edward P. Lazear and Sherwin Rosen, "Rank-Order Tournaments as Optimum Labor Contracts," *Journal of Political Economy* 89, no. 5 (1981): 841, http://ow.ly/L6DEl.

2. Rob Asghar, "Incompetence Rains, Er, Reigns: What the Peter Principle Means Today," *Forbes*, August 14, 2014, http://ow.ly/GqKPR.

3. Interview with Anat Bracha, May 2014.

4. A. Bracha and C. Fershtman. "Competitive Incentives: Working Harder or Working Smarter?" *Management Science*, 2012, http://ow.ly/L6DLA.

5. Hikaru Takeuchi et al., "Regional Gray Matter Density Is Associated with Achievement Motivation: Evidence from Voxel-Based Morphometry," *Brain Structure and Function* 219 (2012): 71–83, http://ow.ly/GqTSK.

6. "Orbitofrontal Cortex," *Wikipedia*, n.d., http://ow.ly/GqKWF.

7. "Army Warrant Officer History," *Warrant Officer Historical Foundation*, n.d., http://ow.ly/GqL79.

8. Interview with Marni Pastor, Former Director of Talent Management at Pittsburgh Public Schools, 2014; "Empowering Effective Teachers / Career Ladders," Pittsburgh Public Schools, accessed January 12, 2015, http://ow.ly/Hd6Ir.

9. IBM, "IBM Fellows Program: 50th Anniversary," YouTube, n.d., http://ow.ly/GqLcu.

10. Gardiner Tucker, "IBM Fellows: Still Ahead of Their Time, 50 Years Later," *Building a Smarter Planet, A Smarter Planet Blog*, April 3, 2013, http://ow.ly/GqLok.

11. IBM, "2013 IBM Fellows—United States" (IBM, January 30, 2013), http://ow.ly/GqVtU.

12. John Markoff, "Computer Wins on 'Jeopardy': Trivial, It's Not," *New York Times*, February 16, 2011, http://ow.ly/GqMRM; "Jeopardy—Watson vs. The Humans Day 1," YouTube, n.d., http://ow.ly/OzKf5.

13. IBM, "2013 IBM Fellows—United States"; "Chandu Visweswariah" (IBM, March 22, 2013), http://ow.ly/GqVzH.

14. IBM, "2013 IBM Fellows—United States." IBM, January 30, 2013, http://ow.ly/GqVtU.

15. Tucker, "IBM Fellows: Still Ahead of Their Time, 50 Years Later. "

16. Interview with Jen Hines, former Chief Operating Officer, October 2014.

17. "National Rankings: Best High Schools," *US News & World Report*, 2015, http://ow.ly/MSyzJ; Katy Stewart, "Best Places to Work: Companies with 501+ Employees," *Houston Businesss Journal*, October 18, 2013, http://ow.ly/MSz0Y.

18. "Careers at the Federal Reserve," accessed February 4, 2015, http://ow.ly/L9jQQ.

19. Kirk Semple, "Judges Give Low Marks to Lawyers in Immigration Cases," December 18, 2011, http://ow.ly/GqNbO; "Our Story," *Immigrant Justice Corps*, accessed December 25, 2014, http://ow.ly/GqNaX.

CHAPTER 12: COMPENSATIONISM

1. Edward P. Lazear, "Performance Pay and Productivity," *American Economic Review* 90, no. 5 (2000): 1346–61, http://ow.ly/OzKtV.

2. E. L. Deci, R. Koestner, and R. M. Ryan, "A Meta-Analytic Review of Experiments Examining the Effects of Extrinsic Rewards on Intrinsic Motivation," *Psychological Bulletin* 125 (1999): 627–68; discussion 692–700, http://ow.ly/L6aiQ.

3. Sumit Agarwal and Faye H. Wang, *Perverse Incentives at the Banks? Evidence from a Natural Experiment* (Working Paper, Federal Reserve Bank of Chicago, 2009), http://ow.ly/GqNkG.

4. Lisa D. Ordóñez, Maurice E. Schweitzer, Adam D. Galinsky, and Max H. Bazerman, "Goals Gone Wild: The Systematic Side Effects of Overprescribing Goal Setting," *Academy of Management Perspectives* 23, no. 1 (2009): 6–16, http://ow.ly/OzKGk; Lawrence M. Fisher, "Sears Auto Centers Halt Commissions After Flap," *New York Times*, June 23, 1992, http://ow.ly/GqNq7.

5. John R. Graham, Campbell R. Harvey, and Shiva Rajgopal, "The Economic Implications of Corporate Financial Reporting," *Journal of Accounting and Economics* 40, no. 1–3 (2005): 3–73, http://ow.ly/L6n5j.

6. Li and Murphy, "A Three-Country Study of Unethical Sales Behaviors."

7. Michael Winerip, "Ex-Schools Chief in Atlanta is Indicted in Testing Charged in Cheating Scandal," *New York Times*, March 29, 2013, http://ow.ly/GqNUG.

8. Ibid.

9. Ibid.

10. Ned Resnikoff, "Atlanta Cheating Scandal Puts National Education Policy on Trial | MSNBC," MSNBC, September 13, 2013, http://ow.ly/GqO42.

11. Winerip, "Ex-Atlanta Schools Chief Charged in Cheating Scandal"; Lois Beckett, "America's Most Outrageous Teacher Cheating Scandals," *ProPublica*, April 1, 2013, http://ow.ly/GqOdw.

12. Dana Goldstein, "What You Need to Know About the Shocking Cheating Indictments in the Atlanta Public Schools," *Slate*, April 2, 2013, http://ow.ly/GqOh1; Heather Vogell, Jaime Sarrio, and Alan Judd, "The Art of War at Atlanta Schools: Indictment Portrays System of Deception," *Atlanta Journal-Constitution*, March 31, 2013, http://ow.ly/GqTFO.

13. Greg Toppo et al., "When Test Scores Seem Too Good to Believe," *USA Today*, February 17, 2011, http://ow.ly/GqOWy.

14. Roland G. Fryer, "Teacher Incentives and Student Achievement: Evidence from New York City Public Schools," *National Bureau of Economic Research Working Paper Series* No. 16850 (2011), http://ow.ly/GqPAo; Matthew G. Springer, Dale Ballou, Laura Hamilton, Vi-Nhuan Le, J. R. Lockwood, Daniel F. McCaffrey, Matthew Pepper, and Brian M. Stecher, *Teacher Pay for Performance: Experimental Evidence from the Project on Incentives in Teaching (POINT)* (Nashville, TN, 2011), http://ow.ly/L9kuq.

15. Results have been mixed in experiments around the world. Studies in Kenya and India showed some lift in performance. Fryer et al., "Teacher Incentives and Student Achievement: Evidence from New York City Public Schools."

16. "Continuum | YES Prep Public Schools," *YES Prep*, accessed December 25, 2014, http://ow.ly/GqPGV.

17. Gagné describes this same conclusion in her meta-analysis: "most studies that have found a positive effect of contingent pay plans on performance have used algorithmic tasks (Bandiera, Barankay, & Rasul, 2007; Cadsby, Song, & Tapon, 2007; Locke, Feren, McCaleb, Shaw, & Denny, 1980), while studies that have found no effect or a negative effect used heuristic tasks (e.g., Amabile et al., 1990)." Marylène Gagné and Jacques Forest. "*The Study of Compensation Systems Through the Lens of Self-Determination Theory: Reconciling 35 Years of Debate.*" Vol. 49. Educational Publishing Foundation, 2008, http://ow.ly/L6FN4.

18. Tom DiDonato, "Stop Basing Pay on Performance Reviews," *Harvard Business Review,* January 2014, http://ow.ly/GqQgS.

19. "100 Best Companies to Work for," *Fortune*, 2015, http://ow.ly/MSDQC.

20. Stacy Perman, "For Some, Paying Sales Commissions No Longer Makes Sense," *New York Times*, November 20, 2013, http://ow.ly/GqQtl.

21. Dan Ostlund, "Why Do We Pay Sales Commissions?," *Fog Creek Blog*, January 4, 2012, http://ow.ly/GqQwr.

CHAPTER 13: THE HUNTING PARTY

1. Paraphrased from quote attributed to Winston Churchill.

2. David A. Kravitz and Barbara Martin. "Ringelmann Rediscovered: The Original Article," *Journal of Personality and Social Psychology* 50 (1986): 936–41, http://ow.ly/L6G2C.

3. Ringelmann shows data related to a number of different studies summarized together. We are applying his data back to the rope experiment for the sake of communications clarity.

4. Steven J. Karau and Kipling D. Williams, "Social Loafing: A Meta-Analytic Review

and Theoretical Integration," *Journal of Personality and Social Psychology* 65 (1993): 681–706, http://ow.ly/L6G93.

5. Information sourced from, and Figure 18 created from data in *Journal of Human Evolution*, 22, R. I. M. Dunbar, "Neocortex Size as a Constraint on Group Size in Primates," 469–93, 1992.

6. Technically, Dunbar tabulated the data for thirty-eight genera, not species.

7. "Neocortex." *Wikipedia*, n.d. http://ow.ly/L9lNY.

8. R. I. M. Dunbar, "You've Got to Have (150) Friends," *New York Times*, December 25, 2010, http://ow.ly/GqThm.

9. The relationship was exponential, hence the logarithmic axes. Ibid.

10. R. I. M. Dunbar, "Coevolution of Neocortical Size, Group Size and Language in Humans," *Behavioral and Brain Sciences* 16 (1993): 681–735, http://ow.ly/L6GpJ.

11. Ibid.

12. Bruno Gonçalves, Nicola Perra, and Alessandro Vespignani, "Modeling Users' Activity on Twitter Networks: Validation of Dunbar's Number," *PLOS ONE* 6 (2011), http://ow.ly/GqTmY.

13. R. A. Hill and R. I. M. Dunbar, "Social Network Size in Humans," *Human Nature* 14 (2003): 53–72, http://ow.ly/L6Gw8.

14. The major shortcoming in our research here was that we asked survey respondents how many people work in their company. While this may be a good proxy for community size for small companies (below five hundred people), at larger sizes the data does not capture the reality that some companies are divided into smaller communities. In future research, we will ask a few different questions to capture the sizes of different types of groups.

15. Dunbar calls hunting parties "sympathy groups" and confidants "cliques." We used words that we find resonate more in the business world.

16. Gregory M. Walton, Geoffrey L. Cohen, David Cwir, and Steven J. Spencer, "Mere Belonging: The Power of Social Connections," *Journal of Personality and Social Psychology* 102, no. 3 (2012): 513–32, http://ow.ly/L6GJK.

17. Verna Allee, "Knowledge Networks and Communities of Practice," *OD Practitioner* (Fall/Winter 2000): 1–15.

18. Vivian Giang, "The 'Two Pizza Rule' Is Jeff Bezos' Secret to Productive Meetings," *Business Insider*, October 29, 2013, http://ow.ly/L6HVU.

19. C. M. Dickens et al., "Lack of a Close Confidant, but Not Depression, Predicts Further Cardiac Events after Myocardial Infarction," *Heart (British Cardiac Society)* 90 (2004): 518–22, http://ow.ly/GqTaW.

20. The experiment is sourced from, and Figure 19 is reprinted from the *Journal of Experiment Social Psychology*, 53, Priyanka B. Carr and Gregory M. Walton, "Cues of Working Together Fuel Intrinsic Motivation," 172, 2014, with permission from Elsevier.

21. Dennis Overbye, "Kenneth I. Appel, Mathematician Who Harnessed Computer Power, Dies at 80," *New York Times*, April 28, 2013, http://ow.ly/GM4kb.

22. Marcus B. Mueller and Geoff P. Lovell, "Relatedness Need Satisfaction in Senior Executives," *European Journal of Business and Social Sciences* 2, no. 7 (2013): 105–35, http://ow.ly/L6LlD.

23. D'Ann White, "Mentoring Program Helps Hillsborough County Keep Good Teachers," *Bloomingdale-Riverview Patch*, August 20, 2012, http://ow.ly/L6Luf.

24. Brook Manville and Josiah Ober, *A Company of Citizens: What the World's First Democracy Teaches Leaders About Creating Great Organizations* (Cambridge: Harvard Business Press, 2003), http://ow.ly/Hd7Xs.

25. Jay Rao, "W. L. Gore: Culture of Innovation—Babson College Business Case," 2012.

26. Gaylen K. Bunker, "Of All Things Precious to Mankind, Freedom to Dream Is the Ultimate Value. Presentation by Gaylen K. Bunker," n.d., http://ow.ly/GqT4Q.

27. Ibid.

28. Jay Rao, "W. L. Gore: Culture of Innovation—Babson College Business Case," 2012.

29. D. Reid Townsend and Joseph Harder, "W. L. Gore & Associates" 2000, (University of Virginia: Darden Business Publishing), http://ow.ly/GqTyF.

30. Yves L. Doz and Keeley Wilson, *Managing Global Innovation: Frameworks for Integrating Capabilities Around the World* (Cambridge: Harvard Business Press, 2012), http://ow.ly/GqTdz.

31. Townsend and Harder, "W. L. Gore & Associates."

32. Alan Deutschman, "The Fabric of Creativity," *Fast Company*, December 2004, http://ow.ly/GqT6L.

33. Rachel Emma Silverman and Kate Linebaugh, "Who's the Boss? There Isn't One," *Wall Street Journal*, June 19, 2012, http://ow.ly/GqTwk.

34. Gaylen K. Bunker, "Of All Things Precious to Mankind, Freedom to Dream Is the Ultimate Value. Presentation by Gaylen K. Bunker," n.d., http://ow.ly/GqT4Q.

35. Jay Rao, "W. L. Gore: Culture of Innovation—Babson College Business Case," 2012.

36. "Workplace Democracy at W. L. Gore & Associates," *Workplace Democracy*, July 14, 2009, http://ow.ly/Hd8oa.

37. Jay Rao, "W. L. Gore: Culture of Innovation—Babson College Business Case," 2012.

CHAPTER 14: THE FIRE WATCHERS

1. Herb Kelleher, "Customer Service: It Starts at Home," *Journal of Lending and Credit Risk Management*, February (1998): 74–78, http://ow.ly/GqSNW.

2. E. S. Bernstein, "The Transparency Paradox: A Role for Privacy in Organizational Learning and Operational Control," *Administrative Science Quarterly* 57, no. 2 (2012): 181–216, http://ow.ly/L6LTV.

3. Adam M. Grant, "Leading with Meaning: Beneficiary Contact, Prosocial Impact, and the Performance Effects of Transformational Leadership," *The Academy of Management Journal* 55, no. 2 (2012): 458–76, http://ow.ly/L6A7x.

4. Nicola Bellé, "Leading to Make a Difference: A Field Experiment on the Performance Effects of Transformational Leadership, Perceived Social Impact, and Public

Service Motivation," *Journal of Public Administration Research and Theory* 24 (2013): 109–36, http://ow.ly/L6M30.

5. Chip Heath and Nancy Staudenmayer, "Coordination Neglect: How Lay Theories of Organizing Complicate Coordination in Organizations," *Research in Organizational Behavior* 22 (2000): 153–91, http://ow.ly/L6Meo.

6. P. O'Hara, "The Illegal Introduction of Rabbit Haemorrhagic Disease Virus in New Zealand," *Revue Scientifique et Technique (International Office of Epizootics)* 25, no. 1 (2006): 119–23, http://ow.ly/GqSWI.

CHAPTER 15: PERFORMANCE CALIBRATION

1. Kurt Eichenwald, "How Microsoft Lost Its Mojo: Steve Ballmer and Corporate America's Most Spectacular Decline," *Vanity Fair*, August 2012, http://ow.ly/GqReo.

2. Terence R. Mitchell and Laura S. Kalb, "Effects of Outcome Knowledge and Outcome Valence on Supervisors' Evaluations," *Journal of Applied Psychology* 66 (1981): 604–12, http://ow.ly/GqSb6.

3. Francesca Gino, Don A. Moore, and Max H. Bazerman, "No Harm, No Foul: The Outcome Bias in Ethical Judgments," *Harvard Business School NOM Working Paper*, no. 08–080 (2009), http://ow.ly/GqRnq.

4. Elaine D. Pulakos, Rose Mueller Hanson, Sharon Arad, and Neta Moye, "Performance Management Can Be Fixed: An On-the-Job Experiential Learning Approach for Complex Behavior Change," *CEB Corproate Leadership Council*, 2014, http://ow.ly/GqRxX.

5. Peter Cohan, "Why Stack Ranking Worked Better at GE Than Microsoft," *Forbes*, July 13, 2012, http://ow.ly/GqS8s.

6. Jena McGregor, "The Corporate Kabuki of Performance Reviews," *Washington Post*, February 14, 2013, http://ow.ly/GqRHT.

7. Ibid.

8. Pulakos et al., "Performance Management Can Be Fixed: An On-the-Job Experiential Learning Approach for Complex Behavior Change"; Tom DiDonato, "Stop Basing Pay on Performance Reviews," *Harvard Business Review,* January 2014, http://ow.ly/GqQgS; Julie Cook Ramirez, "Rethinking the Review," *Human Resource Executive Online*, July 24, 2013, http://ow.ly/GqRNZ.

9. Kevin Roose, "Ray Dalio's Former Assistant Tells All," *New York Times*, March 13, 2012, http://ow.ly/GqRU4.

10. Matthew Goldstein, "SAC Capital, Meet Point72 Asset Management," *New York Times*, April 7, 2014, http://ow.ly/GqScO.

11. Lukas I. Alpert, "Uralkali Expects Potash Prices to Bottom Out," *Wall Street Journal*, October 3, 2013, http://ow.ly/MSzwK.

CHAPTER 16: IGNITING A MOVEMENT

1. Edward L. Deci and Richard Flaste, *Why We Do What We Do: The Dynamics of Personal Autonomy* (New York: G. P. Putnam's Sons, 1995), http://ow.ly/GqSiN.

2. Bennett G. Galef, "The Question of Animal Culture," *Human Nature* 3, no. 2 (1992): 157–78, http://ow.ly/L6N4o.

3. Bronwyn H. Hall, "Innovation and Diffusion," in *The Oxford Handbook of Innovation*, ed. Jan Fagerberg (Oxford, Eng.: Oxford University Press, 2005), 459–85, http://ow.ly/GqSIN.

4. Aldon Morris and Cedric Herring, "Theory and research in social movement: A critical review" (1984).

5. Jeffrey Pfeffer, *The Human Equation: Building Profits by Putting People First* (Cambridge: Harvard Business Press, 1998), http://ow.ly/Gg59Z.

6. Ira Glass and Frank Langfitt, "NUMMI," *This American Life*, WBEZ, 2010, http://ow.ly/Gg6rg.

7. Ibid.

8. Pfeffer, *The Human Equation: Building Profits by Putting People First.*

9. Glass and Langfitt, "NUMMI."

10. Ibid.

APPENDIX: THE SCIENTIST'S TOOTHBRUSH

1. Murray Gell-Mann, "Complex Adaptive Systems," *Complexity: Metaphors, Models and Reality*, (Cambridge, MA: Perseus Books, 1994), 17–45, http://ow.ly/GqSrT.

2. R. M. Ryan and E. L. Deci, "Self-Determination Theory and the Facilitation of Intrinsic Motivation, Social Development, and Well-Being," *American Psychologist* 55 (2000): 68–78, http://ow.ly/GqSxT.

3. J. Richard Hackman et al., "A New Strategy for Job Enrichment," *California Management Review* 17 (1975): 57–71, http://ow.ly/GqGMH.

4. Bernard M. Bass, "From Transactional to Transformational Leadership: Learning to Share the Vision," *Organizational Dynamics* 18 (1990): 19–32, http://ow.ly/L6NKN.

5. Lale Gumusluoglu and Arzu Ilsev, "Transformational Leadership, Creativity, and Organizational Innovation," *Journal of Business Research* 62 (2009): 461–73, http://ow.ly/L6O2p; D. Charbonneau, J. Barling, and E. K. Kelloway, "Transformational Leadership and Sports Performance: The Mediating Role of Intrinsic Motivation," *Journal of Applied Social Psychology* 31, no. 7 (2001): 1521–34, http://ow.ly/L6O7F; Ronald F. Piccolo, and Jason A. Colquitt, "Transformational Leadership and Job Behaviors: The Mediating Role of Core Job Characteristics," *Academy of Management Journal* 49 (2006): 327–40, http://ow.ly/L6OcD; Timothy A. Judge and Ronald F. Piccolo, "Transformational and Transactional Leadership: A Meta-Analytic Test of Their Relative Validity," *The Journal of Applied Psychology* 89 (2004): 755–68, http://ow.ly/Hdaz5; Xiaomeng Zhang and Kathryn M. Bartol, "Linking Empowering Leadership and Employee Creativity: The Influence of Psychological Empowerment, Intrinsic Motivation, and Creative Process Engagement," *Academy of Management Journal* 53 (2010): 107–28, http://ow.ly/HdaHg.

Index

About the Authors

Neel Doshi and Lindsay McGregor have a combined twenty years of practical experience transforming cultures at iconic institutions. They are the cofounders of Vega Factor, a company that helps organizations build high-performing, adaptive cultures through technology, learning programs, and human capital systems. Previously, Neel Doshi was a partner at McKinsey & Company, a founding member of a tech start-up, and an employee of several multinational institutions. Lindsay McGregor led projects at McKinsey & Company with Fortune 500 companies as well as school systems and nonprofits. Lindsay and Neel are married and live in New York City.